Woodstone

1841-1945

– MARGARET BREWSTER –

FASTPRINT PUBLISHING
PETERBOROUGH, ENGLAND

WOODSTONE 1841-1945
Copyright © Margaret Brewster 2009

ISBN 978-184426-615-9

First Published 2009 by
FASTPRINT PUBLISHING
Peterborough, England.

Printed on FSC approved paper by
www.printondemand-worldwide.com

INTRODUCTION

This is a factual account which gives an insight to a great many of the families who lived in Woodston over a period of 100 years. Some of these people stayed in the village all their lives. Many of them brought up their families in the original cottages where they had also grown up with their parents who had since passed away. The family history of Woodstone begins at the time of the 1841 census and follows through at ten year intervals to the 1901 census. The spelling of names may not always seem correct but are shown exactly as the enumerator recorded them at that time.

The last forty years of history was told to me by all the wonderful people I visited or had contact with via the internet. My thanks go out to them also for the pictures that I received and the patience they have had waiting for me to complete this Woodston story.

Other historical facts have been taken from the Peterborough Advertiser.

The family trees I have created may not be complete but show a rough sketch of individual families.

ACKNOWLEDGEMENTS

Ron Abbott, John Ackroyd, Janice de Lima Araujo, Margaret Bates, Alec Bloodworth, George Bott, Christine Briggs, Gwen and Eileen nee Brooksbanks, Margaret Brimble, Betty Chambers, Vanessa Christie, David Clark, Derek Clay, Maurice and Barbara Clayton, Sylvia Coulson, Nell Creamer, Rosemary Cross, Joan Darby, Debi Eatherley (Canada), Fred Few, Stan Foreman, Doreen Foster, Neil Foster, Jean Frith, Bruce Frost, Joan Garner, Shirley George, Gloria Godley (USA) Sheila Gowler, David Gray, Julie Gunn, Dorothy Hamm, Leonard Hankins, Eric Heath, Richard Hillier, George Hockney, Cath Jennings, John Knight, Betty Laws, Alan Laxton, Annette Martin, Neil Mitchell, Michael O'Connor, Marian O'Dell, Colin Pacey, Jenny Paul, George Pickering, Jessie Pitt, Dick Preston, Joan Raines, Margaret Rist, Ethel Roan, Neville Robinson, Alvin & Linda Rowton, Babs Setchell, Eileen Smith, Bob Sowman, Barbara Spiers, Gwen Sprawson, Roy Taylor, Violet Tilley, Pauline Turner, Sandra Vinter, Peter Waszak, Jean Watier (Canada), Roy Weston, Brian White, Joan White, Steve Williams,

Thanks also go to:-
Neil Mitchell for the use of photographs taken from his collection.
John Knight for the use of photographs taken from his collection.
The Museum of English Rural Life at University of Reading - for the copy of the Patent Safety Ladder Company Limited catalogue.
The City of Peterborough offices for information regarding past Mayor's of Peterborough.
The Rector of Woodston for allowing me access to Parish Records.
Keith Ovenden - Peterborough Archives Service
Peterborough Central Library
Northampton Record Office
Huntingdon Record Office

Other areas used in research
www.freebmd.org.uk
www.findmypast.com
www.familysearch.com

I would like to thank Simon Potter for all the advice and help he has given to me in the production of my book, and also to all the staff at Fastprint Publishing.

An extract from "Samuel Lewis Topographical Gazetteer – 1831"
"WOODSTONE, a parish in the hundred of NORMAN CROSS, county of Huntingdon, ¾ mile (SW by W) from Peterborough containing 149 Inhabitants.

The living is a Rectory, in the archdeaconry of Huntingdon, and diocese of Lincoln, rated in the Kings books at £7.11s.3d, and in the patronage of John Bevis Esq.

The Church is dedicated to St Augustine. John and Mary Walsham, in 1728, gave certain land for the establishment of a school and other charitable purposes"

According to statistics in the parish records on 20th May 1821 the population of Woodstone was 149, there being 72 males and 77 females.

William Dean was an overseer at that time.

Ten years later on 30th May 1831 the population totalled 243. There were 111 males and 132 females, these were spread over fifty one families who lived in the forty eight homes in Woodstone. William Dean was then described as the local churchwarden.

By 1894 the Parish of Woodstone was divided into Woodstone Rural which consisted of 984 acres and Woodstone Urban which covered 70 acres. By 1905 Woodstone Rural became part of Old Fletton Urban District until 1938 when it was once again known as Woodston.

1841

At the time of the 1841 census Woodstone comprised of the Lodges inhabited by the farmers Dean, Smith and Jones and covered the area between the first houses which stood next to the 'Cherry Tree' public house right through to the lodge of William Jones.

The other farmers were William Dean, Samuel Smith, Richard Jones and John Cottingham. All but John Cottingham employed male and female servants who lived at their place of work.

Farming was the principal occupation with thirty males working as agricultural labourers from a total of fifty eight households in the whole of Woodstone. Ages ranged from fifteen to seventy five.

TURNPIKE END

Turnpike End (Oundle Road) was the main road through the village. Turnpike stands for a barrier or gate across the road, usually a main road, where a toll is collected. The Old Toll House was on the outskirts of Woodstone approximately half way between the Cross Keys public house at Woodstone Hill and the Gordon Arms public house in Orton Longueville. There were around twenty six families along the Woodstone section of Turnpike End. The majority of the heads of these households were employed as agricultural labourers apart from James Desbrow who was a publican and timber merchant at the Boys Head, Herbert Ashley a shoemaker, William Hill a butcher, John Grey a gardener and Caroline Fox a governess.

Thomas Coulson an agricultural labourer was born in Thurning, his wife Elizabeth was born in Alwalton. They had a four month old son William.

James Desbrow, the publican at the Boys Head Inn, lived there with his wife Mary and their sons Richard and John.
On 27th April 1843 Richard, a carpenter, married Mary Ann Cox at St Augustine's church. They both lived in Woodstone at the time of their marriage, Mary worked as a servant. Her father Thomas was a carpenter.

THE DRAGE FAMILY

The Drage family had lived in Woodstone from around the 1700's. Samuel Drage was born in 1763 and he married Sarah Wright in the 1780's. Their children were William, Thomas, Samuel, Elizabeth, John, Simon, Mary and David and were all baptised at St Augustine's church.

William Drage married Hannah Parkinson on 25th November 1816 at St Augustine's church. The witnesses were Godfrey Parkinson and Elizabeth Drage.
In 1841 William and Hannah lived along the Turnpike End with their two children. William was born in 1826 and Mary born in 1827.

The following details were told to me by Eileen de Ville who is the great great granddaughter of Thomas and Ann Drage.

Thomas Drage married Eleanor Lambley on 2nd August 1818 at Grantham. They made their home at Pickworth in Lincolnshire and had two children. Sarah was christened on 21 October 1823 but died a year later and was buried on 8th November 1824. John was christened on 20th March 1826 but he died and was buried on 17th March 1831.

Eleanor died and was buried in November 1828 aged thirty two.

Thomas remarried on 13th October 1829 to Ann Hollingworth at Pickworth where he had lived for many years. They had nine children who were all christened at Pickworth. Their first daughter was called Alphage, she was born in 1830. Their other children were Sarah born in 1831, Lucy in 1833, Ann in 1836 Thomas in 1838, William in 1843, John in 1844, Harriett in 1846 and Eliza in 1849.

Three generations from left to right Harriett (nee Drage) Naylor, Constance Brayshaw granddaughter of Harriett and Ann Elizabeth (Lizzie) daughter of Harriett.

Elizabeth Drage married William Trenton on 5th November 1821 at St Augustine's church.

Samuel Drage (senior) died in 1826 and was buried on 26th September of that year.

Mary Drage married William Phillips on 12th December 1827 at St Augustine's church. William was born in Glatton and worked as an agricultural labourer. They lived along the Turnpike End with their five children. William was born in 1829, Henry in 1833, Mary in 1836, Johnson in 1839 and George was born in 1840.

Samuel Drage married Susannah Bellamy after their banns were read in April 1834. Susannah came from Connington. They lived along Water End with their two year old daughter called Mary. Living next door was Samuel's widowed mother Sarah and his brother Simon Drage. Simon was an agricultural labourer.

John Wood, born in Woodstone around 1766, lived along the Turnpike End with his wife Ann.
Next door lived Thomas Wood an agricultural labourer, Elizabeth his wife and their son William who was seven. Thomas was born about 1806.

John Palmer, an agricultural labourer, and his wife Ann lived further along with their children John and Richard (twins) aged two and Alice who was one year old.

Next to the Palmer family lived Robert Ashley, a shoemaker, and his wife Mary with their children Mary and William.

William Hill, a butcher, and his wife Susannah lived in the next cottage with their children Peter aged fourteen and William aged seven.

Loammi Barratt lived about three houses along from the Hill family with his daughter Jane and son James. Loammi, a widower, married Susannah Wright, also a widow, on 26th June 1842 in St Augustine's church. At the time of their marriage Loammi was described as a 'Yeoman' and Susannah was described as a widow of a Yeoman.
On the 1st November 1842 also in St Augustine's church Loammi's daughter Jane married Joseph Barr a cattle dealer.
Loammi died during 1850 and Susannah died during 1855.

In the next cottage lived John Grey, a gardener, and his wife Ann.

Mary Ireland aged eighty five shared her home with Juliana Ireland aged thirty five. Lois Arber was their female servant.

The following families lived next to one another;

William and Maria Fox with their children Thomas aged ten, William nine, Ann six and Charles five years old. William and Maria had two servants working for them, Fanney Tiplen and Anne Guildford who were both twenty years old. Sybulli Lendon also twenty lived with the family and was shown on the census as being independent.

William Whitsed was also shown as being independent and lived with his wife Sarah and their family. Jarvis was fifteen, William thirteen, Leonora twelve, Adlenia ten, John nine, Augustus eighteen months and Sarah was five months old. Caroline Fox aged twenty was employed as their governess, Samuel Hunt aged twenty was a male servant, Jane Withers aged twenty five, Maria Withers fifteen and Mary Buswell fifteen were all female servants.

William and Mary Wright had four daughters Sarah aged seven, Amey five, Mary three and Eliza one year old. William was an agricultural labourer.

Richard and Mary Pentlow had two children Charles aged twenty and daughter Emma aged eight. Richard was also an agricultural labourer.

James Short was an agricultural labourer and lived with his wife Charlotte.

Richard Palmer, an agricultural labourer, and his wife Sarah had two sons. William was fifteen and Richard was nine. Mary Pettifer a widow aged seventy also lived with them.

William Burnham, an agricultural labourer and his wife Martha had four sons. George born in 1826 Reuben in 1827 Isaac in 1829 and Levi in 1830, all were born in Woodstone. Also living with them was Elizabeth Henry aged sixty.

Martha died in 1845 aged and William died in 1848.

The last family recorded along Turnpike End was Ann Ward, a widow, and her nine year old son Joseph.

Even though the Rectory is recorded as being dated c.1700 there was no reference to it on the 1841 census. The Rectory was extended in both height and size during the 19th Century.

WATER END

Water End, later known as Wharf Road, turned off from Turnpike End and wound its way down to the river. There were twenty eight households down Water End.

Twelve men were employed as agricultural labourers. Other occupations were
John Jarvis a cooper (maker or repairer of casks or pails), Charles Wright a carpenter, Robert Whyman a bone dealer, John Newton a blacksmith, Henry Fuller a coal dealer and porter, William Hemment a waterman and John King was a farmer.
Some of the families living along Water End were;

William Pacey, a journeyman, lived with his wife Sarah and their children Elizabeth nine, Sarah six and Susannah three years.

William Phillips married Martha Sharwood on 10th November 1825. Martha died not long after her marriage. William, a widower, remarried at the beginning of 1828 after banns were read in Woodstone Church during November and December 1827. His new bride Mary Drage was the daughter of Samuel and Sarah Drage from Woodstone. Their children were William born in 1828, Henry in 1832, Johnson in 1834, Mary in 1836, and George in 1840. At the time of the 1841 census William was an agricultural labourer.

Further along Water End lived Richard Weston, an agricultural labourer and his wife Lucy with their son George who was two years old. Richard was the son of William and Elizabeth Weston. Lucy was born at Burley in Rutland.

William Parkinson from Ailsworth married Elizabeth Barrett on 6th July 1823 their daughter Maria was born around 1826. Elizabeth died and was buried in Woodstone churchyard on 25th January 1832 aged forty five. In 1834 William married Olive Craythorn who was also a widow after the banns had been read during July. Olive came from Warmington. They had a son Charles. Olive also died as William was shown as a widower of the parish of Woodstone when he married Jane Pentlow on 11th March 1835 at St Augustine's church. Their witnesses were George and Harriet Weston.
By 1841 William and Jane were living along Water End with their children. Maria was fifteen, Charles was six, Thomas was four and John was two years old. William worked as an agricultural labourer.

John Wood, an agricultural labourer lived with his wife Priscilla and their five children. The oldest was Sarah aged eleven, then Elizabeth ten, James eight, William four and John one year old. All the children were born in Woodstone as well as their parents, John around 1801 and Priscilla around 1806

Elizabeth Weston was sixty five and lived with her son George who was twenty five but was not shown as having an occupation. Elizabeth married William Weston after their banns were read in November 1808 at St Augustine's church. It is recorded in the parish registers that they had two children baptised, Ann on 1st October 1809 and Richard on 29th December 1811. William Weston was baptised at St Augustine's church on 7th December 1785 and was the son of Richard and Ann (nee Bird). Ann came from Whittlesea and married Richard after banns were read during November 1784.

John Jarvis married Harriet Weston in Woodstone after their banns were read in January 1839. They had a daughter Anne who was one year old.

Charles Wright, a carpenter, and his wife Elizabeth lived next to John Jarvis, with their four children. Emma was eleven, Charles nine, Matilda five and Ellen was two years old.

Robert Whyman was a bone dealer and lived with his wife Susannah and their children. William aged thirty, George twenty, Susannah six and Sarah four years old.

Henry Fuller was a porter and lived with his wife Sarah and their family. William was fifteen, Henry twelve, John ten, Mary eight, Sarah and Samuel six, Charlotte four and George was two years old.

Eliza Pentlow, aged fifteen, lived with Thomas and Susannah Pridmore. Her parents were Richard and Mary Pentlow. On the 15th December 1846 Eliza married William Ashberry at St Augustine's church Woodstone. William was a boatman and Eliza a dressmaker. That was a very short marriage as William died not long after. On 5th August 1850 Eliza Ashberry, a widow, married

Joseph Wallis, a railway porter. Eliza still continued with the dressmaking.

Sarah Hemment was only forty five and recorded as being a widow at the time of the census. Sarah, nee Wood, was born in Woodstone and married William Hemment on 10th November 1819 at Woodstone church. William died 7th January 1841 aged forty five and was buried in St Augustine's churchyard. Their children were Sarah seventeen, William twenty and John fifteen years old, they lived along Water End. They were all born in Woodstone.

There were eighteen servants who lived at their place of work in the village. Ten of them were fifteen years of age so this was possibly their first job from leaving school.

Thirteen people were recorded as living by 'independent means' and one person as a 'pauper'

There were sixty nine children up to the age of ten and thirty two between the ages of eleven to seventeen. Generally by the age of fifteen they would be in full time work.

The oldest residents all aged seventy five were Benjamin Freeman, John Wilson, Frances Afford, John Wood and Jane Speechley from Turnpike End, and Mary Sharman from Water End.

The population of Woodstone was 260 which included 142 males and 118 females. Just over half of the total population were born locally in the County of Huntingdonshire.

1851

Over the next ten years the population increased to 380, there being 188 males and 192 females. This included seventy four children up to the age of ten and fifty one between the ages of eleven and seventeen.

A change of occupations came along when Peterborough became linked with the railways in the 1850's. Nineteen men and boys were employed by the railway company and twenty eight were either agricultural labourers or farm labourers.

Other occupations unlike those of ten years ago included wool merchant – baker - dressmaker - malster (a malt maker) – woodman – laundress – nurse – boatman - bricklayer – coachman – plasterer - hurdle maker - building surveyor - mortgagee - solicitors general clerk - cordwainer (a shoe maker).

NORTH STREET

North Street, previously known as Water End, consisted of thirty nine houses. Two of which were uninhabited at the time of the census.

Sarah Hemment was the innkeeper of the Ferry Boat. Also living there with Sarah was Alice, her daughter in law, whose husband William was a coal merchant, and their two children Sarah who was four and Alice one year old.

Not far from Sarah lived her son John Wood Hemment. He was twenty eight, and a widower. Living with him were his three sons George aged four, Leyton John aged three and Alfred one year old. John's Aunt Elizabeth Richardson was his housekeeper.

When a young person married they often lived next door to their parents, families seemed to stay close together, in particular the Hemment, Pridmore, Drage, Wood and the Weston families.

Thomas Pridmore (senior) and his wife Susan lived not far from the Hemment family. Susan was a school mistress and she lived very near to the school. Also living with them was their daughter-in-law Eliza and three year old granddaughter Eliza. Eliza was the wife of their son Thomas who was a coachman at Woodstone House.

In the next house was Sarah Pridmore who at seventy one was described as a pauper. Sarah Ireson, daughter to Sarah, was living with her mother. Sarah married William Ireson at the end of the year in 1840. William was not shown as being at home at the time of the census.

(*Sarah married John Pridmore, at the time their children were baptised their surname was spelt PRIDGMORE. John and Sarah's children were Elizabeth, William, Mary Ann, Alice, John, Sarah and James.*

Elizabeth married Isaac Goodwin on 14th November 1831 at St Augustine's church. One of their daughter's was Emma, shown in photograph, who married George Slote on 12th November 1862 at Yaxley parish church. George and Emma Slote were my great grandparents which makes John and Sarah Pridmore my Great great great grandparents).

Sarah Drage, born in Woodstone, was the oldest resident aged eighty five years. She lived in North Street, with her son Simon and granddaughter Mary aged twelve. Mary was the daughter of her son Samuel and daughter in law Susannah. Sarah was recorded on the census as being a baker. She died in Woodstone on 19th March 1858 aged ninety. Priscilla Wood was present at her death.

Samuel Drage was shown on the census as being a Chelsea pensioner aged fifty six and lived next door to his mother Sarah. Susannah his wife died in 1842. She gave birth to their son who they named James in October 1842 but sadly he died in November 1842. Living as lodgers with Samuel were John Mercey, a railway policeman, and his wife Katherine.

John Darker was the local tailor he lived with his wife Mary Ann and their four children. Watkin Owen aged nineteen who was also a tailor, Caroline Emma aged eleven. Adelaide Ann aged nine and Louisa Matilda aged seven all attended school.

The Drage Family

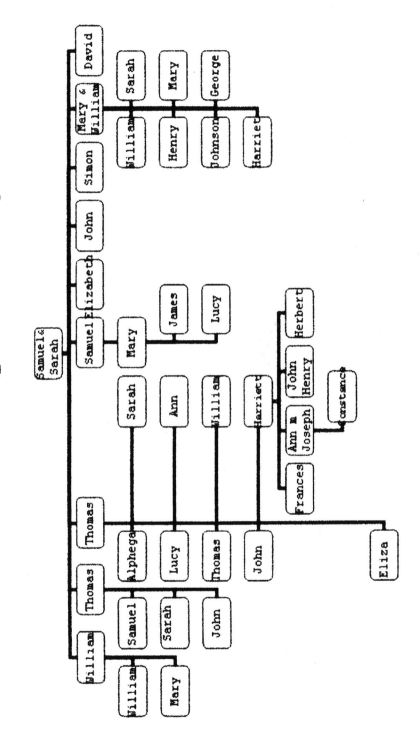

John Wood and his wife Priscilla possibly lived in the same house as at the time of the 1841 census. John by this time had changed his occupation to a butcher. Their oldest children Sarah, Elizabeth and James were not shown as living with the family, but William, John and George still lived at home. William was a butcher's boy who probably worked with his father.

Their daughter Sarah married Henry Hoare on 20th October 1851 at St Augustine's church. John, her father, was shown on her marriage certificate as being a parish clerk. Henry worked as a stoker and Sarah was a servant.

Another of John and Priscilla's daughter Elizabeth married Stephen Brown on 26th December 1854 at St Augustine's church. At the time of her marriage Elizabeth was a dressmaker, and Stephen was an engine driver.

Next to John and Priscilla Wood lived William and Jane Parkinson and five of their children. Charles, Thomas and John all worked as agricultural labourers. Eliza aged eight and Richard aged three attended school.

Joseph Bland was shown on the census as a farming man and lived with his sister Charlotte who worked as a housekeeper. William Phillips, son of William and Mary, lodged with Joseph and Charlotte and worked as an agricultural labourer.

Richard Weston was born in Woodstone in 1812 and the son of Elizabeth. He married Lucy and they lived with their son George Canner Weston who was born in 1839 at March in Cambridgeshire.

Sarah Holding was a servant to George Whyman, an agricultural labourer, who lived in North Street. Sarah had three young children to provide for. They all lived in George's home at the time of the 1851 census.

Unfortunately things must have become too much for Sarah as on Saturday June 22nd 1855 a report was printed in 'The Peterborough Weekly News and Advertiser' which stated:-

"Sarah Holding was charged by Mr Samuel Charles Watson Buckle, Clerk to the Guardians of the Peterborough Union, with having, on the 21st instant, at Woodstone, ran away and left her four illegitimate children chargeable to the said union.

The defendant made no answer to the charge, and was committed to hard labour, at Huntingdon, for two calendar months"

George married Elizabeth Holden in 1843 at Woodstone. Elizabeth died after only being married for a few years.

On 7th February 1860 George married Susannah Smith at Woodstone church. Susannah's parents were Edward and Mary Smith who lived two houses away from George Whyman at the time of the 1851 census although Susannah was not shown as being at home at that time. George's parents were Robert and Susannah Whyman from Woodstone. Robert was a bone dealer. George had two brothers William and Charles and two sisters, Susannah and Sarah.

Joseph Wood aged twenty five was lodging with James and Charlotte Short. Joseph was born in Woodstone and was a railway engine fireman.

Ann Wood, by now seventy five years of age, was a widow and lived along Church Street as a charwoman for William Speechley.

William Phillips, a farm labourer, and his wife Mary lived with four of their children. Sarah was a laundress, Johnson a farm labourer, Mary aged fourteen and George aged ten attended school.

Their daughter Sarah married Joseph Bland on 24th December 1851 at St Augustine's church. Joseph lived a few doors away during the 1851 census. By the time of the 1861 census they were living at Farcet.

A report in 'The Peterborough Weekly News and Advertiser' dated Saturday 9th February 1856 read:-

"Married on Sunday last, at the General Baptist Chapel, (by the Reverend T Barrass) Mr Thomas Webb, foreman to Wm Lawrence Esq., Fletton Towers, to Mary, the youngest daughter of Mr William Phillips of Woodstone".

Two houses away from William and Mary Phillips lived William Pacey a bricklayer/ journeyman, and his wife Sarah. They had two daughters Elizabeth and Susan (baptised as Susannah).

Further along North Street lived George and Elizabeth Weston. They married during 1845 in the district of Peterborough and had two children, John born in 1846 and Ann born in 1847. George was born in Woodstone in 1814 and probably brother to Richard who lived a few houses away.

CHURCH STREET

Church Street was previously known as Turnpike End. There were twenty two houses along Church Street including the Rectory and the Boys Head Inn.

A Terrace, which consisted of seven cottages, had been built around the 1840's which were named Nene Voir Place (92 to 104 Oundle Road). These houses were not recorded clearly on the 1851 census but were recognised by 1861. They were built of brick and had slated roofs that were once described as 'very plain industrial housing'. There was probably a view of the river when Woodstone was surrounded by fields.

By 1851 Thomas and Elizabeth Coleson (Coulson) lived in the same area but it had been renamed from Turnpike End to Church Street. Their son William was ten years old and a scholar. Thomas' brother James was also living with them.

Robert Chamberlain was the Curate of Woodstone and lived with his children, Eliza eight and Thomas five, at the rectory. Robert was born in Leicestershire and was living at Hinckley with his wife Eliza at the time of the 1841 census. By 1851 Robert was a widow. There were three servants who also lived at the rectory to help with the running of the household, Ann May was the cook, Charlotte Payne was the housemaid (who was also their servant during 1841) and Jacob Walker was their house servant. Mary Ann Larkin, born in Sussex, was Robert's aunt–in–law and was the housekeeper.

James Desbrow continued as the innkeeper at the Boys Head. His wife Mary died on 5th December 1849, aged 71, and was buried in St Augustine's churchyard. Living with James was his son John and wife Susannah who married in the district of Peterborough during 1850. They had a young daughter called Elizabeth who was only a few weeks old.

James Desbrow aged twelve lived with his grandparents and worked as a tailor's apprentice. Mary Dexter from Eye was a nurse who lived with the family. John Stanger and William Crowson lodged at the Boys Head.

James Desbrow (senior) died in January 1854 aged 75. He was buried next to his late wife in St Augustine's churchyard.

Thomas Core, a coal merchant's agent, lived at the Manor House with his wife and family. William their son worked as a rail station clerk, his sisters Mary and Sarah attended school. The Manor House was built in the late 17th century. The northern front had bay windows to the ground floor, the upper windows once had stone mullions but later these were removed. Originally the house had two large rooms with a central chimneystack. There was a small wing at the back where the staircase and entrance hall would have been.

Thomas Pridmore, Elizabeth Weston and Mary Ann Pearce were all servants living at Woodstone House. Thomas, a coachman, was born in Woodstone around 1823 and the son of Thomas and Susanna (shown as Susan on the census). Eliza his wife was living with Thomas' parents in North Street. Elizabeth Weston, a widow of the late William Weston, worked as a laundress. Mary Pearce was a housemaid. The building was a cottage, east of the Manor House, which had two storeys. The building, which had a date stone showing 1700, had been altered over the years. Occasionally the cottage was known as the Coach House or Farm cottage in various census recordings.

This was where David Clark of Woodstone spent his childhood. He remembers a spinney where he enjoyed climbing the trees, one of which was the Sycamore which is still there. A Mulberry tree still stands in the grounds which have been converted and renamed Earl Spencer Court.

ORTON ROAD

Included on the census as part of Woodstone was Orton Road on which stood six homes and the Cross Keys public house.

Charles Watts was a carpenter who employed three men. He married Susannah Harris in the district of Peterborough during 1842. Susannah died around 1849 leaving Charles a widower. In 1851 he was a publican and lived at the Cross Keys inn with his son Charles, a carpenter's apprentice, and his brother William a labourer. Bridget Harris, mother to his late wife, worked as the housekeeper. Charles Wright, a carpenter from Norfolk, lodged with the family.

John and Harriett Jarvis had moved from Water End to Orton Road. Anne, their oldest child was eleven. They had two more children, Frances eight and Susannah three years old, all attended school. William Turner a carpenter from Dogsthorpe lodged with the family.

George Burnham, son of William and Martha, married Mary Taylor in the Peterborough district during 1849. By 1851 they were living along the Orton Road with their seven month old daughter Martha.

George's brothers, Levi and Isaac were coal dealers lodging with local families. Isaac was living with Richard and Sarah Palmer who lived along North Street. Levi was next door with James and Charlotte Short.

Another of George's brothers was Reuben who married Jane Briggs on 12th June 1851 at St Augustine's church. Jane was a servant and the daughter of John Briggs who was a farmer.

Isaac married Mary Dexter at the beginning of 1852 in Peterborough.

LONDON ROAD

Robert and Elizabeth Gollings lived at the Brick Yards along London Road. Robert was a brick and tile maker. They had six children, Ambrose, William, Joseph, John, Charlotte and Frederick. Robert employed Eliza Goodyer from Stanground as their house servant. James Barnes and William Freeman both lodged with the family and were labourers.

Thomas Rowell was a farmer who lived at Rowell's Lodge (previously known as Smiths Lodge) with his sister Harriet. Nathaniel Palmer from Longthorpe was employed as a farm labourer. Thomas' farm consisted of 110 acres and he employed five labourers.

John Cottingham, an agricultural labourer, lived in the next lodge, formerly known as Lodge Cottages. Mary his wife was recorded as doing field work as were their daughters Ann and Emma. Their sons Stephen and John were agricultural labourers.

Richard and Lucy Jones lived at Jones Lodge, his farm was 280 acres and he employed eight labourers. Their son Richard who lived at home was also a farmer and owned a farm of 60 acres, he employed two labourers. Three servants were employed by the Jones family, Jane Sharpe from Werrington and Sarah Chamberlain from Yaxley were both house servants and George Lambert also from Yaxley was a farm labourer.

A report in 'The Peterborough Advertiser' dated July 1st 1854
"New Fletton – We congratulate our Fletton and Woodstone friends on the effort they are making for the purpose of building British Schools upon land given by Earl Fitzwilliam. We understand the subscriptions, which are liberal, are nearly completed. The works are likely to commence forthwith, as the Schools are promised to be opened by the autumn of this year",

Another report dated September 1854:-
"8 Albion Terrace Woodstone
Miss Smith having established a School for the Instruction of children from 3 to 12 years of age, embraces the present opportunity of informing Parents and Guardians that all children

entrusted to her care shall receive that attention which shall be most beneficial to them,

Terms 6 shillings   9 shillings   and 12 shillings per Quarter"

<u>A report dated Saturday May 26th 1855 stated</u>:-

"S Searson, Butcher, (late of Peterborough) begs to thank his friends for all their favours, and to apprize them that he is now carrying on the same trade at

No.8 Albion Terrace, New Fletton, where all orders will be thankfully received and punctually attended to."

Note the change from Woodstone to New Fletton.

1861

Moving on, to the time of the 1861 census, Woodstone's population had decreased to 345. This included 167 males and 178 females.

There were sixty eight children who went to school between the ages of three to fourteen. One boy, aged sixteen, was listed as a scholar. Generally from the age of twelve boys would be taken on as labourers whereas girls would still be attending school up to the age of fourteen. One boy was employed as an errand boy and another boy as a foot boy.

Thirty children living in Woodstone did not attend school. The majority of these were from the ages of a few months through to three years, for some reason two children of five and six did not attend school.

WOODSTONE ROAD

Another change in street name once known as Church Street then became Woodstone Road.

William Phillips (junior) married Charlotte Bland during the winter of 1852 at Thrapstone and by 1861 they lived along the Woodstone Road, William worked as a real cartman. John Bland their nephew was also living with them, he was a book keeper.

Thomas and Elizabeth Coulson were shown as living in the house next to 1 Nene Voir Place. Thomas was a farm labourer and William worked as a fireman with the railways.

Further along lived Reuben Turner and his wife Sarah and young family. Reuben was a homeopathic chemist.

A few houses away lived William Robinson and his wife Mary. William was a solicitor (not practising).

Thomas Grey lived at the Parsonage as 'temporary charge of the house'. He was a widower, born in Leicestershire, and his occupation was shown as a butcher and gardener

James Desbrow was shown as an innkeeper and timber merchant who continued to live at the Boys Head Inn with his family.

WATER END ROAD

North Street reverted back to being called Water End Road where there were forty three households.
The village school was also the home of Thomas Pridmore, an agricultural labourer, and his wife Susan who was the schoolmistress. Next door to them lived Sarah Pridmore a widow who carried out the duties of a parochial relief.

Jane Parkinson married John Ford at the beginning of the year in 1861. John Ford was an agricultural labourer and Jane was a char woman. Jane's first husband was William Parkinson who died during 1859. The census recorded the following children John, Eliza, Robert and Richard Parkinson as sons and daughter in law to John Ford. Jane had been living along Water End with William, her late husband, before he died

Along Water End Road were a row of nine houses named Orchard Terrace.
In one of these John Darker and his wife Mary Ann continued to live with their family. John was a tailor, his two daughters followed in his footsteps, Adelaide was a seamstress and Louisa was a milliner and dressmaker. On 1st March 1864 Louisa married William Carter at St Augustine's church.
On 23rd April 1867 Charles Edward Crawley, a whipmaker, married Adelaide Darker at St Augustine's church. Charles' father was William a whipmaker. Adelaide's father, John, died February 1867 aged sixty seven, her mother Mary Ann died March 1870

aged sixty five. They were both buried in St Augustine's churchyard.

Next to John Darker and his family lived Samuel Drage and his daughter Mary. On 9th August 1868 Mary married Charles William Bellshaw at St Augustine's church.

Thomas Pickering was also a tailor who lived with his wife Mary and their three children, Eliza (Ann Elizabeth) baptised as Eliza Elizabeth Pentlow Pickering born 1853, Emma Dashwood Mary baptised Emma Gertrude Mary born 1855 and Herbert Hugh Charles born 1856. Thomas and Mary married at St Augustine's church on 19th September 1852. Mary was born in Woodstone and the daughter of Richard Pentlow. Thomas was the son of John and Rebecca Pickering who lived in Thorney during 1841 where John was a tailor.

Another family living in Orchard Terrace was John Wood and his wife Priscilla. John was sixty two and a retired butcher. George their youngest son aged nineteen was still living at home, he was a parish clerk. On 20th May 1867 George whose occupation had changed to a fireman married Caroline Crawley who was born in Stanground. Caroline's father was Robert whose occupation was a glover.

Sarah Hoare lived at number eight with her very young family. They were Sarah aged six, Henry aged four, Mary Elizabeth aged three and Laura aged two. Sarah did the occasional dressmaking, probably to bring some money into the home to help support her family. Times must have been very difficult for Sarah as her husband Henry died on 22nd December 1858 aged twenty seven. He was buried in the churchyard at St Augustine's. Elizabeth Richardson, a retired housekeeper and born in Woodstone, was boarding with Sarah and her family. The 1851 census showed Elizabeth as aunt to John Hemment.

Sarah Hemment continued as the innkeeper at the public house along Water End. Her son William a coal merchant married Dorothy Alice Sismey during 1845 in the Oundle district. William and Dorothy lived with Sarah with their five children. Sarah born in 1847, Alice in 1850, William Thomas in 1851, Harriet in 1855 and Fanny in 1867 all were born in Woodstone. Sarah senior died 16th November 1868 aged seventy two and was buried in St Augustine's churchyard with her late husband William.

Edmund Richardson, a shepherd, and his wife Elizabeth lived with their daughter Jane who was twenty nine years old.

Next to them lived Peter and Mary Ann Parkins and their new born daughter Ann. Peter married Mary Ann Richardson on 10th February 1861 at St Augustine's church, at that time Peter was a labourer. He was the son of Thomas and Sarah Parkins who lived at Cardington in Bedfordshire where Peter was born. Mary Ann was the daughter of Edmund and Elizabeth Richardson who also lived at Cardington in Bedfordshire where Mary was born.

Richard Weston, a coachman, and his wife Lucy continued to live along Water End. Their son George Canner, a carpenter and joiner, was also living with them with his young wife Annie, who worked as a dressmaker. Annie was born in Ramsey.

John and Harriet Jarvis had moved back to Water End. Susan, their thirteen year old daughter, attended school. Another daughter Ann married John McDonald in 1860. John was born in Scotland and worked as a gardener. Ann and John had a ten month old daughter Fanny and they lived with Ann's parents.
Elizabeth Weston, aged eighty two, was the oldest resident of Woodstone. She was a widow and lived as a boarder with John and Harriet Jarvis. In 1841 Elizabeth lived with her son George, just a few doors away from the Jarvis family.

TURNPIKE ROAD

Shown on the census along the Turnpike Road between the Parsonage and the Boys Head Inn lived George Burnham and his wife Mary. They possibly lived on the opposite side of the road as there were no houses between the parsonage and public inn. George and Mary had five children, Martha was born 1851, Robert born 1852, Ann Elizabeth born 1854, George born 1858 and Mary who was six months old.

William Drage and his wife Hannah both aged seventy lived along the Turnpike Road

Reuben and Jane Burnham lived not far from his brother George. Reuben, an agricultural labourer, and Jane had four children who were William born 1852 James born 1854 Ellen born 1856 and John born in 1858 all were born in Woodstone.

James Ley Row was a wool merchant, born in Lincolnshire, and lived at Woodstone House with his wife Harriet and their five children who were Alice, James, Laura, Emma and Harriet aged between eleven and two years. James and Harriet (nee Dean) married in 1849 in the Peterborough district. All the children were born at Wansford. Ann North was their governess, Emma Palmer was their cook and Ann Parkes was the housemaid. Caroline Crawley was the kitchen maid, until she married George Wood and started their family. May Russell was the Head Nurse with Lucy Ford as her under nurse. John William Sutcliffe, born in Woodstone around 1846, was a stables manservant.

Living in the cottages near to Woodstone House was Thomas and Ann Parkinson, Thomas was a carter, and born in Woodstone, his parents were William and Jane. Ann was the daughter of John and Mary Chambers from Orton Waterville.

In the other cottage lived Alice Worraker and her son George who was a groom.

The Cross Keys Inn was along Turnpike Road; Charles Watts was recorded as being the publican and a builder. He re-married in 1851 to Elizabeth Farey, they had a daughter Elizabeth in 1855. Charles and Elizabeth had taken in two lodgers William Newton a bricklayer and William Hextell a masons labourer.

Not far from the Cross Keys were the nursery gardens where John Bruce lived with his wife Ann and children Mary Ann and John whose full name was John James MacDonald Bruce. John (senior) was born in Scotland and was a master gardener who employed three servants. Ann his wife was born in Orton Longueville.
George Clipson was a journeyman gardener, Everitt Desborough was a garden labourer and Sarah Sprigins was a general servant.

Further along Turnpike Road were four families employed as brick makers, bricklayers and agricultural labourers.
David and Sarah Greenwood both aged twenty seven from Ramsey and Haddon respectively. David was a brick maker.
William and Susannah Lambert lived in the next cottage with their son Joseph who was born in Haddon and worked as a bricklayer like his father. William was born in Orton Waterville and Susannah in Longthorpe.
William Palmer, an agricultural labourer born in Peterborough, and his wife Mary who was born in Fletton
John Cole was also an agricultural labourer and lived with his daughters Hannah and Rachael. John was a widower.

STILTON ROAD
Moving on to Deans Lodge on the Stilton Road lived Martha Whyman and her two servants. Elizabeth Benstead from Peterborough was twenty three and worked as a house servant, Thomas Bew from Sutton was sixteen and was a general servant.
Samuel Sutcliffe an agricultural labourer lived at Deans Cottage with his wife Mary Ann.
The next household was Brick Kilns where Robert Gollings, a brick manufacturer, lived with his wife Elizabeth and eight of their children. Joseph, John, Elizabeth, Frederick, Henry, Mary, Sarah

and Emma, all were at school except Emma who was only two years old.

Thomas Rowell was a farmer; he employed four men and two boys and lived at Smiths Lodge with his wife Helen and their five children. They married during 1853 in the Peterborough district. Also living at Smiths Lodge as servants were Charles Smith a horse keeper and Fanny Mellor a maid of all work. Helen Rowell died in 1869 her burial place is unknown.

Moving further along were Jones Cottages where John Cottingham, a shepherd, and his wife Mary lived with their daughter Emma.

In the other cottage was Henry Barber, a horse keeper, with his wife Elizabeth and their three children William aged six, Amelia three and Thomas one year old.

Not far from them in Jones' Lodge lived Richard Jones, a widower, and his two sons Richard and William. Richard was a farmer of 340 acres of land and employed eight men and five boys. Three servants also lived at the Lodge. Mary Flanders born in Sawtry was a house maid; Mary Glithero the dairy maid and Henry Bellamy was the milk boy. Both Mary Glithero and Henry Bellamy were born in Yaxley.

Whilst workmen were excavating for a new roadway in 1866 they uncovered an Anglo Saxon graveyard. They found skeletons and various artefacts. This site became Palmerstone Road named after Lord Palmerstone who died in 1865.

A total of seven houses were erected, a plaque built into the brickwork shows
'B.J.K. Palmerstone Terrace 1869' the initials could be those of the builder. These houses are now numbered from 28 to 40.

1871

By the time of the 1871 census the population of Woodstone had doubled to 698. This was split between 351 males and 347 females. There were two hundred and thirty seven children between the ages of one month to eleven years. Seventy six of these were pre school age. There were twenty five youngsters between the ages of twelve and fourteen years.

The railways employed eighty of the residents from Woodstone. Apart from the occupations previously mentioned on earlier census' a change in employment was happening which included the following.

Stone Mason – Annuitant – Machinist – Attorney – Seamstress – Grocer - Commercial Traveller – Milliner – Leather Currier – Sales Woman – River Toll Collector – Sawsmith – Coppersmith – Stationers Assistant - Book Maker – Sawyer – Clerk in H.M. Court Peterborough – Police Officer - Solicitors Clerk – Cabinet Maker – Milkman – Dairymaid – Miller – Upholsterer.

OUNDLE ROAD

Along Oundle Road there were five cottages (evenly numbered from 72 to 80) before reaching the Palmerston Arms public house which was owned by William Parnell. James Rowell was the publican/gardener at the Palmerston Arms and he lived there with his wife Elizabeth and their four children Elizabeth twelve, Ann seven, Charles five and James eight months old.

Continuing west stands York Terrace which consists of four cottages, (numbered 84 to 90); next to them are a row of seven houses called Nene Voir Place.

Of all the residents in Nene Voir Place William Coulston was the only head of household who was born in Woodstone. William was the son of Thomas and Elizabeth Coulston. On 11th March 1862 he married Emma Palmer, daughter of Thomas Palmer. In 1861 Emma worked for James Ley Row at Woodstone House where she was their cook. By 1871 William had become a railway engine driver and lived with Emma and their children at 7 Nene View Place. John W. was eight, Elizabeth Ann was six, James was four, and Charles Henry was one year old. By 1881 they had moved to 81 Westwood Street in Peterborough and had two more children, Caroline was born in 1872 and Emily in 1875.

A short distance from the cottages was the Rectory where John Sansome lived with his wife Hannah and their eight year old son John. It was recorded that John was Rector of Bassingthorpe in Lincolnshire. Also living with the family were Thomas Sawer who was a domestic servant/gardener from Lincolnshire and Margaret

Butler aged twelve who was recorded as a temporary domestic servant who was born in Ireland.

James Ley Row, farmer and wool merchant, still lived at Woodstone House, his wife Harriett had passed away as the census showed John as a widower. Elizabeth, his sister, had come to live with the family as a housekeeper. James and Laura were the only two children remaining at home.

Their daughter Alice Dean Row, at the age of nineteen, married in Bath during 1869 to John Harvey Everitt who was born in Spalding.

Another of their daughters Emma Mawby Row married George Fitzroy Dean Gaches at St Augustine's church on 8th October 1873. George was a solicitor as was his father William. By 1881 William was also a Registrar at the Peterborough County Court and Judge of the Court of Pleas Ramsey.

Emma and George Gaches had two daughters and a son. Mary Ethel was born in 1874, Gertrude Frances in 1877 and Vernon Peed Gaches in 1880, sadly their father George died in the mid 1880s leaving Emma, aged only twenty four, to bring up her young family. At the time of the 1881 census they were living at Granville Street in Peterborough.

George and Mary Burnham continued to live in the same cottage. Their eldest daughter Martha was not shown as living at home by 1871. Robert aged eighteen worked as a railway engine cleaner. George aged twelve and Mary ten attended school as did their younger sister Emma who was born in 1865.

The Burnham Family

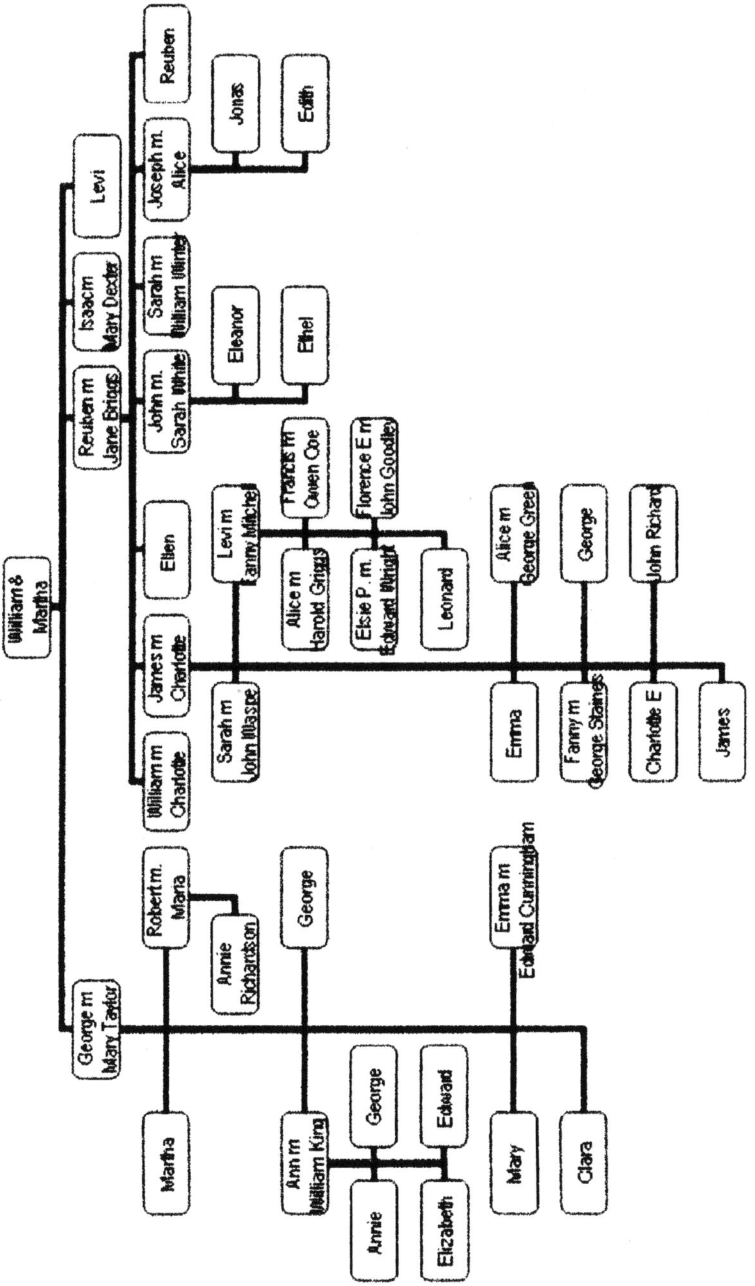

Ruth Cooper, a widow, was shown as an annuitant, she was born in Stanground around 1795. Janet Bigley aged thirteen and born in New Fletton was a domestic servant for Ruth.

Thomas Coulson, an agricultural labourer, and his wife Elizabeth lived next to Ruth Cooper.

At the next house to the Coulson family the census enumerator recorded 'Lodgers absent'.

PALMERSTON ROAD

For some reason it was decided in the 1870's to drop the 'E' and since then has been known as Palmerston Road. Out of the fifty four households in the road there were fifty six men and boys who worked for the railways.
Palmerston Road was quite small, it comprised of fifty four homes. These began from the Palmerston Arms which were numbered (1 and 3 which have been knocked down) 5 to 13 then 21 to 79. Also, on the other side of the road, from 2 to 46 approximately. Research has shown the building since named the Palmerston Arms began as a farm house.
There was a private school recorded as being in Palmerston Road during 1871.
At one time there was a group of twelve houses known as Demontford Terrace on the land where Demontfort Court was built.

Living at number 7 were George Ashling, a tailor, and his wife Mary with their family. Sarah was twenty two and worked as a tailoress, possibly for her father. Elizabeth was seventeen and her occupation was a pupil teacher. Charles was fifteen and worked as a stationers assistant and Ellen their youngest child aged eight attended school. In 1861 George and his family were living in Glinton.

Robert Landin, a bookmaker, and his wife Ann lived next to the Ashling family.

George English, a labourer in a coal yard, and his wife Frances lived with their children at number 10. George aged seventeen was a railway engine cleaner, Charles aged fifteen was a smiths labourer, James aged thirteen was a brickyard labourer, John aged ten and Alice eight attended school and the youngest was Emily aged two years.

At 12 Demontford Terrace was Phillip Henry Darker and his wife Louisa. Phillip was a railway clerk. Emma, their daughter, was fourteen and worked as a dressmaker's apprentice. William, their son was seven years old and attended school. In 1854 Phillip married Louisa Chadd in the Leicester district. Louisa was the daughter of William and Susannah who lived at Barleythorpe in Rutland.
By the time of the 1861 census Phillip and his family were living at 34 Richard Street in Leicester.

Not far from Demontford Terrace were a group of seven houses named Palmerston Terrace. Apart from John Lightfoot who was a woodman's labourer the other six head of the households living in the terrace worked for the railways. They included Joseph Boon, Thomas Beeby, Charles Upton, Joseph Kent, William Kitchen and George Kibbey. Joseph Boon was born in Peterborough but the other families moved to Woodstone from other counties

Some families who lived along Palmerston Road ran businesses in their homes.

William Smith kept a grocer/baker shop and lived there with his wife Annie and their two young children, John Thomas aged three and Magdalen two years old. It is probable that they lived at The Old Bakery which was later numbered 132

At the time of the 1861 census James and Mary Grice lived at Grove Street in New Fletton, they had six children between them. James married Mary Yates at the beginning of the year of 1859 in Leicestershire. Mary was the widow of John Yates. By 1871 James and Mary lived at South House which was also a grocers' shop where Mary was the shopkeeper. This would have been number 84 next to Demontford Terrace. Their children were James aged twenty seven born in Middlesex Hospital, and Mary aged nineteen born in New Fletton who were James children from his first marriage. Matthew aged eleven, Kezia aged nine, Robert aged eight, Joseph aged six, and Richard aged four were all born in New

Fletton. James Grice senior was a railway engine driver as was his son James. Also living with the family were John, Thomas and Mary Yates, these were children from Mary's first marriage. John Yates was a railway engine fireman and Thomas Yates was a railway goods clerk.

Samuel Jamson, a leather currier, lived in the grocers shop along Palmerston Road with his wife Jane and their six children. Samuel married Jane Marson in the Nottingham district during 1854. Their first son Frank was born a year later. They all came to Peterborough around 1857 when John was born. Their first daughter Elizabeth was born in 1859. At this time Samuel, Jane and family lived along Bread Street in New Fletton. Edward was born in 1864 and Hannah baptised Mary Hannah J was born in 1867. Later they had moved to Woodstone and Lucy was born in 1869.

Living in Woodstone Cottage, number 14, was Henry English and his wife Mary Ann. They married in 1870 in the Peterborough district. Henry was the clerk in H.M. Courts of Peterborough. Martha Allen also lived with and worked as their domestic servant. In 1861 when Henry was sixteen he lived with his parents Edward and Sarah English along Bridge Street in Peterborough, Edward was a bank clerk. At that time Henry was a solicitor's general clerk.

William and Ellen Piggott lived at number 28. William worked as a railway wagon inspector. They married during 1857 at Lewisham. Ellen was the daughter of Charles and Elizabeth Wright who lived along Water End in Woodstone where Ellen was born. William and Ellen had four children, Ellen Emma was born in 1859 and George in 1861 both born in New Fletton. Annie was born in 1867 and Lizzie in 1869 both born in Woodstone. During 1861 they lived along Bread Street in New Fletton.

By 1871 William and Charlotte Phillips were living at Vine Cottage, later known as 1 Palmerston Road.
Johnson Phillips, brother to William, married Elizabeth Wilson, from Fletton, on 26th May 1861 at St Augustine's Church. By 1871 they were living along Woodstone Hill with their children George Johnson aged nine, David aged seven, Ruth S five and Sarah Ellen eleven months.

Thomas Peter Webb was born in Glapthorne and worked as a coal and coke dealer. His wife Mary was born in Woodstone about 1837. They had two children, Charlotte aged five, and Arthur Thomas aged three months. Charlotte Warren lived in as a nursemaid, she was fourteen. Hannah Liquorice, born in Woodstone in 1818, was a boarder and worked as a laundress.

Edward Filby Oswick, a railway porter, and his wife Jane lived not far from the Webb family. Their children were Oliver George three years and Arthur Filby two years old. Two young men who worked on the railway were lodging with the Oswick family.

Charles Crawley, a whipmaker, and Adelaide his wife were living at Aboyne Lodge (167). They had a daughter Ellen Elizabeth aged three and John William aged one.

STILTON ROAD/LONDON ROAD
William Whyman, a farmer of 230 acres, lived with his wife Mary and daughters Isabella aged thirteen and Mary aged ten at Westbrook House. He employed five labourers, a boy and a domestic housemaid.
In 1861 William and his family lived at Fletton Lodge where William was a farmer of 600 acres.

There seemed to be another Woodstone Cottage where William Nichols, Mary his wife and their young son George aged eleven months lived. William was a commercial traveller in the beer trade. He employed Elizabeth Laxton as a domestic servant.

In the next cottage lived John Brown, a shepherd, his wife Mary and their son John aged twenty one who was a labourer.

Robert Gollings, recorded as a master brick maker, still lived in the cottage called Brick Yard with Elizabeth his wife. Their six children were mostly in employment and all still lived at home. Joseph was a drapers assistant, John a brick maker (possibly with his father) Frederick was a labourer, Mary a dressmaker, Sarah a servant and Emma attended school. Robert employed Thomas Glithero as a servant who was fifteen and born in Elton.

WATER END

There were no new houses built in Water End since the time of the previous census.

Henry Palmer, a railway signalman, and Matilda his wife, lived along Water End. Matilda was born in Woodstone around 1836. Her parents were Charles and Elizabeth Wright who lived in Water End during 1841. Charles was born in Norfolk and Elizabeth in Whittlesea. Charles had been a carpenter for at least thirty years. In 1871 he was living as a boarder with Henry and Matilda as his wife Elizabeth had died. Henry's oldest daughter Elizabeth aged eleven was born in New Fletton in 1860. The family had moved to Woodstone by 1864 when their second child Matilda was born. In 1866 Emily was born then Charles in 1867 and finally Walter was born in 1870. At the time of the census he was seven months old. Matilda's sister Ellen lived at 28 Palmerston Road with her husband William Piggott.

John and Harriet Jarvis lived in the next cottage, their family grown up and moved away.

George Weston and his wife Annie lived further along with their four children. George Charles Whyman was born in 1861, Kate in 1863, Fred in 1865 and Julia in 1869.

Further along was a group of cottages named Orchard Terrace where the following families lived;
George Wood was still living in the first cottage with his wife Caroline and their young family. Alfred was two and William was three months, both born in Woodstone. Priscilla aged seventy two, by this time a widow and mother to George, was also living with them. She was recorded as being a nurse.

Sarah Hoare continued to live in the second cottage with her children Henry aged fourteen, Mary aged thirteen and Laura aged twelve. Henry was an agricultural labourer and the girls were still at school.

Thomas and Mary Pickering lived further along at 4 Orchard Terrace with two of their children Eliza aged seventeen and

Herbert who at the age of fourteen still attended school. Their daughter Emma died in the spring of 1862 aged seven.

Joseph Bland was a milkman and he married Sarah Phillips on 24th December 1851 at St Augustine's Church. Sarah was the daughter of William Phillips of Woodstone. Joseph and Sarah began their married life in Farcet Fen where their children were born, William in 1856 Robert in 1858 and Joseph in 1861. They had a daughter Elizabeth who died during 1861 aged ten. William worked with his father as a milkman's son, they lived along Water End.

Living at the Dames School was Susan Pridmore, aged eighty four and a widow, again recorded as being the dame's schoolmistress. Also living there was Sarah Stubley aged seventy four, a widow, and recorded as the school nurse.

William Phillips' mother Mary was a widow in 1871 and lived along Water End with her eight year old grand daughter Theodosia Webb born in Woodstone. Theodosia was the daughter of Thomas and Mary Webb who lived along Palmerston Road.

Mary Short was a greengrocer and shared her home with her son James, his wife Caroline and their daughter Sarah who was three months old.
Mary's husband James died at the beginning of the year in 1870 aged sixty two.

Richard Weston, born during 1811 in Woodstone and his wife Lucy, born around 1810 at Burleigh on the Hill in Rutland, were still living along Water End.

Mary Bellshaw (nee Drage) lived next to the Ferry Boat Inn with her step-daughter Lucy aged four. Lucy was shown on census as daughter-in-law to Mary. Her mother, also named Lucy, died during the spring of 1868. Lucy (nee Palmer) married Charles William Bellshaw during the winter of 1865.
The census recording shows Mary as being a 'Sailors wife and husband at sea'. Mary married Charles Bellshaw during the summer of 1868 at St Augustine's church in Woodstone.

Margaret Brewster

Family of William and Mary Phillips

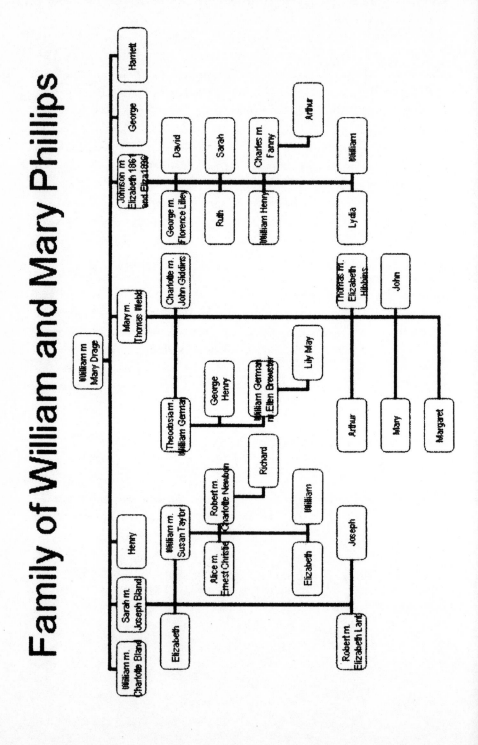

James Hunt had taken over as the innkeeper at the Ferry Boat inn. He lived there with his wife Sarah and their young family.

(According to records belonging to Steve Williams of Peterborough, who has a vast knowledge of the history of Public Houses, many landlords passed through the Ferry Boat.)

After James Hunt left John Jackson took over in 1872 for a short time. George E. Laughton was landlord from 1872 to 1874. When George left Richard Marriott took over for the rest of 1874. Edward and Thomas Manton were landlords from 1875 until 1877 when Benjamin Smith stepped in as landlord. In 1878 Charles Baxter had taken over.

Edmund and Elizabeth Richardson continued to live along Water End. Their daughter Jane married Thomas Odell on 17th June 1862 at St Augustine's church and lived with Edmund and Elizabeth. Also living with them was William their grandson aged fifteen.

William Hemment, the boat builder in Water End and his wife Alice who was known as Dorothy when she married, only had two daughters Harriet and Fanny living at home who both attended school.

Their daughter Sarah married Francis Hiscox on 12th December 1871 at St Augustine's church. Francis was a timber merchant from Peterborough as was his father John.

Their son William Thomas married Mary Ann Garner on 16th April and their daughter Alice married Samuel Rowning Leader two days later on 18th April 1876 at St Augustine's church Woodstone. By 1881 Samuel and Alice Leader were living at 2 St Georges Terrace in Peterborough and had two young children.

William and Mary Hemment were living at 25 Brown Bridge Street in Peterborough by 1881 and had three children. Although when they first married they lived in Woodstone where two of their children were born.

George Weston (Richards' brother) and his wife Elizabeth lived next to the Hemment family with two of their children, Annie aged twenty four and George aged seventeen. Annie was a servant and George was an agricultural labourer.

By the time of the 1871 census Peter and Mary Parkins had moved a few houses away from Mary's parents, Edmund and Elizabeth Richardson. Peter had changed his occupation from a labourer to a railway porter. They lived along Water End with their children. Annie, their first child, was born in 1861. Thomas was born in 1863, Robert in 1864, Edmund in 1867 and Charles Samuel in 1869. John Richardson, who was related to Mary Ann Parkins was also living with them as one of the family. He was twelve years old and worked as a farm boy.

WOODSTONE HILL

Since the 1861 census Turnpike Road had been renamed to Woodstone Hill, where there were fourteen private houses a grocers shop and the Cross Keys Inn.

John Bruce, the gardener, was still living along Woodstone Hill with his wife Ann and their children. Mary aged seventeen and John aged twelve. Also living back home with them was their daughter Margaret, aged twenty three, she was born in Wales. William Pacey was eighteen years of age and was born in Woolsthorpe in Lincolnshire. He lived with the Bruce family and was a gardener's apprentice.

The families who lived in the other houses along the Woodstone Hill, described on the census as private homes, were Johnson Phillips and family, Alice Worraker and son George, Frederick Billington and his family, Richard Murdock and Charlotte his wife, John Newman and his family, Henry Butler, a Chelsea Pensioner/labourer his wife Catherine and their daughter, Abraham and Harriett Butterwick and their young family, Joseph and Ruth Pepperdine and their eight children, Henry Newton, a blacksmith, his wife Alice and Alfred their son, William and Elizabeth Elms, John and Emma Lambert and their four children, Thomas Goulding, a miller, his wife Ann and their four children, John and Mary Anne Carpenter and their four children, and finally William and Mary Palmer.

Elizabeth Watts was the innkeeper at the Cross Keys inn, her husband Charles died in 1869 aged sixty eight. Living with Elizabeth were her daughters Elizabeth and Sarah who were both dressmakers. Also living at the inn were three lodgers, Richard

Bird, a labourer and his daughter Sarah a dressmaker from Oundle, and William Langley a labourer from Fotheringhay.

Thomas Parkinson had changed his occupation from a carter in 1861 to a coal dealer and grocer. He lived at the grocers shop along Woodstone Hill with Ann, his wife and five children. Susan nine, Mary eight, Lucy six, John four and Charlotte two, they were all born in Woodstone.

Living next door to the Parkinson family was John Lambert a bricklayer born in Yaxley and his wife Emma born in Orton Longueville. They had four children John aged eight, Elizabeth aged four, Mary one and Harriett was under one month old.

1881

The population of Woodstone had increased again There were 467 males and 443 females making a total of 910 approximately. There were 261 children between the ages of two months and fourteen years, 114 of them being of pre-school age.

There were 83 Heads of households recorded as working on the railways. Out of all the people living in Woodstone 125 men and boys worked for the railways.

The majority of these workers lived along Palmerston Road. It was apparent how times were changing as the number of agricultural labourers had decreased from thirty in 1841 to seventeen forty years later. All but two of these agricultural labourers lived in Water End, with the other two living in Palmerston Road.

Other occupations were Shoemaker - Compositor - Butcher - Wood Dealer – Chemist Assistant - Dressmaker - School Teacher - Currier - Annuitant - Coal and Coke Dealer Machine Wool Moulder – Tailoress – Carpenter – Joiner – Steam Millwright - Shop Boy – Whip Manufacturer – Woodman – Wood Turner –- Clerk - Master Baker – Wood Sawyer – Coppersmith – Wagon Repairer – Mangle Woman – Upholsterer - Blacksmith – Bricklayer – Gardener – Straw Bonnet Maker – Milliner - Cooper -School Governess – Horse Breaker – Postmaster – Printers Overseer – Miller (Corn)

Groom – House Agent – Lace Maker – Boat Builder – Dairyman – Coachman - Brewers Drayman - Nurse - Laundress – Shepherd – Domestic Confectioner.

Not forgetting the many servants and labourers who covered various tasks.

Four new families were living in the cottages along Oundle Road east of the Palmerston Arms. Henry Gaymor and his family came from Essex, John Cameron, a shoemaker, born in Scotland lived with his sister Margaret from Ireland, William Harlock and his young family came from Huntingdon.

The fourth family were Samuel Ward, a butcher, and Maria his wife with four of their children Dorothy aged twenty two, Fanny aged thirteen, Benjamin aged seven and Albert four years old. Their two daughters Susan and Sarah were living at High Street in Kettering with Benjamin and Rosina Calton who were their uncle and aunt. Benjamin was also a butcher.

In 1871 Samuel and his family were living at Milton Street in Peterborough where Samuel worked as a butcher. Benjamin Catton/Calton was shown as living with the family and was recorded as brother to Maria. At the time of her marriage to Samuel in the Pancras district Maria's maiden name was Calson. There seems to be a slight error when the census was recorded. Samuel and Maria were living at Johnson's Yard in Peterborough in 1861 when Dorothy was two years old.

James Rowell continued to be the publican at the Palmerston Arms with his wife Elizabeth and their family. Ann aged seventeen was a dressmaker, Charles thirteen was a coach builders apprentice and their youngest child James aged ten attended school. Elizabeth, their oldest daughter, had left home and was living at Grove Cottage in Luton where she worked as a domestic housemaid for Amos Ewen and his son Frank. Amos was a manager in the timber and slate trade, his son was a commercial clerk.

On 3rd February 1882 James wife Elizabeth died aged fifty five. She was the first person to be buried in the new cemetery along Woodstone Lane on 7th February 1882.

James died in 1888 aged sixty two and was buried on 30th October next to Elizabeth.

OUNDLE ROAD

On the corner of Palmerston Road, opposite the Palmerston Arms public house, was York Cottage (84a and 84b Oundle Road) where Edmund and Maria Isham lived.

Round the corner on Oundle Road stand a row of four houses named York Terrace (84 to 90 Oundle Road)

Thomas Hart, a postmaster in the civil service, lived at 1 York Terrace (84) with his wife Jane, and sons John and Hugh. Listed in the Huntingdonshire Post Office Directory 1877 and Kelly's Directory Bedfordshire, Huntingdonshire and Northamptonshire for 1903 Thomas Hart was shown as being a grocer and draper.

Number 2 York Terrace was uninhabited.

Samuel Tomblin was born in Leicestershire and worked as a railway guard. Samuel married Elizabeth Hetley Desbrow on 7th December 1875 at St Augustine's church. By 1881 they were living at 3 York Terrace (88) with their daughters Florence Desbrow and Ethel Mary. Elizabeth was the daughter of John and Susannah Desbrow, and granddaughter of James and Mary. James was the publican of The Boys Head inn until he died in 1851. His wife Mary died in 1849 and they were both buried in St Augustine's churchyard. Their son John took over running The Boys Head public house.

Finally living in the end house 90 was Frances Samuell, a printer's overseer, and Caroline his wife, both born in Northampton. They had four children Frances aged six, Earnest aged five, Harold aged one and Maud of three months. They were all born in Woodstone.

Since the 1871 census three of the houses in Nene View Terrace were uninhabited.

At number 1 was George Chamberlain, a carpenter, and his wife Alice. They had lived in the same house at the time of the 1871 census. Also living with them were their grandsons George and Arthur Wright, both born in Woodstone.

Apart from number 2 being uninhabited the next family along living at number 3 was William and Mary Robinson and their unmarried daughter Mary born in 1830. William was a retired solicitor. They were first shown as living in Woodstone on the 1851 census. At that time it was known as Church Street. William and Mary had another daughter Isabella who was born in 1834 although she was not living with her family at the time of the census.

Living at the Rectory was Reverend Reginald Tompson who had been the Rector of Woodstone since 1871. He was married during 1876 at Shepton Mallett to Mary Josephine Pratt from Peterborough. They had two children, Margaret Mary aged four and Reginald Henry aged two years, both were born in Woodstone. Mary Raynham from Middlesex was their nurse. Elizabeth Plowman from Fletton was the rector's house and parlour maid. Kate Wilbourn from Peterborough was their cook.

Henry Humberstone married Susannah Watts in Peterborough in 1866. Henry was a licensed victualler and blacksmith at the Boys Head inn where they both lived. John Watts, their nephew, was living with them and was a blacksmiths apprentice. Hubert Linnell was lodging with the family, he was a clerk.

James Ley Row continued to live at the Manor House (previously known as Woodstone House) James had remarried to Betsy (nee Baines) who was born in Yorkshire. They married at Wetherby during the winter of 1873. Coincidentally James daughter Emma married George Fitzroy Dean Gaches on 8th October 1873 at St Augustine's church in Woodstone. George was a solicitor from the St Marks parish in Peterborough.
James daughter Laura married Frederick Wright Laxton, a warehouseman in London, during 1873 at St Augustine's church.
Living with the Row family was Thomas Roberts their nephew from York. Eliza Scotney from Ramsey was their cook. Martha Clark from Silverston was their housemaid. Edward Morris from Peterborough was their groom.
James senior died in 1898 at Stamford aged seventy nine. James, his son, died in 1894 at Stamford, aged forty two.

Thomas Freeman, an agricultural labourer's foreman, and his wife Betsy were living in the Farm Cottage nearby to the Manor House. They had six sons, five of whom were born in Woodstone, their ages ranged from twelve to two years.

William Roberts, a retired farmer aged fifty one, lived in a house not far from the cottage with his two daughters shown as Mary C aged thirteen and Mary A aged two.

Rebecca Ashley, aged forty nine and born in Woodstone, was their domestic cook. Robert Ashley, the shoemaker, was her grandfather who had lived along the Oundle Road since at least the time of the 1841 census.

George Burnham a malster was still living along Oundle Road with his wife Mary. Since the 1871 census their son Robert, a railway fireman, had married and was living in Battersea with Maria his wife and Annie Richardson who was recorded as their stepchild.

George the younger son was still at home, he was a railway stores porter. Sadly he died during the summer of 1882 at the age of twenty three. He was buried in the cemetery along Cemetery Road Woodstone.

Mary, one of their daughters, was a general servant for Thomas and Ann Southam. Thomas was a surgeon and they lived at Thorpe Road Peterborough.

Clara the youngest child aged thirteen was still at school.

Their daughter Emma was sixteen and worked as a domestic servant. On 31st May 1887 Emma married Edward Cunningham at St Augustine's church.

Their eldest daughter Martha was living at Leckhampton Hall in Cheltenham which was the home of Frederick and Marian Benwell. Frederick was a Lt Col 1st Surrey Militia. They had seven sons and a daughter. Martha was employed as their nurse.

Thomas and Elizabeth Coulson were also still living along Oundle Road, and had done so since 1841. Their son William, an engine driver, his wife Emma and their children had moved from Nene View Place to live at 81 Westwood Street in Peterborough. Two of William and Emma's sons John and James were not at home at the time of the census. Their daughter Elizabeth had left school and was an apprentice dressmaker. Charles attended school as did his sisters Caroline and Emily who were born in 1872 and 1875 respectively.

Thomas' brother James had married since living with the family in 1851. At the time of the 1881 census he was living with his wife and family in Thurning where he was born.

PALMERSTON ROAD

Since the time of the 1871 census many houses had been built in Palmerston Road

.

68 to 74	Rodwell Cottages	1878
110 to 132	Limetree Terrace	1878
134 to 136	Rose Cottages	1878
150 to 156	Linford Cottages 'T.G.'	1880
158	Woodville House	1878
113 and 115	'G.R.'	1881

Some of the families who lived in Palmerston Road during the 1881 census were:

William and Charlotte Phillips were still living at Vine Cottage their family having grown up and left home. William and Charlotte had lived in the same cottage since at least 1871.

Mark Christmas, a wood dealer, his wife Emma and their four young children lived a few cottages along from the Phillips family. Their children were Sarah aged seven born in Fletton, John W aged four, Emma E aged two and Mark aged four months all born in Woodstone.

Thomas and Mary Webb continued to live further along Palmerston Road. They had five children living at home all were born in Woodstone, Charlotte, Thomas Peter, Mary Elizabeth, John William and Margaret, their ages ranged from 15 years to 7 months.
By 1881 their daughter Theodosia was shown on the census as a servant working for James and Martha Norton. James was a railway station master and lived at 1 Station Cottages, Station Road Fletton.

Thomas Yates married Carolina Rosa (nee Clarke) in Peterborough towards the end of the year in 1873. They were shown as living in Woodville House with their two children, Thomas born 1874 and Rosa Caroline born 1877. Woodville House was built in 1878 and known as number 158.

In 1861 Thomas Goulding lived with Richard and Annie Freeman along Town Street in Yaxley. The premises were described on the census as Wind flour mill and bakers shop. Richard was a miller/baker and Thomas aged nineteen was shown as being a servant miller/baker. He married Ann Rist on the 13th September 1863 at Yaxley parish church. Ann was the daughter of Abraham and Elizabeth Rist who lived at Weeks Lane in Yaxley at the time of the 1861 census. Ann and her four sisters and brother all worked as agricultural labourers. In 1871 Thomas and Ann lived along the Woodstone Hill but had moved to 3 Linford Cottages along Palmerston Road by the time of the 1881 census. Thomas was born in March and Ann in Yaxley. Their son William worked as a chemist's assistant, he was fifteen years old. Their other children were Susan Elizabeth aged thirteen, Alice Ann aged ten and the youngest Tom Frederick was five. They all attended school. Also living with the family was Edith A.Rist their niece aged eight, born in Calcutta, she also attended school.

James Waspe was born at Coddenham in Suffolk during 1852. He was the son of Robert and Esther and lived at 21 Street in Coddenham at the time of the 1861 census. James was a railway goods guard and married Amy Guest in the district of Peterborough in 1874. They had three sons James Robert born in 1875, John William born in 1878 and George Oliver in 1880, all were born in Woodstone.

William Bland, son of Joseph and Sarah, was a carpenter and joiner. He married Susan Taylor from Hockwold in Norfolk at the beginning of the year in 1880. By the time of the 1881 census they lived with their three month old daughter Alice along Palmerston Road. In 1861 William was living with his parents at 11 Farcet Terrace in Farcet. Susan was the daughter of Thomas and Susan Taylor who lived at the Ball Inn in Hockwold cum Wilton near Thetford during 1861 where her father was a gamekeeper.

John Claypole, an engineer at the wagon works was born in Whittlesey. He married Grace Skeggs in Reading during 1873. Grace was born in Oundle. They lived in Berkshire where their first son Ernest was born in 1875, then moved to Peterborough and Oliver was born in 1877. Henry Bingley, a railway foreman, was boarding with them.

Robert Biggadike married Harriet Blunt on 8th October 1879 at St Augustine's church. Robert was a baker and they lived at 1, Limetree Terrace with their seven month old daughter Mabel Harriett. Edward Biggadike, brother to Robert was also a baker and boarded with them. Their father was George, a farmer from Whaplode. Frederick Green, aged fourteen, was also living with Robert and Harriet as a servant. The house they lived in was once known as The Old Bakery number 132.

Newman Parrish married Harriett Cornwall in the district of Hull during 1872. They lived at 3 Limetree Terrace with their children Samuel Newman aged seven, Florence Harriett aged five, John William aged three and Elizabeth Annie aged two months. Newman was a coppersmith for the railways.

John Garfield married Sarah Rycraft during 1869 in the Oundle district. Sarah was the daughter of William and Rebecca Rycraft who lived along the High Street in Nassington during 1861. John was the son of William and Ann who lived in Stibbington during 1861 with his six brothers and sisters. John, a railway engine driver, and Sarah lived at number 10 Limetree Terrace, 114, with their four children. John William aged eight, Albert Henry aged six, Emma Gertrude aged four and Ethel Rebecca seven months old.

12 Limetree Terrace was recorded on the census as an uninhabited butchers shop. This was later known as 110 Palmerston Road where Mr Moore had his television repair and workshop.

Set back from the other houses was Demontford Terrace which provided twelve homes mainly to railway workers. Alternate occupations of the other residents were Mary Wallis, a laundress, lived at number 3 where she shared her home with Thomas and Susannah Pettitt and their three children who were boarding with Mary.
George Dobson was an upholsterer and lived with Elizabeth his wife and their five children at number 5.

James and Mary Grice were still living at South House with their children Kezia aged nineteen, Robert aged eighteen and Joseph aged sixteen who were both railway clerks, Richard aged fifteen was still at school.

Their oldest son James married Ellen Jinks at the end of the year in 1871, at the time of the 1881 census they were living at Gladstone Street with their nine year old daughter who they named Adlen Ellen. John Thomas Jinks brother to Ellen also lived with them he worked as a fireman on the railways.

Matthew, another son of James and Mary, married Mary Neale during the second half of the year in 1880. They made their home in Leicester where their daughter Mary was born.

John Yates son of Mary Grice (nee Yates) married Elizabeth Mary Bigley during 1872. Elizabeth was the daughter of Henry and Elizabeth who lived at the school house along Oundle Road in Fletton during 1871. At the time of the 1881 census John Yates (recorded as Gates on the census) was also shown as living at South House and had three children. John aged six, Elizabeth Mary Rodwell aged five and Edith Ethel aged two. These were grandchildren to James and Mary Grice. Edith died in 1882 aged three. Harriett Hibbins was fifteen and born in Eynesbury was a boarder with the family and worked as a pupil teacher.

Mary Grice, wife of James, was born on 4th May 1823 and died on 11th September 1887. She was buried in the cemetery along Woodstone Lane.

Henry Hoare, son of Henry and Sarah from Water End, was a wood sawyer. He married Emma Greensmith at St Augustine's church on 23rd October 1876. At the time of the marriage Henry was shown as being a sexton. By 1881 they lived at 2 Palmerston Terrace with their three children, Ada Emma aged three years, Laura Helen aged two years and John Thomas one month old.

Edward Oswick married Jane Chantrey during the summer of 1866 in Peterborough. Edward, a railway porter, and Jane moved to Palmerston Road around the time their second son, Arthur Filby, was born in 1868. Oliver George, their eldest son, worked as an errand boy. He was born in Fletton during 1867 where they used to live. The other children were Ada Jane born 1872, Joshua born 1876 and Emma Louisa who was nine months old at the time of the 1881 census.

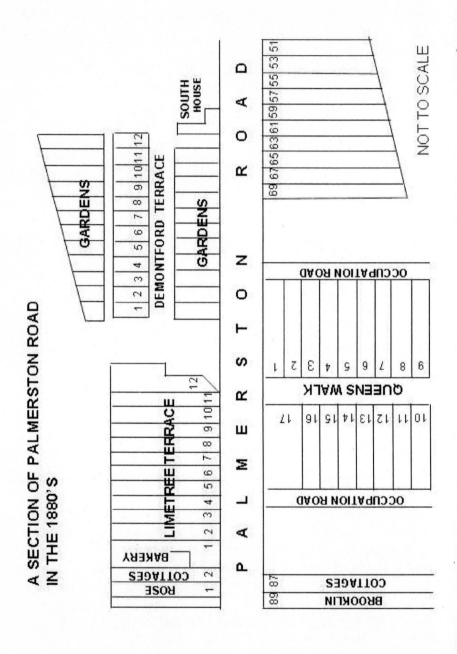

A SECTION OF PALMERSTON ROAD IN THE 1880'S

NOT TO SCALE

Charles Edward Crawley, a whip manufacturer, and his wife Adelaide continued to live at Aboyne Lodge (167). Their family included Ellen Elizabeth who was twelve, John William eleven, Agnes Emily nine, Evelyn Mary six and Charles Edward three years old. They all attended school. Elizabeth Louder aged sixteen worked for the family as a domestic servant.

Next to the Crawley residence was a large house which was uninhabited.

QUEENS WALK

Part of Queens Walk was in Woodstone, there were only eighteen households, three of which were uninhabited at the time of the census. The terrace of cottages were numbered 1 to 9 from Palmerston Road towards the school in Orchard Street (172 to 156) then across the road to the cottages numbered 10 to 18 (155 to 171) back towards Palmerston Road.

Of the fifteen inhabited cottages the occupation of eleven of the men who were head of the household was railway workers.

Living in these cottages were Harry Weldon, a railway clerk, his wife Annie and their five month old daughter Alice.

Edward Rowell, an engine driver, his wife Mary and their five children aged between seven years down to the youngest of two months.

Frederick Vickers, a retired farmer, and his wife Mary and their three school age children.

Charles Jackson, an engine stoker, and his wife Mary were married in Peterborough in 1877. Mary's maiden name was (Eggboro). Living with them was Alfred Eggboro who was shown as their son in law and was a railway clerk.

Richard Wright, a goods porter, lived with Maria his wife, and their grown up children, William, Richard, Charles and Ann their daughter. The sons were general labourers, Ann was a scholar. Frederick and James English came from Yoxford in Suffolk and were boarders with the Wright family. They also worked for the railways as an engine shed labourer and an engine driver in the wagon works.

Arthur James Stimpson was an engine foreman and lived with his wife Eliza who was born in Stanground. They married in the district of Peterborough during 1880.

Thomas Phillipson was a railway fireman and lived with his wife Hannah and their seven children. Both Thomas and Hannah were born in Lincolnshire but were married in the district of Peterborough in 1866. All their children were born in Peterborough except Fanny who was born in Woodstone during 1880.

Fanny Rowell, who lived next to the Phillipson family, was a widow and was shown on the census as 'formerly domestic servant'. Emma her twenty seven year old daughter lived with her as well as two boarders. Henry Frederick Francis from Berkshire who worked as an engine driver and Henry Souter a young widower of twenty four who worked as a shunter/pointsman and came from Cambridge. He married Harriet Shaw Tyler at the beginning of the year in 1879 in Peterborough. Harriet died during the early months of the year in 1880 aged twenty three.

Emma Rowell, daughter of Fanny and the late Robert Rowell, married Henry Frederick Francis at St Augustine's church Woodstone on 26th December 1881.

The last family on that side of the road was Thomas and Mary Banham. Thomas was a signalman. They also had taken in two lodgers, William Crosby a railway pointsman and Emma Crosby, both were from Cambridge.

Across the road number 10 (155) was uninhabited.

In the next cottage lived Sarah Whitney a widow at the age of forty one. Her husband Thomas died at the end of 1880 leaving her to bring up their seven children, the youngest being only one year old. George was the oldest at fifteen years and helping out by working as a carpenter's journeyman. Four of the children were at school, Ernest aged three and Harold the youngest were at home with their mother.

The next two cottages 12 and 13 were also uninhabited.

Living at number 14 (163) was Charles and Grace Peed, Charles was a railway guard for the Midland Railway. They lived in Fletton when their sons James Charles and George were born in 1869 and 1872 respectively. The family moved to Woodstone where Jane Elizabeth, Ellen and William were born, their ages being seven, four and two respectively. Also living with the family as a domestic servant was Amelia Peed, sister to Charles, and his niece Jane Peed who was five months old. Thomas and Rebecca Smith lodged with the Peed family. Thomas was a railway servant.

George and Delilah Fletcher (nee North), married in the district of Peterborough in 1869, lived next to the Peed family. George was an engine driver. Their children, Clara aged eleven, Maria aged eight, Charles aged six and William aged three were all born in Stanground. The family then moved to Woodstone where Georgina was born. At the time of the census she was seven months old.

Living at number 16 (167) was Benjamin and Hannah Barnard, Benjamin was a railway servant. They had one daughter Mary born 1872 in New Fletton. At some stage Benjamin and Hannah took Harriet Collins into their care she was an orphan born in Woodstone during 1872. Her parents were Samuel and Harriett Collins, Samuel was a policeman for G.E.R. Benjamin and Hannah also had three boarders living with them, William Payne from Over, Charles Smith from Histon and John Dowse from Bury. All three of the young men were railway porters.

The last house numbered 17/18 (169) was a grocers shop where Robert and Ann Louder lived. John Smith, aged thirteen years, was the shop boy who ran errands also lived with the family. Elizabeth J Row aged sixty six lodged with the family, she was not married. Elizabeth was born in Bourne so it is possible she was sister to

James Ley Row, also born in Bourne. He was a farmer living at the Manor House on Oundle Road

WATER END

There were a few families who continued to live in Water End, having been there for many years.

Henry Palmer, a railway signalman, and his wife Matilda, who was not at home at the time of the census, were still living in the first house along Water End. (Matilda was shown on the census as visiting Thomas and Susannah Hill who were living at Lambeth in Surrey).

Their oldest children, Emily and Charles, attended school even though they were aged fifteen and thirteen respectively. Henry and Matilda had two more sons, Henry aged six and Alfred aged eleven months, both born in Woodstone.

George Canner Weston and his wife Annie still lived at 4 Water End with seven of their children. Kate aged eighteen was a dressmaker. Fred aged fifteen was a joiner's apprentice. Arthur aged eight, Minnie aged six and Frank aged three all attended school. Archie aged two and Annie who was four months old stayed at home with their mother.

George Weston, born in Woodstone in 1813, and uncle to George Canner was the innkeeper at the Black Swan public house in Farcet in 1881. He lived there with his wife Elizabeth and their son George who was twenty eight years old. All three were born in Woodstone.

Johnson Phillips, and his wife Elizabeth, had moved back to Water End where he grew up. They had three more children, Henry was born 1872, Charles in 1876 and Lydia in 1878 all in Woodstone.

Living next to the Phillips family was Richard Palmer, a widower and retired woodman of the grand age of ninety. He was born in Woodstone during 1791.

At the time of the 1871 census he was living along Water End with his wife, Jane who at that time was sixty seven years old, she was born in Yaxley.

Two families were recorded as living at 7 Water End, they were,

James Hunt aged seventy four and his wife Mary (nee Short) aged sixty one.

Also James and Caroline Short with their three daughters. Sarah aged ten, Elizabeth five and Mary was two years old.

Robert Crayton, born in Woodstone around 1834 also lived in Water End with his wife Eliza and their three children. Robert was an agricultural labourer.

John T. Martin, a school master and organist, lived in one of a group of two cottages called Shore Cottages. He was born in Yorkshire, his wife Mary Ann was born in Peterborough in 1851. John married Mary Ann Hunting on 10th August 1875 in Woodstone church. Mary's father was George Hunting, a coal merchant from Grove Street New Fletton. John and Mary had three children, Frank aged three, Ethel aged one and Bertram who was eight months old, all of whom were born in Woodstone. Sarah Edis, from Peterborough, worked for them as a general domestic servant. Thomas Richard Hunting, aged twenty one and born in Fletton, was boarding with the family he worked as a merchant's clerk and was brother to Mary Ann.

Coincidentally living next door in the other Shores Cottage was William J. Hunting. He was brother to Mary Ann Martin and Thomas Hunting and was born in Fletton in 1853. He married Mary C. Rowell at Whittlesey during 1877. They had two children, Percy William born 1878 and Kate Mary born 1880.

In 1861 William lived at Grove Street with his parents George and Emma and his five brothers and sisters. At the time of the 1871 census when William was eighteen he was working for the railways as a porter and lodged with William and Mary Hudson at Wolverton in Norfolk.

Sarah Hoare was living on her own, her family having moved away. She continued working as a dressmaker. Henry, her son, was living in Palmerston Road with his young family.

Another change of hands had taken place at the Ferry Boat Inn. John Royal was the publican and a wheelwright he lived there with his wife Hannah, they were both from Suffolk. Also living with John and Hannah was Emma, their daughter, with her husband

Thomas Kitchen, and their two young daughters Eleanor and Annie. Thomas was a confectioner.

George and Susannah Whyman were both born in Woodstone. They had three children Susannah, William and Robert. George worked as a boat builder's labourer, his son William was an apprentice boat builder and possibly worked for Mr Hemment along Water End. George's parents were Robert and Susannah, Robert was a bone dealer in 1841. Their other children were William, Charles, Susannah and Sarah. They all grew up in Water End.

Sarah Sykes was a widow who lived at the old dame's school with her son Edmund who worked as a coal porter. Sarah was a mangle woman.

William Hemment, aged sixty, was also born in Woodstone and the same age as George Whyman. They had both lived in Water End since birth. William was a boat builder and barge owner and lived in Water End with his wife Alice. Two of their daughters, Harriet and Fanny, still lived at home. Their son William Thomas also a boat builder married Mary Ann Garner on 16th April 1876 at St Augustine's church. Mary's father was Thomas, he was a railway guard for N.W.R. and the family lived at Fletton. At the time of the 1881 census they were living at Brown Bridge Street, Boat Yard, in Peterborough with their young family. William Thomas and Francis Lewis were born in Woodstone but Alice Eliza was born in Peterborough.

On 18th April 1876 Alice Hemment, daughter of William and Alice, married Samuel Rowning Leader at St Augustine's church, two days after her brothers wedding. Samuel was a builder and his father Samuel was a master mariner.

Alice Hemment, senior, died at the age of 63. She was buried in August 1882 in the new cemetery along Cemetery Road. Harriet their daughter died on the 22nd May 1883 and was buried in the same grave as her mother. William Hemment, senior, died at the boat yard in Peterborough in July 1888 aged 68. He was buried with his late wife and daughter.

Joseph Bland was a dairyman who lived next to the Hemment family with his wife Sarah and their two sons, Robert aged twenty three and Joseph aged nineteen. Both sons were recorded as being sons of a dairyman but they did not have an occupation. Sarah was born in Woodstone. Mary Phillips widow of William and step-mother to Sarah was lodging with Joseph and Sarah. Her son William was married to Charlotte Bland who was sister to Joseph.

Peter and Mary Parkins were still living in Water End with their children. They had an addition to their family since the 1871 census they named him William Albert he was born towards the end of the year in 1871. Annie their daughter was working as a dressmaker. Thomas was a butcher's apprentice he died in 1882 aged nineteen. Robert, Edmund and Charles all worked as agricultural labourers. William attended school.

Thomas Rowell had hit hard times; he was only fifty eight but recorded as a 'farmer out of business.' He once was a farmer of 100 plus acres employing three labourers and two boys at Cowpasture Farm in Woodstone. Living with him along Water End were his two daughters and one son, Emily who probably looked after the home as her mother had passed away, Jessie was a dressmaker and George an agricultural labourer.

WOODSTONE HILL

The enumerator then moved along Oundle Road to the Cross Keys public house along Woodstone Hill. Elizabeth Watts senior died at the beginning of 1881, aged seventy years. Her daughter, Elizabeth, took over her mother's role as innkeeper at the Cross Keys inn. Lilian Baxter, a young girl aged fourteen, was a general servant at the inn. Jane Ford was visiting Elizabeth at the time of the census she was born in Woodstone around 1809. Her husband John Ford, who was born in Woodstone around 1804 and their son in law Charles Parkinson were at home a few houses away.

Thomas Parkinson had changed his occupation again since the last census recordings. In 1881 he was working as a railway wagon repairer and continued living along Woodstone Hill with his family, which had increased since 1871. Ada was nine, Thomas was six, Charles was four and Caroline was one year old.
John, their oldest son was aged fourteen and worked as a railway sheet repairer (waterproof), he lived at home.

Susan, their oldest daughter aged nineteen, was working as a general servant for Margaret Moon, a widow of seventy one, her widowed daughter Mary and her three children. They lived at Ilkley in the West Riding area of Yorkshire.

Lucy, their next oldest daughter aged sixteen, was working as a general servant for Robert and Fanny Canham and their two children who lived at Humberstone Road in Leicester. Robert was born in Wisbech and was a civil service clerk for the Inland Revenue. His wife Fanny was born in New Fletton.

Thomas' brother John Parkinson was married and living along High Street in Yaxley with his wife Lucy and their young family, he worked as a potato merchant.

Thomas Ford, a machine fitter's labourer, his wife Mary and their children John and Henry lived a few doors away from Thomas' parents John and Jane Ford.

Emma Lambert was a widow by the 1881 census. She worked as a dressmaker being the main wage earner in the family. Her father John Cole, also a widow, was living with her. He was seventy nine and was a retired farm labourer. Emma's daughter Elizabeth aged fourteen worked as a general servant for Robert and Isabella Catling who lived along Granville Street in Peterborough. Robert was a shoe salesman. Before Emma's husband had died they had three more children, Emily born in 1873, Charles in 1875 and Alfred in 1878. Emma also died while her children were very young. She was only forty four and was buried on 19th January 1886 in the cemetery along Cemetery Road.

LONDON ROAD

Going back down Oundle Road towards London Road not far from the new cemetery was Westbrook House where William Whyman and his family lived. He was a farmer of 240 acres and employed seven men and one boy.

Robert and Elizabeth Gollings and their family had moved out of the Brick Yard cottages to Fletton Lodge which was also along London Road. This was shown as being in the parish of Fletton. Two of their daughters, Sarah and Emma, were recorded on the census as farmer's daughters.

John aged thirty four, one of their sons, was shown on the census as a widower. He was living back home with the family and worked as a brick maker. Nelly Gollings his daughter was one year old.

Charlotte Elizabeth, their daughter, was also widowed by the time of the census and living back home with the family with her seven year old daughter Ada May. Charlotte married John Thomas Weldon during 1870.

Robert and Elizabeth's daughter Mary A. married George Noble towards the end of the year in 1878 at Peterborough. By 1881 they were living in Cowgate with Albert George their first child aged three months. Jane Elizabeth Noble aged sixteen worked for them as a servant.

Robert and Elizabeth's son Joseph, a manager at the brickworks, married Hannah Noble towards the end of the year in 1880 at Peterborough. In 1881 they were living at 13 Elm Street in Fletton with their first child, Alfred M. aged five months. They employed Hannah Eyton as a servant for them.

Frederick, another of their sons, married Elizabeth Power from Whittlesea in 1874. By 1881 they were living at Swan Lane, Chilvers Coton in Warwickshire. They had four young children. Frederick was a farm bailiff.

Elizabeth died in 1883 and was buried on 16th November. Robert was seventy four when he died and was buried on 6th December 1889. They were placed to rest in a double grave in the cemetery along Cemetery Road.

William Payne, a brickyard labourer from Colsterworth in Lincolnshire, had moved with his family to the London Road Company Brick Yard cottage. In 1871 William was an agricultural labourer and lived with his wife Mary and family along Palmerston Road.

The last homestead was Jones Lodge where Richard Jones and his son William continued to live. They were both farmers. Richard employed Eliza Watts as a domestic cook and Ellen Tomlin as a domestic dairymaid.

The oldest Woodstone born residents were Richard Palmer, of ninety years, and Mary Phillips of seventy three years who both lived along Water End.

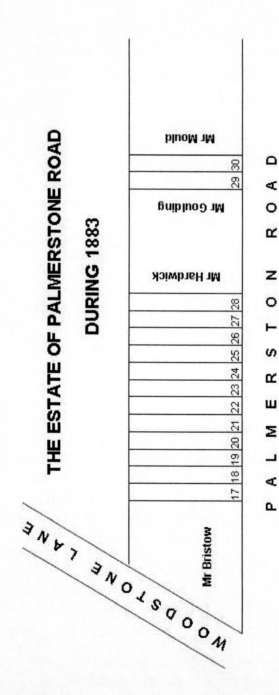

NOT TO SCALE

THE ESTATE OF PALMERSTONE ROAD

DURING 1883

WOODSTONE LANE

PALMERSTON ROAD

Mr Bristow

Mr Hardwick

Mr Goulding

Mr Mould

17 18 19 20 21 22 23 24 25 26 27 28 29 30

Mr C.E.Crawley

Mr J.Clarke

Mr Roper

Reverend R. Tompson

9 10 11 12 13 14 15 16

1 2 3 4 5 6 7 8

OCCUPATION ROAD

QUEENS WALK

T. Mills

1891

Woodstone was covered by the 1891 census and shown as follows:-
The first part of the parish of Woodstone which commenced at the next house to the New Inn on the Oundle Road, all houses in Palmerston Road as far as Bristow's new house. Also houses on the Oundle Road as far and including Terrots, Jubilee Street all the Water End of the village and Pointsmens Boxes on the Railway.
Inhabited – 266.   Uninhabited – 8.   Tenements of less than 5 rooms – 48.
654 Males.   652 Females.
The next part began at Wymans and houses nearby then covering Gollings, Bristow's, Browns and Thompsons Brickyards, Rowells Farm and the houses near Jones Lodge on the left side of road, Jones Lodge and all houses along Cemetery Lane then the houses on Oundle Road from Terrots to Woodstone Hill inclusive.
Inhabited – 110.   Uninhabited – 6   275 Males. 255 Females.
The total population of Woodstone was 1836 which had doubled since the previous census.
There was an increase in Railway workers since 1881 to 327. Agricultural labourers had increased from 17 to 22. There were 10 Brickyard workers and 49 Domestic Servants.
A collection of some of the occupations covered by Woodstone people included hotel porter, coppersmiths, drapers and their assistants, maltster, insurance agents, bus proprietor, cab driver, elastic weaver, newspaper reporter, printer's apprentice, milliner, mill porter, millwright, dressmaker, tailoress, stationers assistant, solicitor, Baptist minister, architect, assurance agent, lexton, nurse, cowmen, builder, whipmaker, shop assistant, gardener, cabinet maker, paper hanger, florist, caretaker in school, bottle washer, chemist, bathing place attendant, agent for singer machine company, boilermaker, music teacher, confectioner's apprentice, bank manager, machinist of nuts and bolts and iron tinplate worker.

There were approximately 734 children recorded on the census made up as follows:-the number of children under the age of one – 42, pre-school children – 290, children attending school 402.
The youngest children recorded were three day old infant son of Abraham and Mary Crick who lived at Gore Corner Cottages along Cemetery Road and one week old infant son of Thomas and Alice Osbourne who lived at 12 Queens Walk.

There were four sets of twins in Woodstone the youngest being one month old William and Caroline Coles from Water End. Edith and William Turner from Palmerston Road were ten months old and Ellen and Phoebe Seaton aged two from Water End.

The oldest twins were Margarett and Rosalie Crow aged eight who were boarders with William and Sarah Livermore at Park View Terrace along Oundle Road. Margarett and Rosali were born at Teddington in Middlesex.

OUNDLE ROAD

All the families who were shown on the 1881 census as living in the five cottages east of the Palmerston Arms had moved.

Newman and Harriet Parrish had moved from Limetree Terrace along Palmerston Road into one of these cottages along Oundle Road. They had seven children at home. Florence aged fifteen, John aged thirteen, Whyman Mary aged eleven, Annie Elizabeth aged ten, Mabel Rebecca aged seven, Ernest aged three and Lilian aged one. None of the children were shown as attending school. Newman continued his work as a coppersmith.

Next to Newman Parrish was an uninhabited shoe makers shop.

The publican at the Palmerston Arms was William Eames from Hertfordshire. His wife Sarah was born in Kimbolton, their daughter Beatie was born in Cirencester.

The Post Office and Shop was also uninhabited.

Living at 2 York Terrace was William Ingram, a railway clerk, his wife Sarah and their two daughters three year old Ella and Gertrude who was one year old.

Frances Samuel continued to live at 4 York Terrace with his wife Caroline and seven children. Frances was still a newspaper printer's overseer, their son Ernest aged fifteen was a newspaper printer's apprentice.

James and Helena Bridgefoot lived at Violet House (83) with their five children. James, a builder and contractor, and his family all grew up in Lincolnshire. Most of the family were working, Angelina was a dressmaker, William as a builder's contractor, and

Nellie and Fanny were both drapers' assistants. Ada the youngest aged thirteen was still at school.

John and Mary Strickson lived at No.1 Kisby Villas (79) with their six children. John was recorded as being an innkeeper. William, the oldest son, was a carpenter. Charles and George both worked as whip makers. Fannie worked as a shop assistant. Elizabeth and Henry at the time had no occupation. In 1881 John and his family lived at 6 Davies Terrace in Fletton.

William and Ellen Piggott lived at May Villa with their youngest son Joseph aged sixteen. William was a railway examiner and Joseph was a joiner's apprentice. In 1881 William and his family lived at 69 Gladstone Street Peterborough although ten years previous shown on the 1871 census they were living along Palmerston Road.

Reginald Tompson, Rector of Woodstone, and Mary his wife were living at the rectory with their four children. Margaret aged fourteen, Reginald aged twelve, Winifred aged eight and Eva aged six. They employed five domestic servants. Henrietta Bontall aged thirty three from Alconbury was the cook, Florence Bates aged twenty four from Horncastle was the house and parlour maid, Sarah Green aged forty seven from Oxford was the head nurse, Susan Spiers aged fifteen from Northamptonshire was the Under Nurse and Marshall Charlotte Page aged seventeen from Alconbury was the Kitchen Maid.

The Boys Head Inn had also seen a change of innkeeper since 1881 with Samuel Bisese having taken over. Living with him were his two daughters and a son Alice aged sixteen, Ann aged fifteen and Harry aged thirteen.

Mrs Alice Maria Terrot and her unmarried daughter Eleanor took over Woodstone House during 1886, formerly known as the Manor House. At the time of the 1891 census Alice employed five servants to help with the running of the house. Francis Goodson and his wife Mary lived at the Coachman's cottage nearby and worked as groom and dairywoman respectively for Mrs Terrot. Alice was born in Paris on 12th November 1819 and was the wife of the late Reverend Charles Pratt Terrot who had been the Vicar of

Wispington in Lincolnshire for the last forty eight years, he died in 1886. Mrs Terrot had a family of five children.

The information that follows comes from Mrs Jenny Paul, a descendent of Alice.

"Woodstone Manor stood in over half an acre of garden. There was a large tiled entrance hall and four large reception rooms. One of which was panelled and all had magnificent fireplaces. There had been ten bedrooms but two had been converted to bathrooms. There were also attic rooms. In the grounds were stables where 'Sailor' the horse was housed and a coachman's cottage.

Mrs Terrot arrived at Woodstone with many belongings and a huge amount of memorabilia, including many of her late husband's watercolour paintings. She spent forty eight years as the wife of the vicar of Wispington. Her late husband was a very Christian, humble man who had a great talent for art and architecture. He painted extensively the countryside of Lincolnshire and was a friend of Peter de Wint. Undoubtedly Alice Maria was the "practical side" of the marriage and the person who organised parochial matters.

Mrs Terrot was a dignified determined lady and although she arrived at Woodstone at a time of great distress to her she had great willpower and quickly integrated into the life and society of Woodstone.

Mrs Terrot lived at Woodstone Manor for sixteen years and then in May 1902 she died after an illness of only two days. Her body was returned to Wispington to lie beside that of her beloved husband.

In her will she left Woodstone Manor to her daughter Eleanor, who continued to live there and take a leading part of life in St Augustine's church and the village. She was a dedicated Sunday school teacher and had a great love of embroidery. She daily took rides out in her carriage drawn by her horse named 'Sailor'. She worked altar frontals which she gave to the church. For companionship she had her dog named 'Jock' and her two parrots. She was also an enthusiastic member of the Primrose League. She allowed meetings to be held in the Manor and in the gardens, which were said to be charming. After she had lived at Woodstone Manor for twenty six years she became seriously ill and had to undergo an operation in London. She returned home to the Manor for one last Christmas but her health was failing and she became confined to her room. She requested to be buried close by her mother in Wispington churchyard and this was done on Ascension Day 16th May 1912. The duties of the Rector of Woodstone, Rev. N.J. Raper, prevented him accompanying the body back to Wispington.

Eleanor Terrot left Woodstone Manor to her niece Elizabeth Cosby. By 1933 it had been divided into two homes, numbers 174 and 176 Oundle Road. In 1968 it was again sold, this time with permission for demolition and a cul-de-sac to be created which was named Earl Spencer Court. "

Thomas and Caroline Yates had moved from Palmerston Road to 1 Cambridge Houses (187). Their son Thomas worked as a railway clerk and Rosa, their daughter was still attending school. Thomas' brother John, a railway engine driver, died in Fulham in September 1892 at the age of forty six. He was buried in the local cemetery in Woodstone.

John Thomas Martin was a schoolmaster and assistant overseer. He had moved from Water End to live at 2 Cambridge Houses (189), with Mary his wife and their six children, all of whom were born in Woodstone. Frank, aged thirteen, was not living at home. He was a scholar at St Johns Boys School in Greenwich, Middlesex. Frank was the nephew of Richard Rooksby who was the schoolmaster. Richard married Harriet Elizabeth Hunting, daughter of George and Emma Hunting on 26th July 1887 at St Augustine's church.

Since the 1881 census John and Mary had four more sons, they were Sydney, Robert, Edward and George.

The Norfolk and Cambridge houses were built in 1888.

Joseph Edward Hunting married Kate Watson during the summer of 1886 after their Banns were read, in Woodstone, and Whittlesea where Kate lived. Joseph, a coal merchants clerk, and Kate lived at 1 Norfolk Houses (191) with their daughter Lily Margaret aged two. Ann Watson a widow and mother to Kate was also living with the family. She was a retired nurse from Whittlesea

James Burnham was born in Woodstone during 1855 his parents were Reuben and Jane. James worked as a maltster and lived along Oundle Road with his wife Charlotte and their seven children. Charlotte was born in Longthorpe as were all their children apart from Charlotte Elizabeth aged three and John Richard aged one who were born in Woodstone.

Levi, aged thirteen, worked as a farm labourer. Emma aged eleven, Alice aged nine, Fanny aged six and George aged five attended school.

Reuben Burnham had changed his occupation since the 1881 census and was a publican, living at 'The Huntsman Inn' in Peterborough with Jane, his wife and two sons Joseph and William.

A row of twelve cottages were built in 1888 along Oundle Road which were named Oriel Terrace. They were numbered from 195 through to 217.

All the males that were the head of each household in these cottages worked for the railways except for Mr Thomas Smith. Thomas was a carpenter from Devon his wife Ellen was born in Somerset. They had a fifteen year old daughter called Ida who attended school and the family lived at 7 Oriel Terrace (211).

Nathaniel Woolley, a railway signalman, and his wife Eliza lived at 2 Oriel Terrace (197). They married during 1889 in Staffordshire where Eliza was born, in 1891 their son James was born in Woodstone.

John Newbon married Mary Elizabeth Garthwaite during the summer of 1890. By 1891 they lived at 3 Oriel Terrace (199), John was a railway guard. In 1881 before John married he worked as a blacksmiths apprentice and lived with his parents John and Sarah Newbon along Lincoln Road in Peterborough. John (senior) was a wheelwright and blacksmith.

Peter Parkins and his family had moved from Water End to number 10 Oriel Terrace (217). Charles Samuel a railway engine cleaner and James who attended school were their only sons still living at home in 1891.
Their daughter Annie married Thomas Cooper on 19th September 1882 at St Augustine's church. Thomas was born in Hereford and the son of Enoch Lloyd and Margaret Cooper who lived in one of the Belvue Cottages in Whitsed Street Peterborough during 1881. Unfortunately Annie died at the beginning of 1885, possibly in childbirth, as Sidney Cooper, born at the beginning of the year in 1885, was living with his grandparents, Peter and Mary Parkins. Annie was buried in the cemetery along Cemetery Road (New Road).
Robert, another of their sons, married Laura Cooper during the winter months of 1889 in Peterborough. Laura was sister to Thomas Cooper and also born in Hereford.
By 1891 Robert, Laura and their eleven month old daughter Winifred Laura were living with Thomas Cooper, a widower, at 38 Whitsed Street in Peterborough the home of his parent's. Enoch also lived with his son and was a retired tailor. Thomas's seven year old son Ernest also lived with his father.
Edmund Richardson Parkins, son of Peter and Mary, married Beatrice in Hackney during 1893.
Finally Charles Parkins married Elizabeth Ellen Perry in Peterborough during 1894. Elizabeth was born in Buckinghamshire.

Mark Walden, his wife Martha and their son and daughters lived in Albion House (221). Mark was a retired baker. Three of their daughters, Emma, Piercey Eliza and Ellen Watts Walden were all school mistresses. Their youngest child Mark aged fourteen attended school. John James Lowe, nephew of Mark and Martha also lived with them, he was a watchmaker.

In 1881 the Walden family lived at 17Albion Terrace Fletton where Mark (senior) worked as a baker and grocer.

Sarah Ann Jaggard from Linton in Cambridgeshire lived at either 229 or 231 Oundle Road in 1891. Living with Sarah were her four sons who all had the surname of Plumb. Albert was thirty and worked as a railway servant, Joseph, who was twenty one, Prophet eighteen and Arthur fourteen all worked as railway labourers. Sarah's husband and father to her children was Charles Plumb they married during 1856 in Linton. Sarah's maiden name was Moore. Charles died in 1868 aged thirty six.

Sarah, nee Plumb, married Joseph Jaggard during 1873 at Linton in Cambridgeshire but by the time of the 1881 census Sarah was shown as being a widow.

Living in the next house along which was named Crick Villa (233) were William Brown, a railway engine driver, and his wife Grace. At the time of the 1881 census Grace was married to Charles Pead, they lived in Queens Walk, but since then Charles died. They had a son Frank who only lived for six days he was recorded as 'Son of Grace Ann Peed, widow' and was buried on 26th July 1884 in the local cemetery. Grace married William Brown during the winter months of 1884 in the Peterborough district. Some of her children from her first marriage were still at home at the time of the 1891 census. George aged nineteen worked as an engine cleaner, Elizabeth, previously known as Jane was a tailoress, William aged twelve and Charles aged nine attended school as did Amelia Brown aged six who was the first child of William and Grace since they married..

Henry Chapman lodged with the family he came from March and was an engine driver. Matthew Peet and George Alfrew both came from Doddington and also lodged with the Brown family.

In 1881 George and Mary Cooper lived at 1 Tower Street Fletton with their children William born in 1868, Alice in 1871, Elizabeth Emma in 1873, Mary Ellen in 1875, George Samuel in 1877 and Martha Ann in 1879. By the time of the 1891 census they had moved to Crick Villa (235). George's wife Mary died aged forty five and was buried in the local cemetery at the end of March 1891.

Their son William worked as a railway fireman. As their mother had died both Elizabeth and Ellen (Mary E) did not have an occupation so probably looked after the house and family. George was working as a baker. Martha aged eleven, Benjamin aged seven and Annie aged five all attended school.

Thomas Honeyball, a railway guard, and his wife Augusta lived in one of the Eastmead Villa's (239). They married during 1876 in Cambridge where Augusta was born. The family moved to Woodstone from 29 Park Street in Fletton where they lived in 1881. Their children were Edith Emily aged twelve, William Frederick aged ten, Clara aged six, Alfred aged four and Thomas aged nine months.

WOODSTONE HILL

William Kisby was the publican at the Cross Keys inn and lived there with Susan his wife. In 1881 they lived in Percival Street in Peterborough where William then worked as a carpenter. William and Susan had twins, born in 1894, they named them Sarah and William. Sarah died in September 1895 aged one and William died in August 1896 aged one year and ten months. They were buried next to each other in the local cemetery.

Joseph and Annie Gamble married during the summer months of 1890 in the Peterborough district. By 1891 they were living not far from William and Susan Kisby. Joseph was the son of William and Sarah who lived along Water End and the brother of Maria who lived further along Woodstone Hill with her husband Joseph Pickering.

Alice Baxter, a seamstress (shirt), lived next to Joseph Gamble with her niece Alice Barnes Baxter, aged twenty one who worked as a tailoress. In 1881 they lived along Bread Street Fletton with Emmanuel Baxter. He was father to Alice senior and grandfather to the younger Alice. Emmanuel died during 1884 aged sixty eight.

Thomas and Mary Ford were still living along Woodstone Hill although their family had moved away. Their nephew Arthur Eason was living with them, he was eighteen years old and worked as an agricultural labourer.

Jane Ford, Thomas' mother lived alone not far from them. Jane died in 1894 and was buried in the local cemetery. Her husband John died in 1888 aged eighty four he was also buried in the cemetery.

Joseph Pickering, a bricklayer's labourer, married Maria Gamble in 1889. They lived along Woodstone Hill with their two children Alpheus William aged three and Clara aged one. Maria, born in Old Fletton, was the daughter of William and Sarah Gamble and sister to Joseph. In 1881 their home was in Lincoln Road. Joseph was born in Swineshead and in 1881 was lodging with Thomas and Mary Howe who lived in Thorney.

John Wright, a platelayer's labourer, his wife Elizabeth and their children Albert aged six and Ethel aged two years. John was the son of William and Mary from Water End.

Thomas and Ann Parkinson lived next to John Wright and had lived along Woodstone Hill since the early 1870's. Thomas was born in Woodstone in 1837 and was the son of William and Jane Parkinson from Water End. Thomas and Ann still had four of their children living at home at the time of the census. Susan, aged twenty nine, had moved back home from Yorkshire and continued working as a domestic servant. Thomas Richard aged sixteen worked as a wagon lifter. Neither Charles Robert aged fourteen, nor Caroline Alice who was eleven, were shown as attending school or as having an occupation.
In the June of 1892 Thomas senior died aged fifty five he was described as having worked as a wagon fitter and market gardener. Lucy their daughter died a few months later in November aged twenty seven. Lucy had been working as a domestic servant in Sloane Square Chelsea. They were both buried in the cemetery along Cemetery Road.
John Parkinson, son of Thomas and Ann, and his wife Jane also lived along the Woodstone Hill, not far from his parents. They had a baby son, Ernest Charles aged ten months. John worked as a railway fireman

John Ward, a railway engine inspector, his wife Elizabeth and their family lived next to John Parkinson. John and Elizabeth were both born in Peterborough. Also living with them were their three sons

George, a general labourer, aged thirty four, John a railway engine fitter aged twenty and Isaac a railway labourer aged eighteen. Also at home was their daughter Caroline aged fifteen who was a general servant and Elizabeth's widowed mother Mary aged eighty nine.

Charles Baker, a carter, married Annie Palmer during 1880, he was born in Stanground and Annie was from Peterborough. They lived at Alma Place Fletton in 1881 until moving to one of the Victoria Cottages (possibly 274) around 1889. They had six children, Arthur ten and Helen nine, Charles seven and Annie five were all born in Fletton. These four children attended school. Emily three and Florence one year old were born in Woodstone. Mary Jane Jackson from Peterborough was a nurse who was visiting the Ward family at the time of the census.

OUNDLE ROAD

John Cockerill, a gardener, and his wife Ann lived along Oundle Road. John was the son of Henry (Harry) and Mary who at the time of the 1841 census lived at High Street Orton Longueville where Henry was an agricultural labourer. During the spring of 1856 John and Ann Taylor married in Peterborough and by the time of the 1861 census they were living in Orton Longville. Ten years later in 1871 they were living at Lodge house not far from the rectory in the same village. In 1881 John was shown on the census as working at Oatlands hotel in Weybridge as a labourer in the grounds and Ann lived there also. By the time of the 1891 census John and Ann had moved back to Peterborough and set up home along Oundle Road in Woodstone. John was working as a gardener.

Richard Murdock, a signalman, and his wife Charlotte lived along Oundle Road at 258. They had nine children Richard aged seventeen a railway servant, William aged fourteen who was an errand boy, both were born in Woodstone. Arthur aged twelve and also an errand boy and Thomas who was ten and attended school, both boys were born in Fletton. Henrietta eight and Beatrice Annie aged six both attended school, Sidney Walter aged five, Albert aged two and Emma aged eleven months all were born in Woodstone.

Jacob Lovell, born in Glapthorne, and his wife Elizabeth who was born in Nassington were lodging with Herbert and Eliza Jackson in Palmerston Road at the time of the 1871 census. It is possible they were friends prior to moving in as Herbert was born in Nassington and Eliza in Glapthorne. Sadly Elizabeth died in 1872 aged twenty three.

Jacob later married Sarah Hatfield during the spring of 1875 in Peterborough. By 1881 they lived in Albert Place in Peterborough. In 1891 Jacob, a railway engine driver, and Sarah lived at 256 Oundle Road with their six children. Sarah their daughter aged nineteen worked as a machinist. William aged thirteen worked as a general labourer, Reginald eleven, Jesse ten and Edith aged eight attended school. Florence was the youngest in the family aged two years.

James and Mary Landin moved from 9 Elm Street, Fletton to Oundle Road after their youngest child Albert was born in 1888. James was a railway engine fireman. They had eight children. Both Rose and Sarah Jane worked as dressmakers. John was a railway porter; George William was a groom, James, Joseph and Alfred attended school and the youngest child was Albert aged three.

Jeremiah Brewster married Susannah Freear during 1888 in Stanground where they both were born. Jeremiah was the son of William and Esther Brewster. His grandparents were Jeremiah and Susannah (nee Barber).The family are descendants of Jeremiah Brewster and Mary (nee Slote) who married on 22nd January 1789 in Whittlesea. They lived in Stanground after the marriage. (*Mary Slote was my Great great great great aunt who was born in 1766 at Deeping St James.*)

Susannah was the daughter of Charles and Caroline Freear, and the niece of William and Esther Brewster.

Jeremiah and Susannah lived at 234 Oundle Road where they owned and ran the bakery. Their first child Gertrude was born in 1890. Esther Brewster, sister to Jeremiah, also lived with them. Charles Morris lodged with the family and worked as a baker's assistant.

Owen Golding, a railway clerk, and his wife Susannah lived at Normanton Villa (212), with their two sons who were both born in March. Charles was fourteen and worked as a printer's boy.

Herbert was twelve and attended school. They also had a son called Frederick but he died during 1888 aged seven. In 1881 the family lived in Cambridge where Owen worked as a number taker at a railway clearing house.

Harriet Atkin was the widow of Thomas Atkin who died during 1888 in Peterborough aged sixty three. In 1891 Harriet lived in one of the Adelaide Villas (208) with her children. Alice was seventeen and worked as a confectioner's assistant, Arthur aged sixteen was employed in a wood yard, Florence aged fifteen was a shopkeepers Assistant and Lily aged eight attended school.

John Bolton was a Baptist minister and he lived at Roseberry Villas (206) with his wife Mary Ann. In 1881 they were living in Lincolnshire.

Benjamin Percival Browne married Ellen Rowell from Stanground in 1876. In 1881 they were living at 41 Ackland Street in Peterborough. Benjamin worked as a railway engine driver. By 1891 they had moved to one of the Roseberry Villas (204) along Oundle Road and had two children, Elizabeth aged thirteen who attended school and Albert aged twelve who was shown on the census as having paralysis of the spine.

WATER END

The following families were long time residents of Water End, many had lived there since 1861 and some since 1851.

Henry and Emma Hoare previously lived at Palmerston Terrace but had moved to live at 2 Acorn Cottages with their children. Ada Emma aged thirteen, Laura Helen aged twelve, John Thomas aged ten, Charles Henry aged eight and Herbert (Henry) aged four.

Henry and Matilda Palmer were still living at 1 Gladstone Cottages. Matilda, their oldest daughter was back home and worked as a milliner (dress). Emily was a dressmaker, Charles was a railway fireman, Henry was a carpenters apprentice and Alfred aged ten attended school.

John and Harriet Jarvis, both seventy four years old, were still living at 2 Gladstone Cottages.

Thomas and Elizabeth Payne continued living at 3 Gladstone Cottages. Their son William lived with his parents and had changed his occupation from an agricultural labourer to a railway platelayer.

George Weston, a joiner, and his wife Annie lived at 4 Gladstone Cottages with their family. Fred aged twenty five was a joiner, Arthur aged fifteen was a railway engine cleaner, Frank aged thirteen was a printers apprentice, Archie aged eleven and George aged six both attended school, Horace and Walter were three and eleven months respectively. All the children were born in Woodstone.

Johnson and Elizabeth Phillips lived at 5 Gladstone Cottages with their family. Sarah aged twenty still lived at home although there was no occupation shown for her. William Henry and Charles both worked as agricultural labourers. Ruth Phillips, aged three months, granddaughter to Johnson and Elizabeth was with the family at the time of the census. William Smith also lived with the Phillips family. He was three years old and nephew to Johnson and Elizabeth. Their daughter Lydia died when she was only four and was buried on 31st August 1882 in the cemetery along Cemetery Road.

James and Caroline Short continued to live at 7 Gladstone Cottages. Mary Ann aged twelve was the only child still at home. Their fifteen year old daughter Elizabeth was a housemaid working and living at The Kings School in Park Road Peterborough. Mary Hunt was shown as lodging with the family her husband James died in 1886 aged eighty.
James and Caroline's daughter Sarah aged twenty was a general servant living with Emma Thompson and her four children at Edmund Street in Horton Bradford.
Sarah married Thurston Bolton, a wool buyer on 7th June 1892 at St Augustine's church. Thurston was the son of Thomas and Hannah Bolton who lived at North Bierley near Shipley, Bradford during 1891. At the time of the census Thurston was a wool sorter. By 1901 Sarah and Thurston were living at North Bierley.

The Weston Family

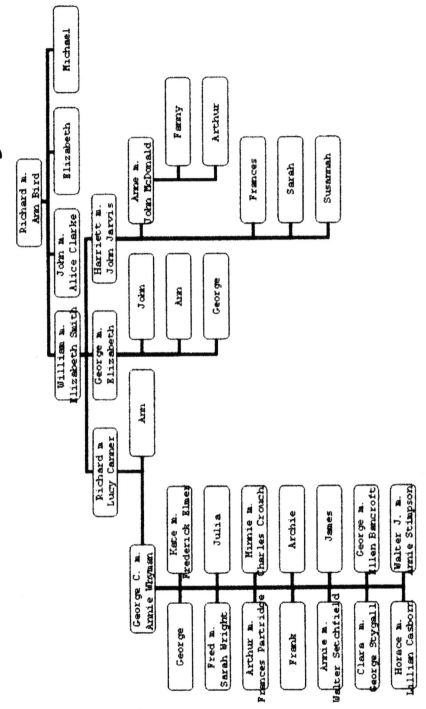

Robert and Eliza Crayton also continued to live at 9 Gladstone Cottages. Their daughter Mary aged twenty one was a domestic cook living with John and Emma Mills at the rectory in Orton Waterville. Their other daughter Annie was a domestic servant for George and Elizabeth Hills who lived in Kensington. George Hills was an assistant secretary for Great Western Railway Co.

Thomas Hubbard, born in Yarwell, and his wife Keziah born in Nassington, had moved to Water End since the 1881 census. They lived in the cottage next to the Crayton family. Thomas worked as a railway labourer. William their oldest son aged nineteen who was born in London also worked for the railways as an engine cleaner. Kate aged sixteen and born in Rotherham was a dressmaker's apprentice. John aged fourteen, also born in Rotherham, and Moses aged twelve born in Nassington were agricultural labourers. Annie aged nine, Fred seven and Robert four all attended school. The youngest child was Charles aged two. All four youngest children were born in Woodstone.

Thomas and Jane Odell had moved to Woodstone from Bedfordshire. They lived at 11 Gladstone Cottages.

Richard and Lucy Weston were still living at number 12. They had three of their grandchildren living with them Minnie was seventeen and worked as a milliner. Annie aged ten and Clara aged seven attended school. Their parents were George and Annie Weston who lived at 4 Gladstone Cottages.

Between Gladstone Cottages and Gothic Villas was the Parochial School.

John Blanchard, a railway guard, lived with his wife Emily and their son and daughter Thomas and Mary at 1 Gothic Villas.
Richard Mason, a railway porter, lived with his wife Mary Ann and their four children at 2 Gothic Villas.
The next group of cottages were Orchard Terrace. Sarah Hoare lived on her own at in the first cottage and was the caretaker at the church.

Mary Pickering was a widow by the time of the census. Thomas her husband died at the end of 1890. He was buried in the cemetery along Cemetery Road on 1st January 1891 aged 62. Eliza Pickering aged thirty six continued to live with her mother at 4 Orchard Terrace.

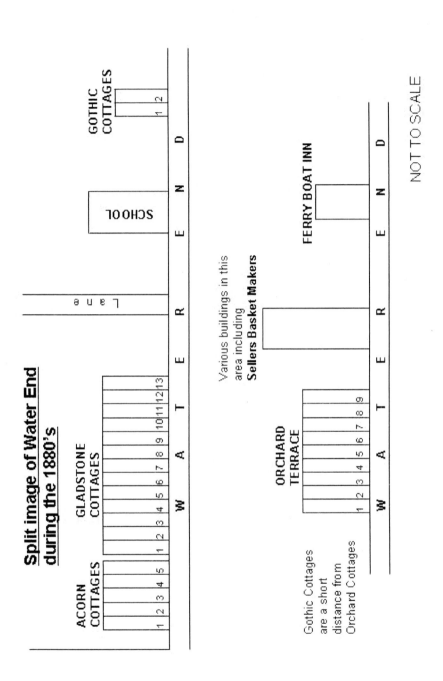

Next door at number 5 lived William and Susan Bland. Since 1881 they had three more children, brothers and sister for Alice. Robert Henry was born in 1882, Elizabeth Sarah in 1883 and William George in 1887. There was also five year old William Davis boarding with the family whose birth place was not known. Sarah Taylor was visiting them, she came from Norfolk.

John and Sarah Lightfoot were living next to the Bland family, John was a sawyer. They had just had a new baby son at the time the census was recorded he was one day old but had not been named at that time.

Ezra Garnham, a railway labourer, and his family came from Suffolk and lived along Water End. His children were Walter, Louisa and Ethel. Mrs Garnham was not at home on the day of the census. Mary Ann Farrow was the housekeeper and her son Allen was a general labourer they both came from Suffolk and lodged with the Garnham family.

A few houses away lived Sarah Sykes, a widow from Upwood. Sarah worked as caretaker for a school. Also living with Sarah was her son in law Frederick Farrow, from Ipswich, his wife Esther and their four year old daughter Adelaide.
Frederick worked as a bricklayer's labourer. Frederick's mother Mary Ann and his brother Allen lived with the Garnham family.
Not far from Sarah lived her son Edmund, his wife Easter and their daughter Florence aged six months.

William Leverett was a publican at the Ferry Boat Inn where he lived with Mary his wife. They both came from Norfolk. William and Mary had five children, William was born in 1882, George Frederick in 1883, Edward in 1885, Clara Gertrude in 1887 and Charles in 1889. Rose Walker aged seventeen was their domestic servant, she came from Woodford in Northamptonshire.

Elizabeth Haynes husband George died during October 1890 and was buried in the local cemetery. Elizabeth worked as a charwoman and lived along Water End with five of her children. Edward aged fifteen was a carpenters apprentice, Harriet aged ten, Alice aged eight, Rebecca aged five and Emma aged three all attended school.

Elizabeth's daughter Sophia was living with her grandparents Edward and Rebecca Cox at East Delph near Whittlesea where Edward was a farmer.

William Thomas Hemment had moved back to Woodstone to live in his late parent's house at Water End with his wife Mary and their young family. William Thomas fourteen, Francis thirteen, Alice Eliza eleven and Ernest eight all attended school. Their youngest daughter Dorothy Mary was one year old and born in Woodstone.

Next to the Hemment family was a signal box. The census shows it was not occupied during the night as the signalman only attended during the daytime.

Robert Bland, son of Joseph and Sarah was married to Elizabeth and they lived next to the signal box with their two year old son Alfred Joseph.
Joseph Bland died in 1891 in his 70th year. He was buried in the cemetery along Cemetery Road. His wife Sarah continued to live along Water End a few houses away from Robert. Sarah's niece, Charlotte Keight, also lived with her. Charlotte was born in Aldwinckle and worked as a dressmaker.
Sarah died in 1893 and was buried alongside her late husband Joseph.

Jane Whitham was a widow by the time she was fifty two and lived along Water End. Her daughters Ellen and Elizabeth worked at a Pea/Corn factory and lived with their mother. They were all born in Peterborough. Edith Whitham aged one year and born in Woodstone was Jane's granddaughter. Edith was recorded as being in her grandmother's home at the time of the census.
Jane had six people lodging at the house, William Bird a bricklayer's labourer and Thomas Bird a fitter's labourer, Hannah Bird was nine and attended school. William Worracker a horse driver. All four were born in Peterborough. John Wilkinson was from Lincolnshire and worked as a farm labourer and Alex Wilkinson was from Chesterton and worked as a bricklayer's labourer.

George and Emma Jane Hunting were living at Manor Farm which was situated between Water End and Jubilee Street. George was a coal merchant and farmer. They had two sons, Frank Edwin who was born in 1868 and Arthur Robert in 1870, both were coal agents. They also had a daughter Agnes Louise who was born in 1872. All three children were born in Fletton. Mary Robinson, at the grand age of ninety one, was aunt to George; she was a widow and lived with the family. Ada Martin aged sixteen was the family's domestic servant born in Fletton.

JUBILEE STREET
Jubilee Street was built in 1887 at the time of Queen Victoria's Jubilee year. By the time of the 1891 census it consisted of twenty five houses. There were thirteen houses down the odd numbered side and twelve down the even numbered side of the street.

Charles Kinns, a railway engine driver, and his wife Emma lived at number 1 with their family. Fred was fifteen and worked as a nurseryman's assistant. Charles William was fourteen and worked as an errand boy. Emily who was twelve, Arthur ten and Thomas seven all attended school. The family were all born in March apart from Thomas who was born in Fletton.

Living at number 7 were James Gunton, born in Chatteris, who worked as a locomotive engineman, his wife Elizabeth (nee Pyle) and their nine children. Arthur Pyle Gunton aged twenty worked as a butcher. James Peters Gunton aged eighteen worked as a moulder. George Robert aged seventeen was a coppersmith. Elizabeth Hannah was fifteen and possibly stayed at home to help her mother with the family. John William was thirteen, Fred eleven, Herbert ten and Charlie who was five all attended school. Both Herbert and Charlie were born in Fletton, the other children were born in Peterborough. The youngest was Frank aged one and born in Woodstone.

In 1881 the family were living at 15 Davies Terrace in Fletton although Elizabeth their daughter was not at home at the time of the census. She was shown as living with her grandparents, William and Hannah Gunton, at Slade Lodge Chatteris. At the time Elizabeth was five and shown on the census as Hannah E.

James Gunton senior died aged forty four and was buried on 11th February 1893 in the cemetery along Cemetery Road.

William Cornwall lived at 17 and worked as a bathing place attendant. His wife Susan died during November 1888 and was buried in the local cemetery. William's unmarried daughter Mary did not have an occupation shown on the census so she possibly looked after the home after her mother died. Lily Cornwell, aged twenty, was William's granddaughter who worked as an assistant schoolmistress and lived with William.

Also living with the family was William Toynton, grandson to William Cornwell; he was nine and attended school. William Toynton was the son of John Thomas and Susan Toynton who lived at 7 Tower Street during 1881. In 1881 William and Susan lived at Victoria Place in Fletton with their ten year old granddaughter Rosalind.

Going back ten years to the 1871 census William and Susan were shown as living in Grove Street at the Ladies School where Ethel, one of their daughter's, was a nursery governess and her sister Florence was a governess.

Joseph William Hankins, a railway engine driver from Warmington, and his wife Caroline from Oundle lived at 23 with their children. Carrie was ten, Ethel was six, Kate was four and George Edward was one year old. Prior to living in Woodstone the family lived at Grove Street Fletton. In 1881 Carrie was shown as Caroline.

The census shows an entry for 27 Jubilee Street which read that the tenants 'Went out on Saturday and have not returned – April 9th 1891'.

George Gillings, a railway engine driver born in Tansor, and Sarah Ann his wife lived at 28 with four of their children. Emily was twelve, John William was nine and Clara aged seven all attended school. The youngest son was Horace George aged three. Elizabeth their daughter was a servant for William and Annie Saunders who lived along Broadway in Peterborough with their five children. William Saunders was a newspaper reporter.
In 1881 George and his family lived along Bread Street in Fletton. Their oldest children Arthur born in 1873 and Elizabeth born in 1875 were also living with them.

Thomas Tunnicliffe a boiler maker born in Gibralter lived at number 6 with his wife Sarah Ann and their children. Alfred Thomas aged seventeen worked as a fitter's apprentice and Kate aged fifteen was a tailoress. In 1881 they were living at Crown Street in Peterborough.

Living at number 4 was Oakey Robert Gowler a railway engine fireman and his wife Amelia. They married at St Augustine's church during July 1885. Oakey was the son of Pedley and Martha Gowler from Houghton in Huntingdonshire. Amelia was the daughter of James and Matilda Dockrill who lived at 14 Davis Terrace in Tower Street Fletton during 1881. Oakey and Amelia had two children William Oakey aged five and Ethel aged three, both born in Woodstone.

Next door to the Gowler family lived Thomas and Sarah Garner who moved from Grove Street where they lived in 1881. There were eight of their children living at home. Charles aged seventeen was a railway clerk, Harry aged fifteen was an errand boy for a chemist. James aged twelve, Olive nine, Sydney seven and Albert who was five all attended school. The youngest children were Frank aged three and David aged two. Lavinia Church, aged twenty four, worked for the family as a domestic servant, she was born in Godmanchester.

Joseph Quincey and his wife Thirza lived in the first house on the even numbers side of Jubilee Street with their two children, Edwin aged two and Thirza was two months. Joseph was an 'out of work butcher'. Eliza Gilbert, cousin to Joseph, was living with the family and worked as a private school teacher.

PALMERSTON ROAD

More houses had been built since 1881 along Palmerston Road.

NUMBER	NAME	BUILT
84a	J.W. Palmerston House	1886
79a to 85	Thorpe Cottages	1887
87 and 89	Brooklin Cottages	1883
105 and 107	Fern Villas	1886
109 and 111	Crown Villas	1884
137 to 143	Lewis Cottages	1884
142 and 144	The Cedars	1886
145 to 151	Florida Terrace	1884
153 and 155	Pix Cottages	1885
168 to 174	St Swithin Villas	1884
180 and 182	Geneva Cottages	1885
184 and 186	Lylas Cottages	1886
188 and 190	Rose Villas	1887
192 and 194	Myrtle Villas	1886
196 and 198	Winshil Villas	1886
200 and 202	Shamrock Cottages	1886
204	Murton House	1887
206	Greta House	1885

All these details were found on plaques built into the brickwork of the houses, the ones missed out were either not marked, been removed or covered over.

A high percentage of men who lived along Palmerston Road worked for the railways.

William Phillips was a widower by the time of the 1891 census but was still living in the same house at number 1 as he had done for twenty years. His wife Charlotte fell asleep on the 15th February 1887 aged sixty seven, and was buried in the cemetery along Cemetery Road. Louisa Bland, niece to William was living with him as his housekeeper, she was also a widow.

The next house along was number 5 where Thomas and Annie Waite lived. Thomas' brother George, a coal hawker, was widowed and also lived there with his thirteen year old daughter Rose. Charles Munden, cousin to Thomas, had lived with them since the 1880's his occupation was a groom.

James Henry Hagger and his family had moved into number 9 the house where Mark Christmas and his family previously lived.

Samuel Jamson, a provision and leather merchant continued to live at 13 with his wife Jane and four of their children. Hannah aged

twenty one and Lucy aged nineteen both worked as milliners. Harry aged eighteen and Robert aged seventeen were both currier and leather salesmen, probably working with their father. John Thomas Jamson, son of Samuel and Jane, died during December 1884 aged twenty seven. He was buried in the cemetery along Cemetery Road. Jane died on 13th

December 1900 aged sixty seven and was buried with her son. On the grave the family had the words engraved 'Kindest of Mothers'.

Further along at 37 lived Mary Webb. Her husband Thomas Peter, a coal dealer, died at the age of sixty two, and was buried on 3rd January 1891 in the local cemetery.

Mary continued working in her husbands business as she was shown on the census as a coal dealer. Mary's children worked to help with the running of the home. Charlotte aged twenty five was a domestic servant, Thomas aged seventeen was a coal labourer, John aged thirteen was an agricultural labourer and Margaret aged ten attended school. The youngest child at home was Frank S. Webb he was two years old and grandson to Mary.

On the 31st January 1892 Theodosia Webb, daughter of Mary and the late Thomas Peter, married William Henry German at St Marks Church in Peterborough. The witnesses' of the wedding were Mary Webb and Theodosia's brother Thomas.

William and Theodosia had a son George Henry who was born in the spring of 1893. They had only been married four years when Theodosia died at the age of thirty two and was buried in the local cemetery on 2nd January 1896.

James and Amy Waspe were still living at 45 with their family. James continued to be a railway guard, their son James Robert worked as a railway cleaner. John William was called William and at the age of thirteen worked as a brewer's assistant. George Oliver born in 1880 attended school with his younger sister Elizabeth Ellen who was born in 1886 their brother Henry was one year old.

George Weldon, a brewer, lived at Palmerston House with his wife Mary Ann. They had two servants living with them. Annie Skinner was a domestic servant and Higgins Ward was a brewer's labourer. George was born in Farcet and was the son of John and Susannah Weldon. During 1871 they all lived at Tower Street in Fletton. John was also a brewer and during 1881 used to live along Palmerston Road with Susannah and their family. John was born on 21st April 1816 and died 25th April 1888. Susannah was born on 5th June 1821 and died 4th April 1899. They were buried side by side in the cemetery along Cemetery Road.

William Bigley lived with his wife Mary and their five children at 87. William was a railway engine driver. Their children were Catherine Annie born in 1872 who worked as a dressmaker. Caroline Milly born in 1877, William Henry in 1879, John Tom in 1881 and Stephen Alfred in 1886, they all attended school. Stephen was the only child who was born in Woodstone, his brother and sisters were born in Fletton. In 1881 the family lived at 15 Grove Street Fletton.

A few houses along at 105 lived Henry Frederick Francis, a railway engine driver, and his wife Emma. Also living with them was Fannie Rowell, mother to Emma, and Emma's brother Alfred who was a railway servant. In 1881 they all lived along Queens Walk.

Elizabeth Kingerley lived at 111 Palmerston Road, her husband Joseph was not at home at the time of the census. He was lodging with George and Eliza Cousins at Walpole St Andrew where he was a dealer in greengrocery. George Cousins was an innkeeper.
Janice de Lima Araujo, great granddaughter of Joseph and Elizabeth, has told me the family moved to Woodstone in the late 1800's from Parson Drove where they had been farming.
Their children were Joseph born 1868 and Walter born in 1873, Millicent born 1876 and Ethel born 1881. Joseph was a railway fireman and Walter was a railway cleaner. Millicent possibly helped her mother in the house as she was not shown as having an occupation. Ethel attended school.

William Beazley was lodging with the Kingerley family and worked as a railway engine cleaner, he came from Cambridge.

In 1841 Joseph Kingerley (senior) aged forty was a farmer who lived on the south side of Town Street towards the Bank (river) at Parsons Drove. Next to him at The Baisk and Swan Inn lived George, aged thirty, and Letitia Kingerley and their two sons Joseph aged five and Henry aged three. George was the innkeeper. Further along lived Robert Kingerley aged twenty five who was also a farmer.

In 1861 they were all still living at Parson Drove along High Street where they all continued farming.

Not far from the Kingerley family lived Phillip Henry Darker with his wife Louisa. The house they lived in was called Clifton House (135). At the time of the 1891 census there had been no houses built between 115 and 135. Phillip and Louisa lived in Leicester during 1861 and by the time of the 1871 census had moved to Demontford Terrace in Woodstone. Phillip was a railway clerk and their daughter Emma Louisa aged fourteen worked as a dressmaker's apprentice. Her brother William aged seven attended school. By the time of the 1881 census Emma was a servant for Walter and Florence Welby who lived at Harlston where Walter was a rector. Phillip and Louisa do not appear to be recorded on the 1881 census. On 25th August 1884 their daughter Emma Louisa married John William Harrison at St Augustine's church. John was a grocer. On 11th March 1885 Emma died aged twenty eight. On 3rd June 1887 Phillip and Louisa's son William Henry also died aged twenty four he worked as a railway clerk. They were both buried in the local cemetery.

A plaque was erected in St Augustine's church by Phillip and Louisa in remembrance of their children.

Francis Girling and his sister Henrietta were also living at Clifton House as part occupiers'. Francis was an assistant curate of Woodstone.

Daniel Nichols continued to live along Palmerston Road at 143 with his wife Hannah. Their family had increased since 1881, Arthur was twelve, Alice eight, Charlie six, Annie five and Joseph was two years old. All children apart from Joseph attended school. Daniel had changed his job from a railway fireman to an engine driver.

John Barrett, a railway signalman, and his wife Eliza were both born at Middleton in Norfolk. At the time of the 1881 census they were living at 7 Elm Street in Fletton. By 1891 they had moved to (145) with their family. Alfred was twenty one and worked as a railway number taker his sister Amelia aged twenty was a draper's cashier. Herbert aged eighteen was not able to work as he was recorded as being a cripple and at the time of the 1881 census he was a patient in the Peterborough Infirmary. The two youngest children were Nellie aged sixteen who was not shown as having an occupation and Walter aged fourteen worked as a baker's assistant.

John and Eliza's married daughter Emma Lucy Holmes was visiting them with her two children Edith and Sydney. Emma married Edward Holmes during 1883 in the Peterborough district. In 1885 Emma and Edward were living in Doncaster with their family.

Another of John and Eliza's daughters Alice married Ernest Willett in the district of Peterborough during 1889. Ernest was the son of James and Emily Willett who lived at 6 Nene Voir Place during 1871 and had moved to 3 Station Cottages Fletton at the time of the 1881 census. By 1891 they had moved again to 39 Park Road, Tring in Hertfordshire.

At the far end of Palmerston Road was Aboyne Lodge home to the Crawley family. Charles Edward Crawley's occupation had changed since 1881 to a wholesale saddler. Adelaide his wife was not at home at the time of the census. Their oldest daughter Ellen Elizabeth married Leonard Burtchaell Foster on 12th September 1889 at St Augustine's Church in Woodstone. Leonard was a bank clerk from the Parish of St Marks in Peterborough, his father George was described as a gentleman.

By 1891 Ellen and Leonard were living at Little Bowden near Market Harborough where Leonard was a bank cashier. They had a young daughter who they named Ethel she was under one year old. Adelaide Crawley, mother to Ellen, was living with them possibly helping out with the new baby.

Charles and Adelaide's other children were still at home. John William, aged twenty one, was a saddlers assistant who probably worked for his father. Agnes Emily aged nineteen was not shown as having an occupation. Evelyn Mary aged fourteen, Charles Edward aged twelve and Percy John aged nine all attended school.

Annie Garwell worked as a domestic servant and Caroline Smith was the cook for the family.

Thomas Richard Hunting, a merchant's clerk, married Rose Jane Bills towards the end of 1881. They lived at Murton House (204) with their five children. Ernest Charles was born in 1882, Mabel Gertrude in 1884 both born in the district of Peterborough. On 25th September 1893 their daughter Elsie Margaret died aged eight months and was buried in the local cemetery. Norman Richard was born in Woodstone during 1885. Frank Bertram was born in 1888 and Marcus Edward in 1890. In December 1894 Rose died aged thirty seven and was buried in the cemetery along Cemetery Road near to her daughter.

Frederick Shepherd married Ann Kinns during 1866 in the district of Peterborough. They then lived in Stanground where Frederick was born. They had six children. William was born in 1867, Harry (Henry) in 1869, Annie in 1871, Herbert in 1873, Frederick in 1875, Arthur in 1877 and Ada in 1880. During the early months of 1880 Ann died aged thirty six. By the time of the 1881 census Frederick and his children were living at Water End in Stanground. Frederick was a railway engine driver and his children all attended school. James Hill, a teacher, lived with the family as did Susan Kinns who was sister to Frederick's late wife.

Frederick and Ann also had a child called Ada who at the time of the 1881 census was shown as a visitor at the household of Thomas and Ann Briggs. They lived not far from the Shepherd family. Henry F. Shepherd was Frederick's grandfather he was eighty four years old, born in London, and listed as being a parish clerk.

By 1891 Frederick had remarried to Susan Kinns, and they lived at 192 Palmerston Road. They had four of the family living at home, Herbert was a draper's apprentice, Frederick was a railway telegraphist, Arthur and Ada attended school.

The following details were given to me by Gloria Godley who lives in the USA. Gloria is the granddaughter of Harry, (occasionally known as Henry).

They have an Indenture Certificate which contains full details of Henri Shepherd, son of Frederick Shepherd of Stanground who puts himself forward as an apprentice to Robert Graver. In 1881 Robert Graver lived in New Road, Peterborough where his grocers shop was.

The Indenture stated Henri was to serve his Apprentice from the first day of March 1884 for four years.

"The Apprentice had to abide by very strict rules, some of which were:-

Not to contract Matrimony within the four year term, nor to play cards or Dice Tables or any unlawful games.

Not to haunt Taverns or Playhouse. Henri was to be paid 2/- per week for the first year with an increase of 1/- per week each year".

Harry Shepherd, known as Henri in the Indenture, immigrated to Chicago sometime around 1890. He married Roza Simka Collins on Christmas Day in 1893. At that time he was a buyer for a large departmental store (Siegel & Cooper) in Chicago and made several trips back to the London area to purchase goods. Roza died in 1939 and Harry in 1940 both in Chicago.

John and Sarah Garfield had moved to 186 Palmerston Road in one of the Lylas Cottages. John William, their eldest son, worked as a railway engine cleaner, Emma was a dressmaker. Ethel attended school as did Ruth and Nellie who had been born since the last census. Herbert was the youngest aged three.

John Currington married Mary Ann Turner Lockwood on 25th December 1879. At that time John was a fireman for LNWR. In 1881 they were living at number 4 High Street in Hardingstone, Northamptonshire with Ethel their first child who was eight months old.

By 1884 the family had moved to Tower Street in Fletton where Bertha was born. John and Mary moved again as in 1887 William Benjamin was born in Woodstone. In 1891 they all lived in one of the Geneva Cottages (180) along Palmerston Road. John had changed his occupation to an engine driver.

Living at Linton House (178) was Thomas and Mary Eveleigh. Thomas was a railway company's goods agent.

In 1881 the family were living at 6 London Road, Belmont Terrace in Fletton with two of their children Emily and Thomas.

Back to 1891 Elizabeth their daughter, born in 1859, was recorded as being an assistant in home duties. Thomas William was born in 1869 and worked as a corn merchant's clerk.

James Garfield and his wife Mary lived not far from his brother John at 162. Their children were Alfred aged ten and Fannie aged eight who attended school. Before moving to Woodstone they lived in Grove Street New Fletton.

Thomas and Ann Goulding continued to live at 150. In 1881 it was known as 3 Linford Cottages. Since 1881 Thomas had been promoted from a miller to a miller's foreman. Two of Thomas and Ann's daughters Susan aged twenty three and Alice aged twenty both worked as dressmakers. Tom aged fifteen was a fitters apprentice and Evelyn who was seven attended school. Edith Rist born in India was Thomas's niece. She was eighteen years of age and like Susan and Alice worked as a dressmaker. Also living with the Goulding family was their five year old grandson George P.L.Cox.

Their oldest son William married Harriet Hicks from Stanground towards the end of the year in 1884. They had a one year old son called Frank and lived in Queens Walk not far from where William's parents lived in Palmerston Road.

Alfred and Mary Tomlin moved from 16 Tower Street Fletton to 146 Palmerston Road around 1884 when Lily was born in Woodstone. Alfred, a railway engine driver and his wife Mary were both born in Fletton. Frank was their oldest son born in 1872 and worked as a tailor's cutter. John born in 1874 was a groom and his brother Alfred who was born in 1876 worked as a shoemaker. Ernest aged twelve, Sarah aged nine, Lily aged seven William aged five and Mabel aged three all attended school. Horace was one year old.

Henry George Petitt, a railway engine driver, his wife Mary and their seven children moved to Woodstone sometime around 1877 when their son Charles Henry was born. They lived at 134 Palmerston Road. Prior to that they lived in Stanground where Florence was born. Florence was their oldest daughter aged fifteen probably helped in the home as she was not shown on the census as having an occupation. Her brothers and sisters who attended school were Charles aged thirteen, Mabel aged twelve, Lily aged ten and Henry aged eight. Thomas was three and Horace was one year old. All the children were shown on the census as being born in Peterborough.

Robert Biggadike, the local baker, continued to live at 132 with Harriet his wife and their two daughters. Mabel Harriett was ten and Gerty (Emily Gertrude) was nine years old, both were born in Woodstone.

William Henry Bonfield, a railway goods porter, married Elizabeth Rowell in 1883. Elizabeth was the daughter of James and Elizabeth Rowell who lived at the Palmerston Arms where James was a gardener and publican. William and Elizabeth lived at 120 Palmerston Road at the time of the 1891 census. They had three children who were Elizabeth Rowell Bonfield aged seven, Charles William aged five and Ives who was two years old. Elizabeth's brother James Rowell, a coal agents clerk and her sister Ann Rowell, a dressmaker also lived with the family.

Joseph Fowler was the local butcher who lived at 110 with his wife Elizabeth. They both came from Lincolnshire.

John Starmore, a sawyer, and his wife Frances lived at 108 with their family. Rosetta aged fifteen and Lillian aged fourteen both worked as domestic servants. William aged twelve and Minnie aged eight attended school. Robert Hendry from Kings Lynn and John Broom from Peterborough were railway engine stokers and lodged with the family.
John Starmore died aged fifty six during October 1896 in Fletton. He was buried in the cemetery along Cemetery Road.

William Cowley King, a carpenter and joiner, and his wife Anne lived at 102.
Anne was the daughter of George and Mary Burnham who lived along Oundle Road in Woodstone. William, a carpenter from Gloucestershire, married Anne on 21st June 1877 at St Augustine's church. In 1881 they were living at Albion Street in Stratton, Gloucestershire. At that time William and Ann had three children Annie Alice aged five, George William aged two and Elizabeth Emily was six months old. Their oldest child Annie was not at home at the time of the 1891 census but George and Elizabeth were. Also living with them was Edward E Burnham, he was born in Woodstone during 1885 and shown as being their adopted son.

James Grice was still living at 84, previously known as South House. Even though he was seventy six years old James continued working as he was shown as having an occupation of a beer retailer. Also living there was James' daughter Kezia but she was not shown as having an occupation. Mary her mother passed away during 1887 so Kezia possibly took over of the running of the home. Richard her brother worked as a railway clerk, John Yates aged sixteen grandson of James Grice also worked as a railway clerk and his sister Elizabeth aged fifteen also possibly helped in the house as she also had no occupation shown on the census.

John Yates, who previously lived at South House during 1881 was shown living at Cheltenham where he worked as a grocer's assistant. His wife Elizabeth was living with her widowed father Henry Bigley at his home 23 Grove Street in Fletton. Elizabeth was their house keeper and possibly helped to look after her sister Catherine who was recorded as being deaf and blind.

Since the 1881 census all families living in the Rodwell Cottages (68 -74) had changed.

Living in the end cottage numbered 74 was Thomas and Alice Turner. Thomas came from Littlebury in Essex and in 1881 when he was seventeen he worked as a railway engine cleaner and was lodging with Thomas and Hannah Stanton in West Ham. Thomas married Alice Hannah Smith in Peterborough. Alice was born at Upwell and at the time of the 1881 census was a domestic servant for Joseph and Agnes Oakden who lived at Granville Street in Peterborough.

In 1885 when Thomas and Alice's first child Mildred Alice was born they lived at Fletton. Annie Daisy their second daughter was also born in Fletton during 1889. The family moved to Woodstone where their twins, Edith Minnie and William Doil were born in 1890. They were ten months old at the time of the census. Edith died during 1891 aged thirteen months and was buried in the cemetery along Cemetery Road. William Doil died during December 1902 aged twelve. His mother Alice died during March 1900 aged thirty five. They were both buried in the same cemetery as Edith.

Stephen Bunyan, a boot maker, and his wife Charlotte lived at number 72 with their daughter Sarah and son Walter.

George Knight who was born in Essex lived with his wife Harriet and family at number 9 Demontfort Terrace in 1881. Harriet died in December 1882 aged thirty nine. Their son John also died, aged sixteen hours, about a month earlier than his mother. Both were buried in the local cemetery.

George worked as a railway guard and remarried in 1884 to Medea Markley who was born in Peterborough during 1853. By 1891 they were living at 68 Palmerston Road in the end cottage of Rodwell Cottages. Florence the oldest daughter of twenty three worked as a dressmaker. Henry was nineteen and worked as a printer's apprentice. Arthur was fourteen and worked as an errand boy. Florence, Henry and Arthur were children of George and Harriet. The family moved to Woodstone from Essex prior to the birth of Arthur in 1876. George and Medea had three more children after their marriage. Eva Medes was born in 1887, Hilda Medes in 1889 and Frederick James was born in 1890 he was six months old at the time of the census.

There were no houses between 68 and 58 along Palmerston Road. The next house was number 58 Raveley Cottages where William Plumb, a railway guard, and his wife Mary lived. William and Mary married in 1881 in the district of Cambridgeshire. They had five children. Alice Gertrude was born in Peterborough in 1882, the family then moved to Woodstone where Miriam Emily was born in 1884. William Charles was born in 1886, Ella Frances in 1887 and Horace Albert in 1889.

William Plumb senior lived at 2 Tower Street Fletton with Benjamin and Sarah Dorrington in 1881. William was born in West Wratting in Cambridgeshire and worked as a railway servant.

William and Mary Hayward were living at 52 Raveley Cottages with their children Charles aged fifteen, Mary aged eleven and Eliza aged seven. William worked as a railway engine driver and the children attended school.

Number 50 Raveley Cottages was uninhabited.

George and Martha Wright had moved from Cleveland Cottages in Palmerston Road where they lived in 1881 to 48 Raveley Cottages also along Palmerston Road. Their four children who lived at home were Arthur who worked as a railway porter, Harry worked as a bricklayer's labourer, Charles Horace aged four attended school and the youngest child was two year old Percy Edward.

Richard Harvey married Eliza Smith in Peterborough during 1884. Richard was a horse driver for the railways. They lived at 40 Palmerston Terrace and had two children Charles aged five and Eliza of eleven months.
In 1881, before he married, Richard lived at 5 Queens Walk (approx 164 Queens Walk) with his mother Maria, stepfather Richard Wright and his brothers and sister.

Ploughright Rolph married Clara Fuller on 24th October 1878 at St Augustine's Church Woodstone. They lived along Woodstone Hill in 1881 with their two children Florence Jane aged two and Thomas William six months. In 1891 the family had moved to 38 Palmerston Terrace. Florence was twelve, Charles William (Thomas) was ten and Ada was eight, they all attended school.
Thomas died on 24th July 1891 aged ten, he was buried in the local cemetery. For some reason Thomas was recorded as Charles at the time of the 1891 census.

Christopher and Mary George married in 1882 and lived at 30 Palmerston Terrace. They had two children, Ethel born in 1887 and Florence Jennie in 1891. Christopher's brother Sydney who was an army reserve lodged with the family.

George Piggott married Annie Bosett during 1885 in the district of Peterborough. Annie was the daughter of Thomas and Jane Bosett who lived in the parish of St Mary's in Peterborough during 1881. George and Annie lived along Palmerston Road with their son Alfred George who was born in 1888 in Woodstone. George was a bricklayer's labourer. In 1881, before George married, he lived at 69 Gladstone Street with his parents William and Ellen. His mother Ellen was born in Woodstone during 1839 and was the daughter of Charles and Elizabeth Wright. George had five brothers and sisters all apart from Joseph were born either in Woodstone or New Fletton. They spent a large amount of their childhood in Woodstone.

Charles Dockrill, a railway platelayer, and Ellen his wife lived at number 20 with their son Ernest. He was sixteen years old and worked as a stable labourer. In 1881 Charles was a journeyman miller (corn) and they lived at Grantchester where Ernest was born. Charles and Ellen were born in Great Shelford in Cambridgeshire.

William Ellis, born at Yaxley Fen, worked as a railway foreman shunter and lived at 6 Palmerston Road with his wife Martha and their family. Herbert was born in 1886 and Emily in 1888 both in Woodstone. William's brother' James also lived with the family and worked as a railway wagon repairer.

James and Matilda Dockerill lived at number 4. They had three young men boarding with them Robert Marshall a gardener, Joseph Thimblebee a railway engine cleaner and Robert Strongleman a railway guard. It was recorded that James was paralysed so they had possibly taken in boarders as a form of income to help with the upkeep of their home. In 1881 before James was paralysed he worked as a railway platelayer. At that time they lived at 14 Davis Terrace Tower Street in Fletton with their four children Eliab, William, Amelia and Sophia. James was born in Shelford Cambridgeshire and was also father to Charles Dockerill who lived at number 20.
Eliab married Johanna Andrew during 1884 in the North Witchford district, Johanna was born in March.
Amelia Dockerill married Oakey Gowler during 1885 in the Peterborough district.

QUEENS WALK
Of all the seventeen houses which made up Queens Walk between numbers 155 through to 169 and over the road between 156 and 172 only three were occupied by the original families recorded on the 1881 census, they were;

Thomas and Hannah Phillipson and their family were still living at 160. Their children were Herbert aged twenty four who worked as a drapers assistant, Louisa aged twenty two was a domestic housemaid, Alfred aged twenty was a railway engine cleaner, Henrietta aged eighteen was a mothers help, Walter aged sixteen was a grocers assistant, Arthur aged thirteen and Fanny aged eleven both attended school.

Benjamin Barnard, a railway signalman, and his wife Hannah lived at 167. Charles Payne their eight year old grandson who was born in Woodstone was living with them at the time of the census.

Their daughter Annie Frances married William Payne during the summer of 1881 in Peterborough. In 1891 William and Annie were living not far from Annie's parents at number 10 (155) Queens Walk. Also at home with William and Annie were their three other children Harold born 1884, Annie born 1885 and Ethel born 1887.

Robert and Ann Louder lived next to the Barnard family at 169 where Robert had a grocer's shop. Edith Mary Perry was sixteen and worked as a domestic servant for the family.

William Burnham married Charlotte Wright on 26th March 1883 at St Augustine's church in Woodstone. They lived at 166 Queens Walk as did their niece Alice Wright who was eight years old and attended school.

William was born in Woodstone in 1852 and was the son of Reuben and Jane Burnham who lived along the Turnpike Road (Oundle Road). Charlotte was also born in Woodstone and was the daughter of William and Mary Ann Wright who lived along Water End.

In 1881 Charlotte was the housemaid for Caroline Cheshire, a Life owner of Real Estate and lived along Cowgate in Peterborough. Caroline was sixty nine and employed four other ladies. Eliza Warwick aged sixty eight was a housekeeper, Mary Robinson aged eighty one as a nurse, Alice Monks aged fifty two as a night nurse and Jane Eagle aged twenty nine as a cook.

In 1881 William Burnham was a lodger with Joseph and Annie Griffin and their family who lived along Grove Street in Fletton. William's brother John also lodged with the Griffin family, sadly both William and John were shown as being widowed.

They both worked as brewers labourers.

James and Sarah Bull were both born in Watford and in 1891 they lived at 156 Queens Walk. In 1881 the family were living at 7 Station Cottages in Fletton where James was a railway guard. Four of their children, Fanny, George, Ernest and Horace were born in Thorpe Northamptonshire. Walter, Mabel, Arthur and Albert were born in Old Fletton. Apart from Fanny and Ernest the rest of the children were still living at home in 1891. George was twenty five and was an iron and tinplate worker. Horace aged twenty one was a railway clerk and store keeper, Walter aged nineteen was a baker, Arthur aged fifteen was a bar boy for L& N.W. railways. Albert was ten and Edith was seven probably attended school although it was not shown on the census.

Edward Filby Oswick had moved since the last census from Palmerston Terrace to 157 Queens Walk. His first wife Jane died in March 1883 at the age of forty one she was buried in the local cemetery.

Edward remarried towards the end of the year in 1884 in the Peterborough district to Elizabeth Foreman. By the time of the 1891 census most of the children had moved away apart from Ada who was nineteen and worked as a dressmakers apprentice and Joshua aged fourteen who was a grocer's assistant.

Their oldest son Oliver George married Lucy Palmer during the first quarter of the year in 1891 in Peterborough. They lived along South Street in the parish of St Mary's in Peterborough where Oliver worked as a copper boilers labourer.

Arthur Filby Oswick (junior) married Elizabeth Fanny Coleman during the summer of 1890 in West Ham. By the time of the 1891 census they were living at 3 Thornton Road Leyton in West Ham.

William Goulding married Harriet Smith in the district of Peterborough towards the end of 1888. They lived at 161 Queens Walk with their one year old son who they named Frank.

William was born in Yaxley and worked as a miller's clerk. He was the son of Thomas and Ann who had lived along the Woodstone Hill since 1868. Harriet was born in Stanground and was the daughter of Edmund and Mary Smith from Farcet Road.

William and Harriett and their family were living in Fletton by the time of the 1901 census where William worked as a basket maker's labourer.

Jesse Starsmore married Elizabeth Reed at the beginning of the year in 1888 in the district of Peterborough. Jesse was the son of Samuel and Ann Starsmore from Yarwell. They lived at 165 Queens Walk. In 1881 Elizabeth was a servant for Andrew and Martha Williamson who had a bakers and grocers shop not far from New Road and Wellington Lane in Peterborough.

LONDON ROAD

Moving away from the main village of Woodstone were a few farm cottages.

Richard and William Jones farmed at Woodstone Lodge. Their parents, Richard and Lucy Jones had lived there in Woodstone since 1834 when their brother John was born. Richard (junior) was born in Billing in Northamptonshire in 1819. Eliza Watts was a general servant for them she was forty five and came from Woodwalton.

George Hillson, a farm servant, and his wife Sarah Ann lived at Jones Cottage with four of their children. William Henry was born in 1877, Bertha and Clara in 1879 and Kate who was two months old at time of census. In 1881 the family lived at Papley Lodge in Warmington where George was a Farm Labourer. They had eleven children who were Ruth, Harriett, Jonathan, Mary Ann, George, Phoebe, William Henry, Annie Marie, Bertha, Clara and Kate.

Ruth married William John Garton on 23rd October 1889. By the time of the 1891 census they were living at Walpole Street in Peterborough with their son George Frederick aged seven months. William Henry married Rosetta Jane Jenkinson on 25th January 1897.

Bertha married John Henry Redhead on 16th July 1900.

Mary Ann married Walter James Quincey on 18th September 1900.

They all married at St Augustine's Church in Woodstone.

Richard Bluck, an architect, and his wife Sarah lived at Woodstone House. They had two children living at home, Richard Robinson Bluck aged twenty two and Rosina aged nineteen although neither had been recorded as having an occupation. Annie Simpson was a general servant for the family, she was born in Gunthorpe.

Living in Woodstone Lodge was Jesse and Jane Mason from Northamptonshire. Jesse was an agricultural labourer.

Not far from Woodstone Lodge were Wymans Farm Cottages. In one of them lived James Foster, an agricultural labourer, and his wife Sarah with five of their children. John Thomas was twenty six and worked as an agricultural labourer as did his brother Albert who was thirteen. Fanny was ten, George was eight and Kate six years old, they attended school. In 1881 the family lived at 2 Selbin Villas in Fletton.

John Brown was born at Fletton Lodge around 1833 he lived with his wife Mary in the other Wymans Cottage next to the Foster family. John was a farmer's foreman. In 1881 they were shown as living in Wymans Lodge on London Road. It was probably the same cottage, at that time John was a shepherd.

William Wyman continued to farm at Westbrook House where he and his wife Isabella lived. Two of their daughters also lived at home, Mary and Emily Jane neither were shown on the census as having an occupation. William Wyman employed a housemaid and a cook.

Isabella, their oldest daughter, married George Edward Abbott during 1886 in Peterborough. At the time of the 1891 census George and Isabella lived along Market Place in Spalding where George was a bank manager. They had four children Annie aged eight, George three, William one and Noel was three months old. George and Isabella employed a governess and three female servants.

CEMETERY ROAD

From around 1884 more cottages were being built between Oundle Road and the cemetery. This road was named Cemetery Road and occasionally known as Cemetery Lane. Table below shows the houses where the date is engraved in the brickwork.

NUMBER	NAME	BUILT
2 & 4	Vaughan Cottages	1885
6 to 16	Woodstone Terrace known as Excelsior Terrace in 1891	1885
18	Rose Villa	1885
20	Rowland Cottage	1885
22 & 24		?
26	Lea Cottage	1885
28	Albert House	?
30	Sidney House	1884
32	May Cottage	1884?
34 & 36	Rutland Villas	1884?

38 & 40	Gore Corner Cottages	1884?
42		?
44	Australian House	1887
46 to 66	Australian Terrace	1890
68 to 86	St Leonard Terrace	1893
88 & 90	Sidney Cottages	1897
100 & 102	Avery Cottages	?
104 & 106	St James Cottages	?
108 & 110	Lime Tree Cottages	1886
112 & 114	Dolphin Cottages	1890
116	Fern Cottage	?
131 to 137	Brookhall Terrace	1894
139 to 145	New Cross Terrace	1892
147 & 149	Diamond Jubilee Houses	?
51 to 53	W.E.	1897
89 to 93	Providence Villas	1897

Fern Cottage, the first house next to the cemetery was where William Patrick, a bus proprietor, and his wife Lizzie lived with their young family. Lizzie was born in Sawtry around 1865. Their children were William Herbert who was born in 1887, Eliza Mary in 1888 and John Thomas in 1889, all in Woodstone.

Eliza Smith, a widow, lived at 114 Dolphin Cottages in the house next to her daughter Lizzie Patrick. Eliza was born in Sawtry where she lived in 1881 with her father Thomas Spriggs. At that time Eliza had five children to support and worked as a mangle woman. Her children were Lizzie, Walter, Herbert, Harriet and Rowland.
Eliza's son Thomas was a farmers' servant lodging at the Cross Keys Inn' at St Ives with William and Hannah Thompson during 1881.
In 1891 Thomas, twenty nine, worked as a cab driver (groom). Herbert was twenty one with no occupation shown, Rowland aged sixteen was a railway servant.

John Thomas Ford married Jane Elizabeth Didymus during the winter months of 1889 at Fareham Hants. John was a railway servant and they made their home at 112 Dolphin Cottages. Johns' father and grandfather were both born in Woodstone

James and Sarah Hooke lived with their two children at 110 Lime Tree Cottages, James was a wagon builder.

James and Ellen Wright lived at 108 Lime Tree Cottages with their eight month old son William. James worked for the railways as a goods porter.

James Sewter, a miller, married Betsy Chambers during the beginning of the year in 1888 in the district of Peterborough. In 1891 they lived at 106 St James Cottage. James was born in Paston his parents were George and Mary who lived at Church Street Werrington in 1881. Betsy was the daughter of John and Hannah Chambers and grew up in Nassington where she was born.

Thomas Setchfield married Eliza Ann Stafford in Whittlesey during the end of the year in 1890. Thomas was a carpenter and by 1891 he lived with his wife at 104 St James Cottage. Harry Paget who was seven years old and shown on the census as brother in law to Thomas also lived with them. At the time of the 1881 census Thomas was lodging with William and Elizabeth Paget who came from Whittlesey but were living at 2 Selbin Villas in Fletton. James Foster who was living at Whymans Farm cottage was also shown as living in this cottage during 1881.

Clement Charles Clay, a joiner, married Emma Ann Knighton in Peterborough during the winter months of 1886 and lived at either 100 or 102 Cemetery Road. They had two children Winifred Gertrude born during the first quarter of 1888 and Robert Edwin during the summer of 1889.
Clement was the son of Joseph and Susan Clay from Stanground. In 1881 Clement was a millwright's apprentice. Emma was the daughter of Robert and Sophia Knighton who lived at Monument Street Peterborough in 1881.
By 1901 Clement and his family had moved to the St John's parish in Peterborough where he worked as a joiner in a flour mill.
A report in the Peterborough Advertiser dated 29th August 1930 stated:-
"The mystery of the disappearance of a retired Peterborough millwright, Mr Clement Charles Clay, aged 70, of Star Road Peterborough, which had engaged the attention of the Police, the B.B.C. and several newspapers at intervals during the past five

weeks, was solved on Monday evening when his body was found on the edge of a cornfield at Belchamp St. Pauls, eighteen miles from Braintree, Essex.

The body was in a decomposed condition and was discovered when the field of corn was about to be cut. Identification was difficult, but was definitely established with the aid of a watch and the clothing. The end appeared to have been peaceful. Mr Clay was missed on July 22nd while on holiday with his wife at the residence of his daughter, Mrs H Mason.

Retired Millwright Found Dead at Braintree.

The mystery of the disappearance of a retired Peterborough millwright, Mr. Clement Charles Clay, aged 70, of Star Road, Peterborough, which had engaged the attention of the Police, the B.B.C. and several newspapers at intervals during the past five weeks, was solved on Monday evening, when his body was found on the edge of a cornfield at Belchamp St. Pauls, eighteen miles from Braintree, Essex.

The body was in a decomposed condition and was discovered when the field of corn was about to be cut. Identification was

THE LATE MR. CLAY.

difficult, but was definitely established with the aid of a watch and the clothing. The end appeared to have been peaceful.

Mrs Clay told an "Advertiser" reporter that Mr Clay had been ill for about six months and was inclined to suffer from loss of memory. They were due to return home to Peterborough soon after Mr Clay was missed, and she believed that home was so impressed upon his mind that he was making his way to Peterborough when he became lost and sat down in the field. He had then covered eighteen miles and was in rather a lonely spot.

Thomas and Louisa Cornish lived at 66 Australian Terrace with their young family. Grace Helena Udell was born in 1877, Olga Louise Ashman born in 1878, Ernest Alexander Daniel born in 1880, Bertha Florence Maud born in 1882, Ethel Marion Hilda born in 1884 and Elfrida Constance Victoria was born in 1887. The family moved from Somerset where Thomas worked as a railway carpenter and he continued his trade in Woodstone.

William Plowman, a brickyard labourer, and his wife Jane lived at 58 Australian Terrace. They had two children Amelia born in 1886 and Ernest in 1889. Williams' brother Samuel and their widowed father Robert also lived with the family. Samuel was a railway shunter (points) and Robert worked as an agricultural labourer, both were born in Morborne as was William. Williams' mother

Martha died in 1878 aged thirty eight.
Celta Road sheep dip with R.Plowman working.

William Sharpe, an insurance agent, and his wife Bertha lived at 54 Australian Terrace with their two children. William Joseph aged one year and nine months born in Stanground and Robert Ernest was three months old and born in Woodstone.

Charlie Haynes, a carpenter, and his wife Mary lived at 44 Australian Terrace. Charles was born in Peterborough he lived at Albert Place with his family in 1881. At the age of seventeen he worked in the wagon shop on the railways. His parents were Frederick and Sarah Haynes.

John Anker married Elizabeth Randall towards the end of the year in 1887 in the Peterborough district. John was born in Whittlesea and Elizabeth in Alwalton.

They had five children, Albert Edward aged eight, Agnes Emma aged seven, Horace William aged five, Ernest John aged four and Mary Cornelia Randall Anker aged six. They lived at the shop called Australian House where John was a general dealer.

William Julyan boarded with the family and worked as an agricultural labourer. He was born in Alwalton during 1841.

Edith Lavinia Daynes aged fifteen worked for the Anker family as their domestic servant.

Abraham Crick married Mary Plowman in 1873 and by the time of the 1891 census they were living at 40 Gore Corner Cottage along Cemetery Road. Abraham was a wagon repairer although in 1881 he was a railway servant and they lived along the Woodstone Hill.

Two of their daughters, Eliza aged seventeen and Florence aged fifteen, were not at home at the time of the census. Eliza was a servant for Alfred and Emily Plant at 237 Gladstone Street Peterborough where Alfred was a draper and baker.

Florence was a servant for Jennet Hetley and her sister Elizabeth Swift both were widows and lived along Oundle Road in Alwalton. Jennet's husband Richard died during 1884 he was a farmer in Alwalton.

Abraham and Mary's daughter Sarah Elizabeth died in July 1883 aged five, also Agnes Maud died in December 1886 aged one year and eleven months both were buried in the cemetery along Cemetery Road.

Abraham and Mary had four children living at home they were Martha Mary born in 1880, Lillian born in 1887, Harry Ploughman (Plowman) Crick born in 1889 and their baby son of three days. He was shown as an Infant the family had not decided on a name at that time.

On 23rd July 1900 Abraham and Mary's daughter Florence married John Hilliard at St Augustine's church.

George Burnham, a retired malster, and his wife Mary had moved from Oundle Road to 26 Lea Cottage along Cemetery Road. Their daughter Emma married Edward John Cunningham on 31st May 1887 at St Augustine's Church in Woodstone. Emma and her son Edward aged one were also living at Lea Cottage during 1891. Edward was born in Woolwich as was his father.

George and Mary's daughter Martha was living at 42 Ladbroke Grove in Kensington where she was a maid for Mary Anderson who was eighteen and paralysed from birth.

John Bye married Sarah Larratt during the beginning of 1884 in the Peterborough district. John and Sarah lived at 24 Cemetery Road with their three children, Florrie born in 1886, Charles George in 1888 and Millie Hannah in 1890.
Before Sarah married she worked as an elastic weaver and in 1881 lived with Mary Mewse at 1 Princess Terrace in Gladstone Street. Both Sarah and Emma Larratt were shown as being daughters in law to Mary at that time. Also in 1881 John Bye, a railway fireman, was living as a boarder with William and Elizabeth Bye in Pipe Lane Peterborough. Both William and John were born in Littleport.

Richard Southwell married Emma Larratt during 1885 in the Peterborough district. They lived at 22 Cemetery Road with their young family. Richard George was born in 1887 and Daniel Harry in 1890 both in Woodstone.
Mary Ann Mewse was visiting the family. Mary, nee Jarratt, married Thomas Mewse in the Peterborough district during 1866. Thomas died in 1870 aged sixty two.
Richard was the son of Richard and Louisa Southwell from Ramsey.

Jesse Woodward married Elizabeth Hale in 1885. Elizabeth died during 1887 aged twenty five. Jesse remarried in 1888 to Mary Jinks. They lived at 20 Rowland Cottage with their two children, Edith Sarah aged three and Albert Jesse aged one.
Jesse and Elizabeth had three more children after the census, Ethel Mary born 1891, Charles Alfred born 1896 and William was born in 1898. Around the time of Williams' birth the family moved to Carlton in Nottinghamshire.

David and Elizabeth Nash married in Whittlesea in 1883 and lived at 14 Woodstone Terrace along Cemetery Road. In 1881 David was lodging with Jonah and Elizabeth Tingey at 18 Grove Street Fletton, he worked as a railway engine cleaner. Elizabeth lived with her parents at Arnolds Lane Whittlesea.

David, a railway servant, and Elizabeth had four children, Lily was born in 1885 and Kate in 1886 both in Fletton, Albert was born in 1888 and Ernest in 1890 both in Woodstone.

John Mason, a platelayer, and Lydia his wife lived at number 6 Excelsior Terrace (end cottage on Woodstone Terrace). Their three children, all born in Woodstone, were Ernest Harry born 1883, Walter William born 1885 and Albert Charles born in 1890. George Harry Allen from Orton lodged with the family he was eighteen years old and worked as a grocer's assistant.

1901

Woodstone continued to grow as more houses were being built. The population had increased by a thousand over ten years to around 2,817 in 1901. This included 1,462 males and 1,355 females. Approximately 974 children lived in Woodstone, the figure being made up of 653 scholars, 250 pre-school and 71 children under one year old. The youngest aged 2 weeks were baby Apthorpe son of Richard and Sarah from Belsize Avenue and baby Woods daughter of Arthur and Mary also from Belsize Avenue.

There were five sets of twins in Woodstone at the time of the census, they were:-

Boy and girl aged four months, not yet named, children of Tom and Lizzie Fuller who were visiting Joseph and Jane Cracknell at 86 Palmerston Road. Tom was from Fletton and Lizzie from Yaxley.

Nellie and Harry Holman aged five children of George and Sarah from Water End.

Rose and Daisy Pape aged nine children of John and Julia from Palmerston Road.

Agnes and Grace Seaton aged ten children of Charles and Mary from New Road.

Margaret and Rosalie Crow aged eighteen wards of Sarah Liversmore from Nene View Oundle Road.

Approximately 240 people from Woodstone were employed by the railways. The brickyard company employed over 300 a large increase since 1891 when there were about 10. Other occupations not shown before included:-

House decorator, drilling machinist, iron moulder, sewing machinist, timber yard manager, basket makers, pawnbrokers assistant, auctioneers clerk, barbers apprentice, fancy shop assistant, watchmaker/jeweller, architect, cycle merchant, law student, outfitter, postman, dentist's assistant, horse collar maker, cashier in shop, stonemason, water works clerk, van driver, barman, fish merchant, clerk in chapters office, police constable, grain blower, furniture dealer, and hay merchant.

The teaching profession had increased from 11 in 1891 to 23 by 1901. Included in these figures were school teachers, for both Elementary and Church of England, daily governess, pupil teachers and some held the title of monitoress.

The census began at Belsize Avenue which was a new development since the 1891 census. The name was derived after the Ecclesiastical Commissioners farm called Belsize Grange in Marholm.

BELSIZE AVENUE

These houses were built mainly to provide homes for brickyard workers. The first deeds to be signed bore the name of Mr J.C. Hill; he was the owner of the majority of the local brickworks.

Fred Hall, a brickyard machine man born in Stanground, lived at 90 with his wife Emma and their two sons. Francis was five and Fred Cooper Hall was three years old. Emma and their sons were born in Eye near Peterborough.

Living at 92 was Emma's brother George Cooper, a brickyard labourer, his wife Eliza and their three year old daughter Gertrude born in Thorney.

Before Emma and George married they lived in Eye with their parents George and Harriett Cooper.

Samuel and Florence Wade lived at 98. Samuel was a blacksmith's assistant and born in the Peterborough district, Florence was born in Leicester.

John Peach married Martha Bunnage from Ramsey in 1894. By 1896 they were living in Stanground where their children were all born. Elsie Jane was born in 1895, Florence Rose in 1897, John James in 1899 and Martha Dorothy in 1900. John senior was a brickyard labourer and lived with his family at 114 Belsize Avenue. He was the son of John and Elizabeth Peach from Abbotts Ripton.

Living at 120 was Richard Smith, a brickyard labourer, his wife Susan and their granddaughter Rose Elger who was eleven years old born in Somersham.

In 1891 Richard and Susan were living at 20 Westwood Street in Peterborough with their son Henry, a railway labourer, and their granddaughter Rose Elger who was then only one year old.

At 130 was the butcher's shop where Charles Warwick lived and worked as a butcher and cattle dealer. He lived there with his wife Ann. Elizabeth Cleaver aged thirteen was their domestic servant, she was born at Chatteris.

Next to the butchers was a grocers shop at 132 where Herbert Davis lived and worked with his wife Kate. They had an eight year old daughter called Isabel. Also living there was Francis and Dinah Smith, who were Kate's parents. Francis was a baker.

Herbert employed Jessie Saunders aged fifteen as a domestic servant.

Number 134 was unoccupied.

Further along at 138 lived Jesse Peacock, a brickyard labourer, and his wife Sophia. Jesse was born at Tilbrook in Bedfordshire and Sophia at Oundle in Northamptonshire. As a family they had moved around the country. Their first child Albert was born in 1894 at Thorney, Beatrice was born in 1896 in Brampton Ash near Rutland and Ethel was born in 1898 at Deptford in London.

Also living at 138 was James and Ann Atkins, parents of Sophia and her two brothers Alfred James, a General Labourer and Arthur a Brickyard Labourer. James and Arthur were born at Elton; Ann was born in Benefield and Alfred in Oundle.

James Henry Swiffen, a brickyard labourer, and his wife Ellen lived at 140. James was the son of William and Eliza Swiffen and in 1881 they lived at Jaunceys Yard in Albert Place Peterborough. They then moved to Stanground for a few years, then to Fletton before settling in Woodstone towards the end of the 1890's.

James married Ellen Popple in 1900, possibly at Deeping St James where Ellen was born. Ellen was the daughter of William Moses and Susannah Popple.

In June of 1901 James and Ellen's son Cecil Edward was baptised at St Augustine's church. In April 1906 their daughter Maria Irene was baptised at Fletton church, around that time they lived at 7 Duke Street Fletton.

Joseph and Maria Pickering had moved from Woodstone Hill where they lived during the period of 1881 through to 1891, to 142 Belsize Avenue by the time of the 1901 census. Their family included Pauline aged fifteen and Alfred aged thirteen who worked as a brickyard labourer, both were stepchildren to Joseph. Clara aged eleven, Henry aged six, Ada aged three and Florrie aged four months. All children were born in Woodstone. William Gamble, Maria's father who worked as a railway labourer, also lived with the family, his wife Sarah died in 1894 aged sixty seven and was buried in the local cemetery. In 1881 William and Sarah lived along Water End Woodstone, Pauline their granddaughter lived with them at that time.

Tom Peach, a coal carter, and his wife Susan, nee Sales, lived at 150. They married during 1900 in the district of Peterborough. Tom, born in Elton was the son of Henry and Mary Ann Peach from The Oaks public house in Woodnewton.

Living at 154 was Albertha Bloodworth with her children. In 1886 Albertha (nee Tinkler) married John Charles Woolley in the

Peterborough district. They had two children William and Albertha. By the time of the 1891 census they lived at 116 Palmerston Road. In 1896 John, a mill porter, died aged thirty seven and was buried in the local cemetery in Woodstone. During 1898 Albertha married William Bloodworth in the Peterborough district. They then had two children Elizabeth Annie born in 1899 and Mildred Victoria born during 1900 both in Woodstone. Albertha's husband William was not at home at the time of the census.

Christopher Brookbanks, a brickyard labourer, and Elizabeth his wife lived at 158 with their four children. Ernest was eight and born in Stanground, Emma was six, Gertrude was four both born in Woodstone Alice was three and born in Old Fletton. Christopher was the son of John and Martha Brookbanks. During 1881 they lived along Church Street in Yaxley and had moved to 10 Love Lane in Fletton by 1891.

Thomas Strickson, a house decorator, lived at 162 nearby to the Brookbanks family, with his wife Elizabeth and their three children. Alfred was born in 1892, Frederick in 1895 and Gertrude Victoria in 1897.

George Elger, a Brickyard Labourer, lived at 164 with his wife Sarah and their three children. John William was born in 1892, May in 1895 and Ernest Charles in 1897. George was born in Colne and Sarah in Somersham.

Joseph and Louisa Cooke married in Peterborough in 1882. By 1901 they were living at 170 Belsize Avenue with their six children. Joseph was born in Orton and worked as a brickyard labourer. Louisa was born in Lincoln and was the daughter of James Treliving. In 1881 Louisa was living at Overton Staunch (Orton) where her father was the toll keeper (collector) of the River Nene. Her mother had died and Louisa, aged eighteen, looked after the family. Her brothers and sisters were Edgar aged nine, Sidney aged eight, Ethel aged two and Joseph aged one.
Joseph and Louisa's children were James Tucker Cooke aged thirteen who was a drilling machine worker, Alfred Edgar was nine, Ethel Jane seven, William Montague five, Emma three and Fred was one year old. All but Fred were born in Orton.

George Hillson married Mary Ann Moulding during 1899 in Peterborough. By the 1901 census they were living at 172 Belsize Avenue with their three month old daughter Dora. George was the son of George and Sarah Hillson who lived in Warmington during 1881.

Charles Elger, a brickyard labourer, and his wife Mary lived at 180 with their three children. Mary Jane was born in Somersham during 1891, Thomas born 1893 in Peterborough and George Frederick was born during 1896 in New Fletton.

Charles was brother to George Elger who lived at 164. Their parents were William and Susan Elger who in 1881 lived at the Water Mill in Pidley cum Fenton where William was an agricultural labourer in charge of the mill.

Homes from 198 through to 218 (evens only) were not occupied. There were also three buildings recorded as being at the end of these homes.

The enumerators then crossed the road where the odd numbered households were and began the recording from 55 Belsize Avenue. This was where Arthur and Mary Woods from Great Gidding lived. Arthur worked as a brickyard labourer and their children were Herbert aged four, Hilda aged three, Ivy aged two and a baby daughter aged two weeks. Their niece Maggie Rowell also from Great Gidding lived with them.

Joseph James, a brickyard labourer, married Ellen Weston during 1898 in the Huntingdonshire district. By the time of the 1901 census they lived at number 67 Belsize Avenue. John was the son of George and Sally James they all lived at Steeple Gidding in Huntingdonshire during 1881 where Joseph was born. Ellen was born at Lutton in Northamptonshire and was the daughter of John and Lucy Weston who were shown as living at No 6 Cottage in Washingley during 1881.

The census shows Arthur Aspittle, a brickyard labourer, and his wife Eliza who were both born in Great Gidding living at 71 Belsize Avenue with their children, Cecil was two and Violet was eleven months, they were both born in Woodstone. Walter Woods worked as a brickyard labourer and was boarding with the Aspittle

family. He was also born in Great Gidding and brother to Arthur
Woods at number 55.

Having contacted someone who has vast knowledge of families in
Great Gidding I was told the family were originally called
'Hospital'. Unfortunately the person filling out the census
misheard the pronunciation of their name.

Arthur Hospital married Eliza Woods in the Peterborough district
towards the end of 1897. Eliza was the granddaughter of Henry
and Sarah Woods and was living with them during the 1881 census
at Great Gidding. Henry and Sarah were also the parents of Arthur
and Walter.

Also during 1881 Arthur was living with his elderly aunt Sarah
Dunkley, a spinster, and her family in Great Gidding. One of
Sarah's sisters was Hephzibah and she married John Hospital at the
end of 1855. Hephzibah was a widow when she died in Woodstone
in January 1905 and was buried in New Road cemetery. Her
surname was recorded as 'Aspittle'.

John Turner, a carpenter, and his family came from Rutland,
although his wife Emma was born in Melton Mowbray. They lived
at 101 Belsize Avenue. Their eldest daughter Edith worked as a
milliner at home. Her sister Louise was a sewing maid and also
worked from home. Four of the sons worked for the brickyards,
William, Joseph and Thomas were all labourers and Herbert was a
carter. Christine, Nellie, Alfred and Reginald were of school age
and Agnes, Gertrude and Leonard were three years, two years and
three months respectively.

Ezra Hall, a brickyard labourer, married Sarah Dunkley during
1865. They both grew up in Great Gidding. By the time of the
1881 census Ezra, Sarah and their seven children continued to live
in Great Gidding. By 1901 they were living at 111 Belsize Avenue.
Their sons Charles and Percy both worked as brickyard labourers.
Emma their oldest daughter married John Ridgewell in 1887 and
was shown as living with her parents at the time of the census.
They had two children, Elsie was seven and Bertie was four. Ezra's
wife Sarah was not at home at the time of the census but was
visiting Arthur and Susannah Dunkley who lived in Steeple
Gidding.

In the next house numbered 113 lived John Hall also from Great Gidding. He was the son of Ezra and Sarah but was recorded as Frederick John when he married Virtue Laurance during 1894 in the Peterborough district. Virtue was born in Holme and was the daughter of Reuben and Elizabeth.

Charles Murfitt a brickyard labourer married Adelaide Peckett on 23rd September 1896 at St George's parish church in Littleport Cambridgeshire. They were both born in Littleport. By 1901 they were living at 123 Belsize Avenue with their one year old son Victor who was born in Peterborough.
Charles was the son of William and Elizabeth Murfitt. Adelaide was the daughter of Eaton and Eliza Peckett.

Daniel Slater was a shepherd and lived at 129 with his wife Hannah and four of their grown up children. William and Thomas were horsemen on a farm, Harriett and Caroline were at home. In 1881 they lived at Oundle where Daniel was an agricultural labourer.

William Wade lived at 149 with his brother John and sister Minnie. Both William and John were brickyard labourers, aged twenty five and seventeen respectively. Minnie was fourteen and stayed at home with Harriett Graham who the family employed as their domestic housekeeper.
William, John and Minnie were the children of Samuel and Mary Ann Wade who in 1881 lived at Albert Place in Peterborough and by 1891 they had moved to 13 Baker Street in Peterborough where William worked as a labourer in a street store.

William and Jane Plowman had moved from 58 Australian Terrace along Cemetery Road where they were living in 1891 to 153 Belsize Avenue by 1901. William continued to work as a brickyard labourer. In April 1892 their daughter Amelia died aged five and was buried in an unmarked grave in the cemetery. Ernest their oldest child was eleven. Annie was born in Woodstone around the time of her sister Amelia's death. The family then moved to the Orton district where Percy was born towards the end of the year in 1897.
William's father Robert Plowman lived with them as did Ann Starsmore, mother to Jane. They were both widowed. Jane's father

was the late Samuel Starsmore who died in 1900, at the time of the 1881 census he lived in Yarwell with his family.

Jane had a brother Jesse who married Elizabeth Reed on 13th March 1888 at St Augustine's church in Woodstone. They lived at 15 Queens Walk in Woodstone.

Another family who had moved to Woodstone from the Giddings and lived at 155 Belsize Avenue was John Robert James. He married Susannah Leach in 1898 in Huntingdonshire, Susannah was born in Upton. They had a daughter Emily Hannah who was one year old. John was the son of John and Sarah James from Steeple Gidding.

John Thomas Setchell, a brickyard labourer, and his wife Mary lived at 167 with their son John who was twenty four and also worked as a brickyard labourer.

Caleb Holland, a brickyard labourer, and his wife Martha lived at 189 with their two sons. Alfred was three and Laurence was one year old.

Thomas Chambers and his wife Sarah who were both born in Nassington lived at 199 with their five children. Their oldest daughter Emma was also born in Nassington around 1887. John aged eight and Jennie aged six were born in Liverpool, Frank aged two was born in Ellington in Huntingdonshire and Thomas aged nine months was born in Woodstone.

Sarah Ann Jaggard was a widow and lived at 209 with Arthur her son who worked as a brickyard labourer. Sarah was born in 1836 at Linton and Arthur in West Wratting in Cambridgeshire.

In the last house along Belsize Avenue which was numbered 215 lived Sarah Jaggard's son Joseph Plumb. In 1881 he lived with his mother and siblings along Oundle Road. He married Nellie Watson towards the end of the year in 1895 in the Peterborough district. Joseph's full name was Joseph Jaggard Plumb he worked as a sand and gravel labourer.

Joseph and Nellie had three children, Annie Edith born in 1896, Joseph Victor in 1897 and Eliza Alice in 1900, all in Woodstone.

OUNDLE ROAD

Nathaniel Woolley married Eliza Bridgwood during 1889 in Stafford where Eliza was born. Nathaniel, a railway signalman, and Eliza had lived at 2 Oriel Terrace (197) along Oundle Road since around the time of the 1891 census. At that time their first born son James Nathaniel was three months old, he was born in Woodstone. James died at the age of three years and eleven months and was buried in the cemetery along Cemetery Road.

In 1901 Nathaniel and Eliza had three more children, Edith Eliza born 1892, John Thomas born 1893 and Florence Irene born in 1900 was eight months old.

Mabel Gush, a school teacher from Lambeth, was a boarder with the family.

Sarah Stimson was born in Thrapston and lived at 4 Oriel Terrace (201) with four of her children. Horace was sixteen and worked as a pupil teacher. Beatrice was fourteen and worked as a milliner's apprentice. Tom aged eleven and Amy aged eight both attended school.

Sarah's other son John William married Mary Jane Treliving during 1898. They had made their home along Woodstone Hill near Mary's brothers James and Sydney Treliving.

Sarah's husband Samuel died in July 1893 aged thirty nine and was buried in the cemetery along Cemetery Road.

During 1881 Samuel and Sarah lived at Rogers Street in Peterborough where Samuel worked as a railway wagon inspector. By the time of the 1891 census they were living at Oriel Terrace where Samuel continued to work for the railways as a carriage examiner.

Charles Palmer was born in Woodstone in 1867 he married Betsy Ann Blackman during 1892 in the district of Peterborough. In 1901 Charles was working as a railway fireman and they lived at 7 Oriel Terrace (207) with their children. Frank was born in 1893, Charles in 1894, Walter in 1897 and Ivy in 1900. Betsy's father Jonathan Blackman was widowed and living with them. He was seventy four but shown on the census as having an occupation of a Thatcher.

Peter Parkins, a railway pensioner and his wife Mary continued living at 10 Oriel Terrace (213). James their son was nineteen and worked as a storekeeper and timekeeper (engines). Sidney Cooper, their grandson, was sixteen and worked as a Shunters apprentice. Rupert Parkins their grandson, aged three and born in 1897 at Little Irchester in Northamptonshire was living with the family at the time of the census. He was baptised as Alistair Rupert.

Alfred Sparne aged seventeen was boarding with Peter and his family. Alfred was a golf professional from Norfolk. Alfred's surname was not clearly written so it may not be correct.

Two doors away at number 12 (217) lived their son Charles Parkins and his wife Elizabeth. They married on 6th August 1894 at St Augustine's church. They had three children Annie born in 1895, Elsie in 1898 and John William in 1899. Elizabeth was the daughter of John and Mary Perry who lived at 11 Limetree Terrace along Palmerston Road during 1881. By 1891 they had moved to Cemetery Road.

Mark Walden, a retired baker, and his wife Martha had lived at Albion House (221) along Oundle Road since around 1891. However at the time of the 1881 they were living at 17 Albion Terrace in Fletton. They married during 1856 in the Peterborough district Martha was the daughter of James and Mary Watts who lived in Orton Longueville.

Mark and Martha had two of their daughters still living with them. Emma was a school mistress at a Public Elementary school and Piercey was a teacher of music, she taught from home.

John Braybrook married Emma Elizabeth Garfoot in the district of Peterborough at the beginning of the year in 1899. They lived at 223 Oundle Road in Cottesmore House with Hilda their ten month old daughter.

John was the son of George and Elizabeth Braybrook who lived at 12 Tower Terrace Fletton in 1881

Emma lived with her Aunt Elizabeth and Uncle George Watts in Hampshire when she was six years old during 1881, and was born at St Stephens Bow in London.

Living at Cottesmore House in 1891 was Ann Garfoot, a widow, born in Wiltshire in 1851. Her daughter Mary Ann aged nineteen worked as a school teacher and lived with her mother. Mary Ann was born at North Bow in London. By 1901 Ann was living in the urban district of Fletton.

Peterborough Co-op Oundle Road

Post Office Oundle Road.

Woodstone church before the Lych gate.

Woodman's cycle shop.

William and Mary Plumb had moved from Palmerston Road where they lived in 1891 to number 2 Hope Villa at 225 Oundle Road.

Three of their children went out to work, Both Alice and Miriam worked as drapers assistants and William was a grocer's assistant. Ella, Horace and Robert attended school and Mabel was the youngest child aged ten months.

George Canner Weston and his wife Annie moved from Gladstone Cottages in Water End where they lived in 1891 to a few houses away from the Plumb family. George continued working as a joiner, their son Arthur was a railway foreman, Annie aged twenty was not shown as having an occupation. Clara was a drapers apprentice, George (junior) was a clerk for an engineer and Horace was an errand boy (post). James aged ten attended school.

Their daughter Minnie married Charles William Crouch on 18th March 1894 at St Augustine's church in Woodstone. At that time Charles was a jeweller from Rushden. By the time of the 1901 census Charles and Minnie were living in Aylesbury and Charles was shown as being a watchmaker. His business progressed into a Jewellers and fine Antiques establishment which still exists to date.

Arthur Robert Hunting married Annie Maria Taylor in the Peterborough district during 1892. In 1901 they were living along Oundle Road. Arthur was a colliery agent and was the son of George and Emma Hunting. In 1881 Arthur's father was the innkeeper and coal merchant at the Swiss Cottage Inn of Fletton.

Annie was the daughter of Samuel and Mary Taylor from South Street in Stanground. Hetty Taylor, sister of Annie, was also living with them and worked as a dressmaker.

Arthur Tebbutt, a dairyman/carter and plumber, married Annie Elizabeth Reed during 1888 in the Peterborough district. They lived at 1 Eastmead Villa (239) with their two sons Sidney aged seven and Bertie aged three.

Annie was the daughter of Isaac and Azubah Reed who lived at 3 Tower Street Fletton in 1881. Azubah died at the beginning of 1881 just before the census was recorded. After her mothers death Annie stayed at home as the housekeeper for her father who went out to work as a blacksmith. Her brother James was a butcher's apprentice. Annie also had a two year old brother called Frank.

Ann Knowles, grandmother to Annie, lived with the family and was a Recipient of Parochial Relief.

WOODSTONE HILL

Thomas Trevor, a hay and corn merchant, lived at Vine House Woodstone Hill (later known as 241 Oundle Road), with his wife Annie and their four children. Charles aged eighteen worked as an apprentice to an ironmonger. Florence was sixteen and Robert was thirteen. They also had a son who was shown as being under one month old.

Sydney Montague Treliving married Mabel Smith towards the end of the year in 1900 in the Peterborough district. Sidney was a brickyard labourer and they lived in one of the houses along the Woodstone Hill.

Living next to Sydney was his brother James Treliving who married Florrie Baines towards the end of the year in 1898 in the Peterborough district. They had a one year old daughter called Bertha born in Old Fletton. Florrie was the daughter of James and Fanny Baines from Stanground.
Sydney and James' father who was also called James was born in Cornwall and shown as living at Overton Staunch in 1881 which was renamed Orton Staunch by 1891. James senior was widowed and worked as the toll keeper of the River Nene.

In the next house lived John William Stimson, a postman, who married Mary Jane Treliving during 1898 in the Peterborough district. Mary was the daughter of James and the late Mary Treliving. John and Mary had a young daughter Beatrice aged one year.

Charles Binckes was the publican at the Cross Keys Inn where he lived with his wife Clare. Charles was born in Peterborough and the son of William and Annie. At the time of the 1881 census he lived with his parents and siblings at the Black Swan Inn along Narrow Bridge Street in Peterborough. His father was a tailor. At that time Charles was a musical school tuner.

Allen Farrow was first shown as living in Woodstone during 1891 when he and his mother Mary lodged with Ezra Garnham and his family along Water End. Mary was their housekeeper. Allen married Maria Bird during 1894 in the Peterborough district. Maria died in 1897 leaving Allen to look after their three children, Christopher, Kate and Thomas. During the spring of 1898 Allen married Sophia Haynes in the Peterborough district. Sophia was the daughter of Elizabeth Haynes and her late husband George who lived along Water End during 1881. Sophia's widowed mother Elizabeth was still living a few houses away from Ezra Garnham in 1891. By the time of the 1901 census Allen and Sophia lived along the 'Woodstone Hill'.

Johnson Phillips first wife Elizabeth died in 1892 and was buried in the local cemetery. At that time Johnson worked as a stableman, they made their home in Woodstone when they married in 1861. By 1901 their children had all left home. Johnson married Eliza Ann Scott during 1896 in the Peterborough district. In 1898 Eliza gave birth to their son William.

Edward Lightfoot married Nellie (Ellen) Whitham during 1896 in the Peterborough district. They made their home along Woodstone Hill with their daughter Edith and their son Cecil. Ellen was the daughter of Jane, her father died before the 1881 census. At that time Jane lived with Nellie and her other daughter Elizabeth at the Kings Head Yard in Peterborough where Jane was a lodging house keeper. By the time of the 1891 census they were living along the Water End in Woodstone. Jane continued to be a lodging house keeper and Ellen worked at a pea factory as did her sister Elizabeth.

OUNDLE ROAD

Charles Baker had changed his occupation from a carter in 1891 to a farmer and gravel merchant by 1901. Charles and his wife Annie had moved from Victoria Cottages to a few houses along at 296 Oundle Road. This was a large detached house with gravel pits at the back.

Their son Arthur was lodging with Thomas Odell with four other lodgers at 131 Brookhall Terrace along New Road in Woodstone.

Their other children were Helen aged eighteen, Charles aged seventeen who was a carter on the farm, Annie aged sixteen, Emily aged twelve, Florence aged eleven, Pattie aged nine, Albert aged eight, Alice aged five, Frank aged four and George aged two.

James Baines was born in Stanground and worked as a brickyard labourer. He was the son of John and Martha Baines. James married Annie Covell during 1900 in the Peterborough district and they lived at 294 Oundle Road known then as Park View. Annie was the daughter of David and Mary Covell from Fletton.

Elijah Crowson was a dentist's assistant who lived with his wife Hannah at 288 this was one of the Thorpe View cottages. They had three daughters Norah aged four, Josephine aged two and Millicent was seven months old. James Riches a railway signalman lodged with them.

David Waite an agricultural labourer lived at 280 Thorpe View with his wife Martha and their children. Arthur was twenty two and worked as a railway porter, Frederick aged sixteen and Charles aged fourteen were both agricultural labourers.
In 1891 David and Martha lived at Ashton near Oundle with their four sons, the oldest was Benjamin. By 1901 he was married and lived at Denford in Northamptonshire.

George Peed married Fanny Langford in the Stamford district during 1899 they made their home at 278 Thorpe View Oundle Road next to David and Martha Waite. George was born in Fletton and was the son of Grace and the late Charles Peed. In 1891 George was living at Crick Villas on the other side of Oundle Road.

There was a shop at number 276 which was 'To Let' at the time of the 1901 census.

George and Maria Wright lived in one of the Victoria Cottages with their six children, Sarah Elizabeth aged twelve, Browitt Henry aged eleven, Gertrude Annie aged nine, Sidney Walter aged seven, George Eden aged five and Frederick William was two years old. George's occupation was a horse collar worker.
At the time of the 1891 census George and Maria lived at Islip with their young son Browitt who was one year old. Their daughter Sarah was shown as living with her grandparents Ebenezer and Sarah Meadows at High Street in Islip. Ebenezer was a furnaceman. Before Sarah (senior) married Ebenezer her name was Wright.

121

In 1881 George was living at Islip with Ebenezer and Sarah Meadows and was shown as being stepson to Ebenezer.

James Winham, a labourer on the railways, and his wife Mary lived at The Sands (266) along Oundle Road with their family. Esther aged twenty three was not shown as having an occupation so possibly helped her mother with the home and family. James aged twenty was a railway fireman and his nineteen year old brother Arthur worked as a railway engine cleaner.

William and Grace Brown moved from Crick Villas where they lived in 1891 to 264 The Sands. Amelia their youngest daughter aged fifteen was a dressmaker. Grace's children from her first marriage were Ellen Pead who possibly helped in the home as no occupation was recorded, William Pead worked as a baker and Charles Pead was a railway engine cleaner.
Arthur Francis, Ernest Henson and William Lane all worked for the railways and boarded with the Brown family.
Charles Pead married Emma Dale during 1905 in the Peterborough district.
The photographs show Charles and Emma's wedding and Ellen Freda Pead who was always known as Freda.

Living in the next house, The Limes, number 262 lived Henry Chapman who worked on the railways as an engine driver. In 1891 he was a lodger with William and Grace Brown. On 26th December 1896 Henry married Jane Elizabeth Pead at St Augustine's church in Woodstone. Ellen Freda their daughter was born in 1899. Jane was the daughter of Grace (Brown) and the late Charles Pead.

Thomas and Kezia Hubbard had lived along Water End since around 1881. By 1901 they had moved along Oundle Road with their eight children. Thomas was thirty two and worked as a railway engine driver, John aged twenty four was unemployed and Moses aged twenty two worked as a brickyard labourer. Annie aged nineteen had no occupation but possibly helped her mother in the home. Fred aged seventeen was a professional golfer, Robert aged fifteen worked as a brickyards labourer, Charlie aged twelve and Frank aged eight attended school.

John Henry Landin was a carpenter and joiner born in Fletton. He was the son of James and Mary Landin who lived at Woodnewton before moving to Woodstone prior to the 1891 census and lived at 236 Oundle Road. John married Ethel Harrald in the district of Market Harborough during the winter of 1898. They made their home in Woodstone where George their one year old son was born.
James and Mary Landin lived a few houses away at 240 Oundle Road.

Jeremiah and Gertrude Brewster continued to live at 234 Oundle Road where they kept the bakers shop. Since the 1891 census they had three more children, Annie aged nine, May aged seven and William aged four. These were brother and sisters for Gertrude.
George Harris and James Pell both boarded with the family and were journeyman bakers.

Frederick Beaumont a railway yard foreman married Mary Ann Venters during 1889 in the Peterborough district. They made their home at 230 Oundle Road in one of the Heaton Villas. Their first daughter Agnes was born in Fletton after which they moved to Woodstone where their other children were born. Francis was nine Arthur six and Jesse was two years old. They had also taken in two boarders Richard Pryor and Edward Nunn both worked on the railways as guards.

Newman and Harriett Parrish had moved from one of the cottages near the Palmerston Arms to 228 Elizabeth Villas along Oundle Road, they had four of their children living at home. Annie was nineteen and worked as a dressmaker at home. Mabel was seventeen and worked as a tailoress. Ernest aged thirteen was an errand boy and Lillian aged eleven attended school.
Their son John William married Florence Elderkin, from Stanground, towards the end of 1900. By 1901 they were living at Sculcoates in Hull where he worked as a coppersmith, Florence was a dressmaker.
Their daughter Whyman was twenty one and worked and lived in Peterborough as a domestic housemaid. (It is possible her name came from her grandmother who was Mary Whyman before she married Samuel Parrish.)

William Bland, a carpenter, and his wife Susan were living next to the Parrish family having moved from Palmerston Road where they first lived in 1881. Alice their oldest daughter aged twenty was an elementary school teacher. Robert who was nineteen worked as a railway clerk, Elizabeth aged seventeen was a drapers cashier, William aged fifteen was a stonemason's apprentice.
At the time of the 1891 census they were living at 5 Orchard Terrace along Water End.

George Simpson was a gravel merchant's foreman and lived with his wife Sarah and their children at 210 Oundle Road in one of the Adelaide Villas. George their oldest son aged twenty was an elementary school teacher. John was eighteen and worked as an engineer's clerk, Harry aged sixteen was a brick manufacturer's clerk. Herbert was nine and Kate six both attended school. Their youngest child was two year old Alec.

Benjamin and Ellen Brown were still living at 204 Oundle Road in the end house named Roseberry Villas they had lived there since the previous census was taken. Elizabeth their daughter was still living with them. Daisy Fry was an apprentice dressmaker who also lived with the family she was sixteen and niece of Benjamin and Ellen.

Their son Alex died during May 1894 aged fifteen and was buried in the local cemetery. He was baptised as Alex although the 1881 census showed him as Albert.

CEMETERY ROAD

In the first house on Cemetery Road 2 Vaughan Cottages lived John Hall, a railway signalman, his wife Harriet and their two children. John was five and Florence was ten months old.

Still living at number 6 Excelsior Terrace was John and Lydia Mason and their three children. John was a railway platelayer. Both sons worked for the railways Ernest was an engine cleaner and Walter was a post messenger. Albert aged ten attended school.

Two of the cottages in the terrace, numbers 10 and 12, were not occupied.

David Nash, a railway engine fireman, and his wife Elizabeth lived at number 14. They had two daughters and three sons. Lily aged fifteen and Kate aged fourteen were both domestic servants recorded as (day girl) both were born in Fletton. Albert was twelve, Ernest was eleven and Harold was nine years old all born in Woodstone.

Frederick Morris was a carpenter and lived with his wife Mary and their nine children in the end cottage at 16 Excelsior Terrace where they had lived since the 1891 census. Gertrude the oldest daughter was twenty and possibly helped in the home. Frederick Ambrose worked as a railway engine cleaner and was nineteen years old, Horace aged fourteen was a brickyard labourer. Bertie aged eleven, Bertha aged nine and Frank aged five attended school. Herbert was one year and Hilda was six months old. All the children were born in Woodstone.

George and Mary Burnham, both in their seventies, continued living at 26 Lea Cottage.

As like George and Mary Burnham, John and Margaret Clarke were also still living next door at 28 Albert House and had done so since 1889. John was a railway guard. Their oldest child Albert aged eighteen worked as a grocers apprentice and Fannie aged sixteen was a dressmaker. Nellie aged fourteen was shown on the 1891 census as Beatrice Nellie and Carrie aged twelve was then named Caroline Mary. Maggie was nine, Elsie was seven and John was three years old.

William Kisby, a carpenter who worked from home, lived at 30 Sidney House with his wife Minnie and their children. Ellen was seven, Sarah was five, Minnie was four, Maud was two and Florence was eleven months. Williams mother Sarah was widowed and lived with them she was recorded as being a Monthly nurse.
"Lying-in hospitals came into being around the late 18th and early 19th century and were usually supported by charities. Some hospitals concentrated on the training of doctors and midwives although this training was often too expensive for midwives to afford. Consequently it led to many midwives being given a poor reputation as being drunken, illiterate and unclean. This is around the time when the 'Monthly Nurse' began as she would attend the mother after giving birth and helped with establishing breastfeeding, often staying many months into the child's life."

John and Mary Currington were living at 180 Palmerston Road at the time of the 1891 census. By 1901 they had moved to 36 Rutland Villa. Ethel their oldest daughter aged twenty possibly helped her mother around the house as no occupation was shown. Bertha aged seventeen was a milliner. William aged thirteen and Arthur aged seven attended school. The youngest child was Ralph (known by his descendants as Bernard) aged seven months.

Mary Crick was living at 40 Gore Corner Cottage where she and her husband Abraham lived during the last census. Abraham died in 1894 aged forty nine and was buried in the local cemetery. At the time of the 1901 census Mary worked as a charwoman possibly to bring money into the home to help with bringing up her children. Lilian was thirteen and Harry was twelve. Martha their daughter was working as a domestic servant in Peterborough. Mary had also taken in two boarders, James Fountain and Harry Curtis both were general labourers from March and Doddington respectively.

Mary's daughter Eliza married Alfred Eagle during the winter of 1899 and made their home in Walton.

Her other daughter Florence married John Hilliard on 23rd July 1900 at St Augustine's church and lived in the first house after the shop in Australian Terrace not far from her mother. Australian Terrace was recorded as being in Rose Lane and not in Cemetery Road although they followed on from one another.

John Edmund Baines, the son of Edmund and Levinia lived in Midland Road during 1881. Edmund was a malster and John was a cabinet maker. John married Emily Wallis/Wallace during 1888 in the Peterborough district. In 1881 Emily lived with her parents and siblings at Percival Street in Peterborough all children were born in New Fletton between 1858 and 1877.

By the time of the 1901 census John, a general dealer, and Emily lived at Australian House and worked in the shop below. At that time their surname was shown as Bains. They had five children living at home at the time of the census who were John William born in 1890, Christopher Carr born in 1892, Florence born in 1893/4, Reginald born in 1895 and Dora born in 1898. At the time of Florence's birth John's occupation was shown as a French polisher.

John and Emily's oldest son Walter aged eleven was staying with his grandparents Edmund and Levinia at the time of the 1901 census. They were living in St John the Baptist Church district of Peterborough.

John Waspe married Sarah Jane Burnham on 3rd April 1899 at St Augustine's church. John was the son of James and Amy Waspe who lived along Palmerston Road in 1891. Sarah was the daughter of James and Charlotte Burnham and was born in Longthorpe where they lived. John and Sarah made their home at 48 Australian Terrace along Rose Lane.

John Anker's occupation was a sand and gravel merchant, he lived at 66 Australian Terrace with Elizabeth his wife and their family. Agnes was seventeen and worked as a general servant, Mary aged sixteen was a dressmaker, Ernest aged fourteen was a milk boy and Leonard aged nine attended school.

William Alcock married Annie Elizabeth Staines in Grantham towards the end of the year in 1881. William, who worked as a railway signalman, and his wife Annie lived at 6 St Leonard Terrace (70) Rose Lane. They had three sons George William aged eighteen worked as a railway carriage oiler, Ernest aged fourteen was a wagon painter and Walter Staines aged ten attended school. Gertrude Annie aged seventeen was visiting James and Annie Bird who lived seven houses away. All William and Annie's children were born in Grantham.

Henry Alcock, an army Sergeant, was visiting William and his family. Also with Henry was his wife Anna who was born in Ireland as was their oldest son William aged thirteen. Henry was ten and born in Derbyshire, Albert aged eight, Millicent aged six and Harold aged three were all born in India as British Subjects.

William was shown on the 1861 census aged one as the son of Henry and Mary Alcock who lived 48 Tenter Buildings Newark on Trent.

Henry, born around the 1830's was the son of William and Ann Alcock who were living along Cow Lane in Newark at the time of the 1841 census. William was a coal seller.

This could mean that William and Henry were most likely cousins, they were both born in Newark Nottinghamshire.

William Ford, born in Woodstone during 1835 was a farm labourer (carter) and lived at 9 St Leonard Terrace (86) with his wife Sarah and children. Oswald aged nineteen worked as a railway engine driver and his sister Agnes was fourteen years of age.

John Thomas Dowse, a railway shunter had lived at 2 Sidney Cottage (90) with Mary his wife and their four children since around the time of the 1891 census. The oldest was William aged fourteen who worked as a grocers assistant, Charles aged thirteen, Alfred aged ten and Florence aged eight all were born in Woodstone. They also had a son Harry who died in 1895 aged five years and nine months he was buried in the local cemetery.

At 1 Avery Cottage (100) lived James Bird, a railway gas fitter, and Annie his wife. James was born in March Cambridgeshire and Annie in Sheffield. They had three children Claud Ernest was aged six and May Letitia aged four were both born in Downham Market. John Thomas was born in 1900 in Woodstone. Gertrude Annie Alcock, daughter of William and Annie was visiting the family at the time of the census.

Gruesome news from April 3rd, 1909

A GAP ACCIDENT befell Oswald Ford, a Great Eastern Railway fireman, of New Road, Woodstone, at Ely, on Saturday. It appears that Ford, who is only 25 years of age, was changing the headlights in front of his engine at Ely in the early hours of Saturday morning, when he slipped and fell on the line. The engine was moving slowly at the time, and one of the front wheels passed over both the man's legs, crushing them badly. The members of the station ambulance corps at once removed the injured man to the waiting room, and Dr Beckett was summoned. The doctor, who was at the station, within half-an-hour, ordered the injured man's removal to Addenbrooke's Hospital, Cambridge. A special train was hurriedly prepared, and Cambridge was reached by 7.15, Dr Beckett taking charge on the journey. It was found necessary to amputate one foot of one leg, and to sever the other leg completely.

Walter George Jackson, a brickyard setter, married Florence Jane Rolph on 24th October 1899 at St Augustine's church in Woodstone. They lived at 2 St James Cottages (106) Rose Lane. Florence was the daughter of Ploughright and Clara Rolph who lived along the Woodstone Hill. Walter was the son of Herbert and Eliza Jackson who had lived along South Street in Stanground since 1874.

Next to Walter and Florence lived Tom and Elizabeth Richardson, from Lincolnshire, at 1 Limetree Cottages (108). They had a son and a daughter Bertie aged five and Dora aged four. Tom was a brickyard worker.

Harry Huckle, a police constable, and his wife Deborah lived at 2 Limetree Cottages (110) with their five year old daughter Annie. Walter Huckle, brother to Harry, also lived with them and was a watch maker and jeweller.

Thomas Pickin, a brickyard labourer, and his wife Hannah lived at 3 Limetree Cottages (112) with their three sons and three daughters. (Although shown on census as Limetree Cottage 112 is named as Dolphin Cottage - Thomas' descendent has told me she believes they only ever lived at 110). William was aged seventeen and was a Telegraphist for the railways, Alfred aged fifteen was an errand boy for a saddlers and Thomas aged fourteen worked for a solicitors as an office boy. Rose aged twelve and Lillie aged eleven attended school and Maud was the baby of the family aged two years. Alfred Pickin in photograph below.

Eliza Smith, a widow, continued to live at 114 Dolphin Cottage along Rose Lane with two of her sons Thomas and Rowland. Thomas worked as a gardener and Rowland was a carpenter.

Eliza died on 16th October 1912 and was buried in the local cemetery.

James and Betsy Sewter lived at Fern Cottage (116) where James was a journeyman miller and Betsy was a grocer and provisions dealer. The front room of their home was a shop where Betsy ran the business. James and Betsy had three children Horace aged nine, Archie aged eight and Bessie aged two they were all born in Woodstone.

Sarah Chambers who was Betsy's sister lived with them and worked in the shop as an assistant grocer. Will Deer, aged twenty four was a brickyard labourer and was a boarder with the family.
In 1891 James and Betsy lived at a short distance away along Rose Lane at 106 St James Cottage.

William and Isabella Whyman continued to live at Westbrook House. By 1901 when William was sixty seven he was shown on the census as a retired farmer. Two of their daughters Mary and Emily were unmarried and lived with William and Isabella.
Their other daughter Isabella married George Edward Abbott, born in Colsterworth, on 27th April 1886 in St Augustine's church. At the time of the wedding George was a bank cashier but by 1901 he had progressed to a bank manager. They lived in Northampton in the Parish of All Saints.
William and Isabella Wyman employed two domestic servants, Ellinor Henson was the cook from Northamptonshire and Emma Brewster was their housemaid. Emma was the daughter of James Thomas and Emma Brewster who lived at Cardigan Cottages along Queens Road in Fletton.

STILTON ROAD
Along Stilton Road were two Wymans Lodges one of which was not occupied.
In the other one lived Robert and Mary Shrives and their three children, all the family were born in Elton. Robert was a stockman on a cattle farm.

There were four more cottages along Stilton Road where the following families lived.
James Heath, a carter in the brickyard, married Edith Duncombe in the Peterborough during 1898. James was the son of Charles and Sarah Heath who lived at Dullingham near Newmarket. Edith was the daughter of James and Catherine Duncombe who in 1891 were living in the village of Holme where James was a farm labourer.

Next to James Heath lived William Worraker, a brickyard labourer and Ada his wife with their six month old daughter Elizabeth Harriet.

Alfred Crane was a brickyard foreman he lived in the next cottage with Louisa his wife and their three children, Francis Daisy aged eleven, Clarance Amelia aged seven and Wilfred Gladstone aged two.

Finally in the end cottage lived Robert Woods a brickyard foreman with Susan his wife. In 1891 they were living at 4 Love Lane in Fletton, at that time Robert was an engine driver.

Further along was Cowpasture Farm where James Hilliard was a yardman on the farm. He married Letitia Warren during the summer of 1889 in the Oundle district. By 1891 they were living at Highgate in Elton with their two sons Ernest Warren aged ten and George Warren aged seven and their youngest child Albert Hilliard aged one.
Letitia's mother, Esther Warren, was a widow and lived with the family. As far back as the 1861 census Letitia was living with her parents John and Esther and her brothers and sisters at Highgate in Elton.

Stilwell Brick Yard consisted of two cottages where Alfred Lofts, a brickworks manager and his wife Laura lived with their seven children.
Next door in the other cottage lived Ernest Tyers, a groom in the brickyard, his wife Susannah and their two children.

Abraham Patston was a farmer and lived at Woodstone Lodge Farm with his sister Mary and his fifteen year old nephew Charles Bertram. Ann Hinch from Peterborough was a domestic servant at the farm.

The last two cottages along the Stilton Road in Woodstone were Patston Cottages where Fred Neal, a farm labourer/yardman, lived with his wife Phoebe and their six children.
In the other cottage was Susannah Barnes, a widow, and her two sons Alfred and John who both worked on the farm.

OUNDLE ROAD
The census then moved back to Oundle Road in the parish of Woodstone Urban Entire.

John Turner, a painter and paperhanger, lived at 74 with Margaret his wife and their son Archie who was thirteen and attended school.

James Whitehead continued working as a railway porter and lived at 76 with his wife Margaret and their children. They had lived there since the 1891 census. Harry their oldest son was fourteen and worked as a barbers apprentice, Florence aged eleven and Thomas aged five attended school. The youngest children were George aged three and Beatrice aged one. Margaret Dilworth a monthly nurse born in Worcestershire was visiting the family.

George Piggott had changed his occupation since the 1891 census from a bricklayer's labourer to a fish merchant. He lived at 78 Oundle Road with his wife Annie and their son Alfred who attended school. George worked from home where he began his fish business. At the time of the 1891 census they were living at 28 Palmerston Road.

William James Whitehand was a tailor who lived and worked from his home at 80 Oundle Road. He was married to Sarah and they had four children. All the family were born in Norfolk. William aged fifteen was a railway clerk and Frederick aged fourteen was a wagon builder's clerk for the railways. Harry aged thirteen and Albert aged twelve attended school.

Sarah Eames was the inn keeper at the Palmerston Arms. Her husband William died on 2nd February 1900 and was buried in the local cemetery. On his grave was inscribed 'His suffering o'er, His end was Peace.
Their daughter Beatrice married Thomas George Palmer in 1900 and lived with her mother. Thomas worked as a railway clerk.
Sarah died on 18 December 1907 and was buried with her late husband William Eames. William and Sarah first took over the Palmerston Arms around 1890.

Frank Ward married Amy Smith from Stanground at the beginning of 1899. Frank was a butcher's manager and lived along the Oundle Road in one of the houses between numbers 84 and 90. He was the son of George and Alice Ward from Wisbech St

Peters where George was also a butcher. Amy was the daughter of Edmund and Mary Smith from Farcet Road in Stanground.

George and Alice Chamberlain had lived at 1 Nene Voir Place (92) since around 1874. George was a retired carpenter. Their granddaughter Mary Isabella Wright married Arthur John Nunn during 1900 and they both lived with George and Alice.
Arthur worked as a railway shunter.

Mary Core Robinson was unmarried and lived at 3 Nene Voir Place where her late parents William and Mary had lived since around the time of the 1851census. William had been a solicitor and died in 1894 aged eighty eight, his wife Mary died in 1882 aged seventy eight. Mary Core died in 1909 and was buried with her parents in the local cemetery.
William and Mary also had a daughter called Isabella who married William Streatfield during 1888 in the district of Peterborough. By the time of the 1901 census they were living at 7 Nene Voir Place in the end cottage. William Streatfield was a retired civil servant.

Reginald Tompson, rector of Woodstone in 1891, had moved to Ipswich by 1901.
The new rector was William Croome he was born in Gloucestershire. His wife was Louisa and they also had their niece Rachel Morrell living with them. Susannah Edwards was their domestic cook Bertha Jarvis their housemaid and Annie Coles was the parlourmaid.

Charles Dawson, a publican and blacksmith, and his wife Betsy had moved into the Boys Head Inn since the last census. They had three children Percy aged twelve, Grace seven and Reginald aged two years. Angelina Cunnington, mother to Betsy, was also living with them. Annie Kingston was their domestic servant, William Jacques was a blacksmith and Harry Armitage was a blacksmiths labourer.
During 1881 Charles Dawson was a labourer in an iron works in Deptford.

Alice Maria Terrot continued to be the head of Woodstone House and had her daughter Eleanor living with her. Their nephew Henry Monckton aged eleven also lived there and attended school.

William Shepherd from Somerset was their Page, Eleanor Page from Norfolk was their housemaid, Alphonsine Herbert from France was their ladysmaid and Elizabeth Jarvis from Huntingdonshire was their cook.
As told during the 1891 census details Alice died in 1902.

William Marshall was a coachman and groom for Alice Terrot. He lived in the Coachman's Cottage with his wife Jane and their daughter Elizabeth. Elizabeth worked as a mothers help.

The census then continued over the road beginning at the Norfolk Houses which were built in 1888. Number 1 (193) was uninhabited.
James Hill born in Stanground was a railway clerk and lived at number 2 (191) with his wife Mary and their two year old daughter Gladys.

John Thomas Martin, a schoolmaster, and his wife Mary were still living at 2 Cambridge House (189). They had seven children living at home all were born in Woodstone. Ethel was not shown as having an occupation so possibly helped out in the home. Bertram was a coal merchants clerk, Sydney was a tobacconist's assistant, Edward, George, Gilbert and Donald they all attended school and were all born in Woodstone.

Thomas and Caroline Yates continued to live at 1 Cambridge House (187). Their daughter Rosa was still living at home but their son Thomas married in 1899 and lived with his wife Annie at Heydon Villa, Blinco Grove at Cherry Hinton in Cambridgeshire by the time of the 1901 census.

William Eatherley was born in Peakirk during 1835 and was a retired ironmonger. He lived with his second wife Louisa at number 1 Mount View (169). They married in the district of Islington during 1885 Louisa's maiden name was Louisa Cave Leggett.
In 1862 William married Ann Jenevera English in the Peterborough district. By the time of the 1881 census William was a widower as Ann died during 1880 aged forty two. William then lived at 42 Narrow Bridge Street in Peterborough where he was an ironmonger. He had six children to support. They were Robert,

Charles, Walter, Ernest, Herbert and Elizabeth their ages ranged from twenty to four.

Arthur Dickinson, a railway canvasser, lived at Preston Villa (167) with his daughter Elsie aged eighteen and sons Fred aged fifteen who was a pupil teacher and Cyril aged nine who attended school. Their mother Mary died on 9th March 1898 and was buried in the local cemetery. Elsie probably took over from her mother and looked after the home as she was not shown as having an occupation.

Edwin Mackinder, a widower, was a manufacturer of mineral water. His wife Anne died on 1st August 1899 and buried in the local cemetery. Edwin's two daughters Alice and Edith lived with him at 2 Claremount Villa (163).

Thomas Phillips, a coal merchant's manager, lived at Granville House (159) with his wife Hannah and their family. Horace aged seventeen worked as a clerk in the Chapters office, Elizabeth aged fifteen was a drapers apprentice and Dorothy aged thirteen all were born in Fletton. Evelyn aged twelve, John aged seven and Charles aged six were all born in Woodstone.

George and Emma Hunting had moved along Oundle Road to Vernon House (161) at that time George was seventy two years old and was shown as being a farmer.
Their son Arthur married Annie Taylor after their banns were read in the September of 1892. They were living in one of the cottages next to the Eastmead Villas along Oundle Road. During the 1891 census Annie was living with her mother Mary and brothers and sisters at Carter Row in Stanground..
George and Emma's daughter Agnes married William Philip Turner on 20th April 1892 at St Augustine's church. By 1901 they were living at Hunston in Suffolk where William was a farmer.
Their son Frank married Nellie Bridgefoot on 18th July 1893 at St Augustine's church. Nellie was the daughter of James and Helena who lived along Oundle Road in Woodstone. By 1901 Frank and Nellie had moved into Manor Farm where his parents were living in 1891.
Frank went to school at Woodstone and then to Deacons school in Peterborough. During 1895 he succeeded his uncle Joseph as

manager of the firm G. & J. Hunting Coal Merchants'. Frank was elected on to the Peterborough Council in 1907 and in 1921 he was appointed as Mayor for the town. By 1925 Frank was elected as an Alderman. He died during 1941 seventeen years after his wife Nellie passed away.

Not far from the Hunting family lived James and Charlotte Burnham although the census shows James as being George. (A possible slip of the enumerators' pen) They had four of their children still living at home George aged fifteen worked as a grain blower, Charlotte aged thirteen, John aged eleven and James aged nine attended school.

Their oldest daughter Sarah Jane married John William Waspe on 3rd April 1899 at St Augustine's church. They lived at 2 Australian Terrace along Rose Lane in Woodstone.

Another daughter Alice was a domestic servant for Levi and Sarah Butler who lived at 158 Palmerston Road. Levi, a retired metal broker, was born in Woodstone during 1838.

Alice married George William Green on 10th May 1909 at St Augustine's church.

James and Charlotte's son Levi married Fanny Mitchell during 1898 in the district of Peterborough. By the time of the 1901 census they were living in the St John the Baptist parish of Peterborough and had two young children, Alice aged one year and the baby Frances who was shown as under one year old.

James and Charlotte's daughter Emma aged twenty one was a domestic house maid at Shanklin on the Isle of Wight at the time of the 1901 census.

By the time of the 1901 census James/George and Charlotte's daughter Martha was living at Greenwich in London where she worked as a dressmaker.

Walter Buckler, a gardener, and his wife Sarah Ann lived at Resting Cottage on Oundle Road with their daughter Evelyn who was nine years old.

The next house on the census was Violet House (83) where James and Eleanor Bridgefoot lived and had been there since around 1891. They had two grown up daughters living at home who were Fannie aged twenty six and Ada aged twenty three. Their father was a contractor and builder.

John Strickson, a foreman at a timber yard lived at 1 Kisby Villa (79) with Mary his wife and their four grown up children. William was forty five and worked as a railway wagon builder, Charles aged thirty eight was a railway wagon examiner, Elizabeth aged thirty was not shown as having an occupation and Henry aged twenty seven was a bootmaker.

Frederick H Hunting was the son of Frederick and Rebecca who lived at Eye Green near Peterborough at the time of the 1881 census. Frederick senior was a brewer and publican. By 1891 they were shown as living at the Greyhound Inn on Eye Green. Frederick junior's occupation was a butcher. He married Agnes Violetta Stanley during 1893 in the district of Peterborough. They lived at 73 Oundle Road where Frederick had a butchers business. They had three children, Harry Stanley born in 1896, Eva Violetta born in 1899 and Tom (Thomas Vernon) was born in 1900 all in Woodstone. Frederick employed three people, Hugh Sponden from Sutton on Sea was a butcher, George Giish from Wales was a butcher's apprentice and Sarah Pocklington was a domestic servant.

Francis William George married Emily Cole in the district of Peterborough during 1900. They were living along Oundle Road where Francis was a hairdresser.

Edward Partridge was a cabinet maker and house decorator and was born in New Fletton during 1858. Edward married Mary Ann Davison during the winter months in 1880 in the Oundle district. By the 1881 census they were living along Grove Street in Fletton, Thomas who was Edward's brother also lived with them and he worked as a painter and writer.
By 1891 Edward and Mary were living at Himalayan House (possibly 71) where they had taken on Edward's cousin William Sharpe aged sixteen who worked as a paper hangers' apprentice.
At the time of the 1901 census Edward and Mary were still living at Himalayan House. Francis Hockerston was a boarder with the family, his occupation was a carpenter. Herbert Lavender, a gardener, and his wife Ann were visiting Edward and Mary.

Fred Jackson was born in New Fletton during 1862. In 1881 when he was nineteen he worked as a shoemaker and lived with his widowed mother Louisa and his three brothers at 13 Tower Street Fletton. Fred and his wife Mary Ann lived at 9 Tower Street Fletton in 1891 where Fred was a boot and shoe maker. By 1901 they had moved to a house along Oundle Road near to Jubilee Street. Fred was a bootmaker and poultry and pigeon judge (Reporter). Also living with them was Fred's mother Louisa and his second cousin Fred Freeman aged five and born in Spalding. In 1891 Louisa lived with her son in law and daughter Walter and Louisa Clarke at Halfway House along Thorpe Road in Peterborough.

JUBILEE STREET

Next on the census came Jubilee Street. In the first cottage named Laurel Cottage lived Arthur Kinns. He was twenty and worked as a grocers' assistant. Also living in the cottage was his sister Emily who was twenty two years old and worked as a school teacher. Their parents were Charles and Emma Kinns who at the time of the 1901 census were shown as being in St Helens parish in Lancaster. Ernest Christmas worked as a grocers assistant and was a boarder with Arthur and Emily

The Kinns family had lived at Laurel Cottage since around the time of the 1891 census.

Elizabeth Gunton had been living at 7 Jubilee Street since the 1891 census. Her husband James died in 1893 aged forty four and was buried in the local cemetery.

Five of her children still living at home were John aged twenty three who was a clerk at the Co-op Society, Fred aged twenty one was a clerk in a brewery and Herbert aged twenty was an apprentice in a confectioners. Charlie aged fifteen and Frank aged eleven both attended school. Some of Elizabeth's children had married and moved away.

Arthur Gunton married Eliza who was born in Islington and they were living in East Ham by the time of the 1901 census. Arthur worked as a potato salesman and they had two children Arthur and Elsie.

James Gunton married Mary who was born in Chatteris and they were living in Bedfordshire at the time of the 1901 census. They also had two children Ernest and Jessie. James occupation was shown as an iron moulder.

George Gunton was at Gillingham in Kent where he was an engine room artificer in the Royal Navy.

William Cornwall, a bathing place attendant and boatman died during 1896 and was buried in the local cemetery next to Susan his late wife.

Rosalind Cornwall, a church school teacher, was living at 17 Jubilee Street the home of her late grandparents William and Susan Cornwell. (At the time of the 1881 census Rosalind aged ten lived with her grandparents at Victoria Place in Fletton.)

Mary Cornwall, aunt to Rosalind and daughter of the late William and Susan, lived with Rosalind. Rosalind was shown on the census as being head of the household.

Caroline Hankins continued living at 23 Jubilee Street, her husband Joseph William died during 1892 aged thirty seven and was buried in the local cemetery. Caroline had two sons to bring up on her own, George aged eleven and Ernest aged nine. Caroline's oldest daughter Carrie was a domestic servant working in Bourne.

George Strickson, a whipmaker, and his wife Phoebe lived at 25 Jubilee Street with their one year old daughter Evelyn. They married in the Paddington district during 1896. George was the son of John and Mary Strickson who lived at 6 Davies Terrace Fletton in 1881.

From this point on the census it was not possible to state which number the residents lived at along Jubilee Street.

Henry George Kingerley, a brickyard labourer, and his wife Mary lived along Jubilee Street with their twenty one year old son George who was a policeman. They lived at Parsons Drove at the time of the 1881 census. In 1891 Henry and Mary had moved to Bedford Street in Peterborough with their sons Jesse aged eighteen and George aged eleven. Henry's widowed mother Letitia also lived with them at that time.

Henry died 20th June 1906 aged 69 and Mary died during 1909 aged 68.

Living about four houses away from Henry was his son Jesse and wife Louisa. Jesse married Louisa Langford during 1897 in the district of Peterborough. They had a son Jesse John who was born in Essex during 1898. Louisa was the daughter of Thomas and Amy Langford who lived at Southwick in 1881.

Arthur Baines, a brickburner, married Sarah Wiles during 1895 in the district of Peterborough. He was the son of John and Martha who, according to the 1881 census, lived in the Houses on the Hill at Water End in Stanground.

Sarah was the daughter of Eliza, a lacemaker, who lived at Spaldwick during 1881. Sarah's father had passed away by then. Arthur and Sarah lived along Jubilee Street with their sons Harold aged four and Arthur Edwin aged three years, both were born in Woodstone.

On 7th July 1911 Arthur senior passed away aged 40. The words on his gravestone read:-

'I hear the words of love,
I gaze upon the blood,
I see the mighty sacrifice,
And I have peace with God'.

On 4th February 1911 Arthur Edwin passed away aged 16. The words on his gravestone read:-

'Lead me in thy truth,
And teach me; for thou art the God of my salvation'.

Sarah passed away during 1922.

William Piggott, a railway wagon painter, and his wife Ellen lived along Jubilee Street. Their son George was a fish merchant who lived along Oundle Road. At the time of the 1881 census William and his family were living at 69 Gladstone Street in Peterborough.

The rest of their family were Ellen Emma who married John Robinson during 1881, Annie who married Arthur Lockington in 1888. They all married in the district of Peterborough.

Lizzie married Richard Thomas Smith on 4th February 1891 at St Augustine's church in Woodstone..

William and Ellen had taken in three boarders. One was Freeman Pettit a grocer's assistant who was also shown as a boarder during 1891 with William Piggott. Freeman was the son of Thomas and Susannah Pettit who lived at 3 Demontford Terrace during 1881 where they lodged with Mary Wallis.

The other two Boarders were Frank and Samuel Gynn/Ginn who were both born at Woodnewton. Samuel was a railway fireman, Frank was a railway driver and in 1891 they were Boarders with Walter and Susan Bullock who lived at 69 Palmerston Road.

Alice Gretton was a domestic servant for William and Ellen's family.

Thomas and Sarah Garner had been living at 2 Jubilee Street since the time of the 1891 census. They had six of their children living at home. Olive aged nineteen was a wife's help, Sidney aged seventeen was a railway engine cleaner, Albert aged fifteen was a railway telegraph clerk, Frank aged thirteen was a grocer's errand boy, David aged twelve and Alexander aged nine both attended school.

Their son Charles Frederick married Susannah Rudd during 1900 in the district of Peterborough.

The majority of families who were living in Jubilee Street during the 1891 census had moved.

WATER END

Water End was shown on the 1901 census as Wharf Road/Water End.

The first home was 1 Acorn Cottage where William Major, a brickmakers clerk born in Spalding, and his wife Matilda lived with their five year old daughter Dorothy. They married during 1893 in the Peterborough district.

Matilda was the daughter of Henry and Matilda Palmer and was born in Woodstone during 1865. They also lived in the first cottage along Water End in 1871 which is where Matilda grew up. During 1881 Matilda was visiting Thomas and Susannah Hill who lived at 25 Glynn Street at Lambeth in Surrey.

William Major was the son of William and Sarah who lived at 63 Westwood Street Peterborough in 1891. At that time William junior was a post office sorting clerk.

Henry Hoare, a wood sawyer, his wife Emma and their children continued living at 2 Water End. Most of their children were living at home. Ada aged twenty three was not shown as having an occupation so possibly helped her mother in the home. Three of their sons worked for the railways, John aged twenty was a lifters wagon labourer, Charles aged eighteen was an assistant truck builder and Herbert aged fourteen was an assistant in the fitters shop. Margaret and Stephen both aged eight attended school.

Their daughter Laura was a domestic nursemaid for a family living in the parish of St Peters Peterborough at the time of the 1901 census. Laura married Harry Long on 26th December 1906 at St

Augustine's church in Woodstone. Harry was a railway clerk and the son of Harry and Hannah Long who lived along Palmerston Road and had done so since around the time of the 1881 census. Harry and Laura both grew up in Woodstone.

In the next cottage lived Mark and Emma Christmas with two of their daughters. Annie aged eleven and Lizzie aged five who both attended school.

Their oldest daughter Sarah was a domestic cook living at Watford in Hertfordshire. John aged twenty four and Mark aged twenty were living and working in Rotherham John as a machine winder in a Wind Mill and Mark as a wood yard labourer. Another of their daughter's Emma Eliza married Reuben Coulson on 27th December 1898 at St Augustine's church in Woodstone. In 1901 they were living in the parish of St Johns in Peterborough. Reuben was the son of Samuel and Lucy from Whittlesey.

William Henry Exton married Elizabeth Mary Palmer on 25th December 1882 at St Augustine's church Woodstone. Elizabeth was the daughter of Henry and Matilda Palmer. Her sister Matilda lived a few houses away with her husband William Major. William Exton was a carpenter and was the son of William and Ruth Exton who had lived along Lincoln Road Peterborough from around 1881.

William and Elizabeth had three children Elizabeth was seventeen and worked as a milliner, Ernest aged fifteen was a shop apprentice and Evelyn aged fourteen attended school. They had lived at 4 Acorn Cottages in Water End since the time of the 1891 census.

Henry and Matilda Palmer were still living along Water End about two houses away from their daughter Elizabeth. Both were in their sixties but Henry continued to work for the railways as a pointsman. Alfred their youngest son lived with them but was unemployed at the time of the census.

Harriet Jarvis also lived along Water End and had been there with her husband since at least the time of the 1841 census. Her husband John died in 1897 aged eighty. Harriet died during 1905 aged eighty nine they were both buried in the local cemetery.

George Holman had changed his occupation since the 1891 census from a baker to a milkman. He lived along Water End with Sarah his wife and their three children. George was eight and both Nellie and Harry were five.

Robert and Eliza Crayton both aged sixty seven continued to live along Water End in 1901. Their daughter Mary married Roderick Arnsby on 16th April 1900 at St Augustine's church. Roderick was a tailor from Theddingsworth in Leicestershire. Eliza Crayton died in April 1909 and Robert died in March 1910. They were both buried in the local cemetery in a double grave.

George and Sarah Hillson had moved from Jones Cottage where they lived in 1891 to a cottage along Water End by the time of the 1901 census. Their children were grown up and married.
Ruth was living in the parish of St Johns in Peterborough with her husband William Garton and their ten year old son George Frederick.
Bertha was living along Belsize Avenue with her husband John Redhead who was a coal wharf foreman.
Mary Ann was living in Helpston with her husband Walter Quincey who was a carter on a farm.
Three more of George and Sarah's daughters married at St Augustine's church after the 1901 census. Elizabeth married Henry Ellington on 18th July 1901, Annie Marie married William Church on 26th December 1903 and Kate married Horace Lettice on 17th October 1904.

Lucy Weston had lived in Woodstone since around the time of the 1841 census. Her husband Richard who was born in Woodstone died in August 1894 aged eighty three and was buried in the local cemetery. Lucy lived on her own in her cottage along Water End at the time of the 1901 census but died at the beginning of the year in 1902 aged ninety two. Lucy was also buried in the local cemetery.

Sarah Sykes was a widow, and had been since she moved to Woodstone around the time of the 1881 census. She also lived on her own in the next cottage to Lucy Weston although her son Edmund Sykes lived not far away with his family. Sarah died during the winter of 1905 aged eighty nine and was buried in the local cemetery.

Sarah Mould and her family had moved into Water End by the time of the 1901 census. Sarah worked from home as a dressmaker. In 1881 she lived at Old Yard, Cumbergate in Peterborough with her husband William and their children. William was a basket maker before he died in 1894.

Their son Arthur, a basket maker, married Annie Meadows during 1896 in the Parish of St Pauls Peterborough. On 14th November 1900 Annie died aged thirty and was buried in the local cemetery. Arthur was living with his mother in 1901.

Another son Walter, a basket maker, married Henrietta Burditt in the Parish of Lutton during the winter of 1895. They had a daughter Ethel aged four and were all living with Sarah.

Sarah's daughter Julia married Frederick Strawson during the winter months of 1890 in the district of Peterborough. They had three children Daisy aged nine, George aged four and Lilly aged one. They also lived with Sarah.

Finally Sarah's youngest son Reginald lived at home with his mother he was seventeen and was also a basket maker.

Harry Marriott, a brickyard labourer, married Mary Ellen Worth during 1896 in Cornwell where Mary was born. Harry and Mary had two children Beatrice aged four and Ashley aged two. They all lived in Water End.

Harry was born in Woodstone and the son of William and Sarah Marriott who had lived at Orton Waterville since around 1881 and continued to live there by the time of the 1901 census.

Mary was the daughter of William and Mary Worth from St Tudy in Cornwall. By 1891 Mary was a housekeeper for her widowed grandfather John Worth who also lived at St Tudy.

Not far from Mr and Mrs Marriott was the Church of England school.

Sarah Hoare had lived along Water End since the 1860's and was a caretaker for the church. Her son Henry and his family lived further along Water End.

Joseph Sellers was the son of Ebenezer. In 1881 they lived in New Road Peterborough at the basket makers shop, Joseph's grandmother Elizabeth also lived with them and was the housekeeper and a cane worker.

Joseph, a basket maker and employer, married Florence Jane Darling during 1894 in the district of Peterborough. Florence was the daughter of William and Matilda Darling who lived at Pipe Lane in Peterborough during 1891.

Thomas Burton was a basket maker born in Norfolk who worked for Joseph Sellers. He lived in the next cottage to Joseph with his wife Lily and their three children. In 1891 they lived along City Road in Peterborough. In 1881 Thomas, a basket maker was a boarder with George Rawlinson and his family at 5 City Road in Peterborough.

John Wilcox, another basket worker, lived in the next cottage with his wife Lizzie and their son George who was also a basket maker. Arthur Butler from Derby was a boarder with the family he also worked as a basket maker.

Timothy Sellers, a basket maker, and his wife Fanny lived at 11 Cumbergate which was in Brusters Yard in Peterborough during 1881 and were still there at the time of the 1891 census. Their grandson Thomas aged three was also living with them. By 1901 Timothy and Fanny were living in the next cottage to John Wilcox along Water End. Their thirteen year old grandson, whose name was shortened to Tom continued living with them and attended school. Mary Jenkinson from Tallington was their domestic servant.

Edward Burton, a basket maker, and his wife Mary lived in the next cottage with their eleven year old son William. Edward was the son of Thomas and Emily Burton who lived at Willingham near Cambridge. Both Edward and his father were basket makers.

William Leverett was still the publican at the Ferry Boat Inn with his wife Mary. Their oldest son William died at the end of the year in 1891 aged ten. He was buried in the local cemetery. Their other children were George aged eighteen, no occupation shown, Edward sixteen an apprentice to an engineers, Clara Gertrude aged fourteen, Charles eleven, Gaston (Gascoigne) nine and Gracie aged six all attended school.

Walter Garnham, a brickyard labourer, married Alice Maud Jenkinson on 20th December 1899 at St Augustine's church in Woodstone. They lived along Water End. Walter was the son of Ezra Garnham and Alice was the daughter of John and Rosetta Jenkinson who lived further along Water End.

One of her sisters' Mary was a domestic servant for Timothy Sellers who lived nearby.

Another of Alice's sisters Rosetta Jane married William Henry Hillson on 25th January 1897 at St Augustine's church. They lived in one of the cottages named Rutland Terrace along New Road in Woodstone.

Robert Whyman married Margaret Pearson on 1st August 1898 in the parish of Northborough where she was born. Robert was the son of George and Susannah who lived along Water End during 1881. Susannah was still living there in 1891, she worked as a laundress. Her son Robert also lived with her and worked as an agricultural labourer.

Robert and Margaret had two children Cecil was two years old and Reginald was four months. Robert's widowed mother Susannah also lived with them along Water End.

Edmund and Easter Sykes were still living along Water End where they had been since the 1891 census. At that time they only had one daughter Florence. By 1901 Florence was ten and had two sisters and a brother. Arthur was six, Kate three and Hannah was one year old. All were born in Woodstone.

Joseph Freeman, son of Thomas and Betsy who lived at the Farm Cottage along Oundle Road in 1881, was a boarder with Edmund and Easter. His mother Betsy lived in the next cottage and worked as a charwoman.

Frederick Farrow and Esther had moved into a home of their own along Water End since the last census when they lived with Esther's mother Sarah Sykes. Their oldest daughter Adelaide was living in the urban district of Fletton where she worked as a domestic servant.

Frederick and Esther had four other children Nellie was nine, Herbert was seven, Alfred was five and Sarah was two years old.

John Jenkinson married Rosetta Olerenshaw on 18th July 1870 at St George's church in Campden. In 1901 they lived along Water End with two of their grown up children. John was twenty one and worked as a general labourer as did Edwin who was fifteen. Their daughter's Alice, Mary and Rosetta lived not far away.

In 1891 John and his family lived at the Rose and Crown Inn along Bridge Street in Peterborough where John was the licensed victualler.

Mary Webb had moved from 37 Palmerston Road, where she lived during 1891, to Water End by the time of the 1901 census. Mary was the caretaker of the School, her son John aged twenty three and her grandson Frank aged twelve were also living with her. Mary's daughter Charlotte married John Giddings, a publican, at the beginning of the year in 1892 in Whittlesey. By 1901 they were living in Whittlesey and had two children.

Mary's other daughter Margaret was shown on the census as living in Hampstead and working as a domestic cook.

PALMERSTON ROAD

Living at number 1 was Charles Lucas, a baker, and his wife Annie (nee Berry). They married during 1900 in the Peterborough district, Annie was the daughter of Ann and stepdaughter of Alfred Hemsley who lived at 21 Palmerston Road during 1881 and had moved to 10 Palmerston Road by 1891. At that time Annie was a dressmaker. Charles was the son of Charles and Susan Lucas and in 1891 they lived along Grove Street in Fletton not far from Annie.

Since the 1891 census 3 Palmerston Road had been built, this was where Albert Hare, a police constable, lived with his wife Rachel and their two daughters Nora and Phyllis.

Albert married Rachel Marriott in the spring of 1891 in the district of Peterborough. At the time of the 1891 census Albert was living with his sister Susannah Palmer who was a widow and lived 4 Victoria Place along Oundle Road in Fletton. Susannah's late husband was Richard Palmer.

Thomas and Annie Waite continued to live at number 5 and had done so since 1881. Annie died towards the end of the year in 1909 aged sixty five. Thomas died towards the end of the year in

1922 aged eighty two. They were both buried in the local cemetery.

John Thomas Setchfield, a wheelwright and carpenter, lived at 15 Palmerston Road with his wife Eliza and their two children. Elsie was nine and Sydney was one year old. John and Eliza were both born in Whittlesea.

The houses numbered 17 to 21 inclusive had been built since the 1891 census.
Henry Strickson, a saddler born in Stibbington, married Ella Harrison towards the end of the year in 1898 and made their home at 17 Palmerston Road.

Frances Starmore had moved into number 37 and worked as a bottle washer at home. Her husband John died in 1896 aged 56 and was buried in the local cemetery. They had been in Woodstone since around the time of the 1881 census and at that time lived at 130 Limetree Terrace in Palmerston Road.
Frances also had two of her daughters living with her in 1901, Ellen aged twenty eight and Minnie aged eighteen both were bottle washers like their mother.
George Webb and Herbert May worked as railway engine stokers and were boarders with Frances. George Winham from New Fletton worked as a confectioner's assistant and also boarded with Frances.
The fourth Boarder was Thomas Charles a goods shed porter aged twenty nine.
On 8th April 1901 Ellen Starmore and Thomas Charles married at St Augustine's church in Woodstone.
Frances' daughter Fanny married Albert Edward Riddle during 1894 in the Peterborough district. In 1901 they were living in the house where Fanny's' parents had previously lived at number 108 Palmerston Road. Albert was a railway checker in a goods shed and the son of Edward and Elizabeth who lived in Tansor. At the time of the 1891 census Albert was a boarder with John and Fanny Freeman who lived at Warkworth in Oxfordshire where Albert was a railway porter.
Minnie Gertrude Starmore married Thomas Frederick Page on 26th December 1905. They made their home at 280 Oundle Road in Woodstone. Thomas was born in Market Harborough and was

the son of Thomas and Elizabeth Page who at the time of the 1901 census lived at Great Bowden in Leicestershire. Thomas Frederick, pictured below, worked as a marker out at a corset factory.

Edgar John Allen married Annie Maria Kennell towards the end of 1889 in the Hartismere district of Suffolk. Annie was the daughter of John and Maria Kennell, her father was a boot and shoe maker. Edgar was the son of Samuel and Elizabeth from Braiseworth in Suffolk, Samuel was an agricultural labourer.

Edgar, an acting railway guard, and Annie had three children. Ada was eleven, Edgar was nine and Albert was nine months old, they were all born in Woodstone. The family lived at 39 Palmerston Road.

Thomas Dixon was a platelayer at the time of the 1891 census but by the 1901 census he had changed his job to a railway Per'mt way inspector' (As recorded on census). Thomas continued to live at 41 Palmerston Road with his wife Naomi and their children. Walter was twenty and worked as a store keeper for the railway wagon works, Harry aged eighteen was a grocer's assistant, Fanny aged sixteen stayed at home, possibly helped her mother, and Lilian aged eleven attended school.

Thomas and Naomi had another son Herbert aged twenty three. At the time of the 1901 census he was shown as living at Chatteris where he worked as an iron founder.

James and Sarah Waspe also continued to live in the same house as they were in 1891 at 45 Palmerston Road. George their son aged twenty one was a grocer's assistant and Frederick aged nineteen was a van man for a furniture dealers. Lizzie aged fourteen and Henry ten attended school.

Their oldest son James Robert married Emily Agnes Atkin in the district of Cambridge during 1898. By the time of the 1901 census James was a furniture warehouseman and they were living at 5 Grove Street in Fletton with their daughter Marjorie who was eight months old.

James and Sarah's other son John William married Sarah Jane Burnham on 3rd April 1899 at St Augustine's church in Woodstone and lived along Rose Lane.

William Henry German, a widower, married Ellen Annie Brewster on 10th September 1899 at St Augustine's church in Woodstone. Ellen was the daughter of William and Emma Brewster from Seaton in Rutland, and twin to Thomas William Brewster who lived in New Road Woodstone. William was the son of Thomas and Sarah German who lived in Brook Street Peterborough during 1881 and Monument Street by 1891.

William, a railway parcels porter, and Ellen were living at 57 Palmerston Road with Williams' son George Henry aged eight, son of the late Theodosia German.

William Newbon, a railway engine stoker, and his wife Arabella lived at 71 with their one year old son William. During 1891 they were living along Queens Walk

George Andrews, a police constable born in Suffolk, lived at 73 Palmerston Road with his wife Annie and their children. George was eight and Florence was five, both were born in Woodstone.

Living at 79 Palmerston Road, the last cottage before Queens Walk, was William Johnson, a drawer of bricks, with his wife Emily and their son William who was one year old.

QUEENS WALK

Lizzie Patrick, the wife of the late William Patrick, lived in the first cottage along Queens Walk from Palmerston Road end (172). William died in 1898 aged forty three, their son William died in

1894 aged seven and both were buried in the local cemetery. Lizzie looked after their other children, Mary aged twelve, John aged eleven, George aged nine, Elsie aged seven, and Arthur aged four. All the children were born in Woodstone. Lizzie also had three young men boarding with them, all worked at the railways.

Christopher George married Mary Ann Hardiment during 1892 in the Peterborough district. During 1881 Christopher was living as a boarder with William and Susannah Willson at 5 Limetree Terrace in Palmerston Road. Frederick George was also living there and was possibly brother to Christopher, they worked as railway engine cleaners and both were born in Old Fletton. By the time of the 1891 census Frederick was married to Hannah from Holbeach and they were living at Archibald Terrace, Wanstead in West Ham with their two young children Sidney aged three and Ernest aged two.

At the time of the 1881 census when she was eighteen years old Mary Ann Hardiment was a cook for William and Susan Thayer at St Stephens Villas in London.

Jane George aged twenty one was a housemaid for the same family: she was born in Old Fletton and possibly related to Christopher and Frederick.

Christopher, a railway engine driver, and Mary lived at 30 Palmerston Road in 1891 but had moved to number 5 (164) Queens Walk by 1901. Their children living at home were Ethel aged thirteen, Florence aged ten, Beatrice aged seven, Olive aged five, Victoria aged three, Horace aged two and Ambrose Sydney aged two months.

James Bull, an insurance agent, and his wife Sarah were still living at 156 Queens Walk and had done so since the last census. Also living at home were four of their grown up family, Arthur was twenty five and worked for the railways as an engine stoker, Albert aged twenty was a beer brewer, Mabel aged twenty seven was a mother's help and Edith aged seventeen was a general domestic servant.

Some of James and Sarah's children had married by the time of the 1901 census.

George Edward, an iron tin platelayer, married Florence Mary Marler in Hertfordshire during 1898. At the time of the 1901 census they were living in Fletton with their son George Ernest who was born during the summer of 1900.

Horace James, a railway engine stoker, married Sarah Elizabeth Stafford during the summer of 1896 in the Peterborough district. At the time of the 1901 census they were living at 148 Palmerston Road.

Walter David Bull, a railway wagon lifter, married Emily Bothamley during the spring of 1893 in the district of Peterborough. They were living at 155 Queens Walk, over the road from his parents, at the time of the 1901 census. They had three sons, Wilfred aged six, Percy aged four and Herbert aged two.

Edward Filby Oswick, a railway cloakroom porter, was still living at 157 Queens Walk with his wife Elizabeth and their son Joshua. Joshua was twenty four and worked for the railways as an engine stoker. His sister Ada was working in Hackney, London as a domestic housemaid. Ada married James Finedon during the winter of 1902 in the district of West Ham.

Joshua married Edith M Perry during 1913, at the time of the 1901 census Edith was living at Fletton where she worked as a domestic cook.

Jesse and Elizabeth Starsmore were also still living in the same cottage as they were in 1891 at 165 Queens Walk with their three children. Edith aged nine, Agnes aged six and William aged one year. At the time of the 1891 census they also had a son Jesse who was one year old. There was no sign of him on the 1901 census nor was he shown in the death records between the two census dates.

Another resident from 1891 was Benjamin Barnard who lived at 167 Queens Walk, his wife Hannah passed away during March in 1901 and was buried in the local cemetery. Their granddaughter Annie Payne, aged fifteen, was visiting at the time the census was read. Annie's parents, William and Annie and her seven brothers and sisters were living in Fletton by 1901. They used to live at 155 Queens Walk in 1891.

Living in the end cottage was George Freeman, a grocer, who worked from his home. He lived there with his wife Annie and their daughter Nora aged one year.

William Payne aged seventeen who was born in Peterborough worked for George Freeman as a grocer and also lived in as a boarder.

PALMERSTON ROAD

Moving back along Palmerston Road at number 83 lived George and Ellen Crowson and their daughter Mabel. George and Ellen (nee Bigley) married at the beginning of the year in 1893 in the Peterborough district. At the age of fifteen Ellen was a domestic nurse for George Payne, a doctor, and his wife Francis who lived at 3 Broad Bridge Street in Peterborough during the time of the 1881 census. Elizabeth Crayton who was also born in Woodstone worked for the family as a cook.

Next to George lived Harry and Hannah Long at number 85. Harry was a foreman at the wagon works, they had four children. Harry aged twenty worked as a railway clerk, (Harry married Laura Hoare on 26 December 1906 at St Augustine's church in Woodstone. Laura was the daughter of Henry and Emma Hoare.) Harry and Hannah's other children were Isabella aged eleven, Annie aged nine and Ernest was six, all four of their children were born in Woodstone.

At number 87 lived William Bigley, a railway engine driver, with his wife Mary Ann and their family who had lived in the same house since 1891. Their family were Catherine aged twenty eight who was a dressmaker working from home. William aged twenty one was a railway clerk, John aged nineteen was a carpenter and Stephen aged fifteen worked as a coal office clerk.

A new house had been built since the last census and was numbered 91. Living there was Fredrick Butcher, a retired inspector for the railway police, his wife Clara and their son Arthur. Arthur was twenty nine and worked as a solicitor's clerk. In 1891 they lived at 31 Park Street in Fletton.

Robert Bland, a farmer, and his wife Elizabeth had moved from Waters End where they lived in 1891 to Victoria House (95) in Palmerston Road by the time of the 1901 census. Their children were Alfred aged twelve and Elsie aged two.

Joseph and Elizabeth Kingerley were also still living in the same house at 111 Palmerston Road as in they did in 1891. Three of their children were living at home Walter was twenty eight and worked as a railway fireman, Millicent aged twenty five and Ethel aged twenty both worked as dressmakers from home.

Their son Joseph married Susan Apthorpe (birth registered as Maria Susan) at the beginning of the year in 1901 before the census was recorded and were living in Fletton.

Joseph passed away on 17th September 1908 aged seventy four, Elizabeth passed away during August 1913 they were both laid to rest in the local cemetery.

Phillip Henry Darker and his wife Louisa were still living at Clifton House (115) in Palmerston Road.

The cottages numbered 123 and 125 named Tydd Villas were built around 1902.

The next house along Palmerston Road was 131 known as Norton House where Willie Wright, a railway guard, and his wife Hannah lived. Willie was born in Oundle and Hannah in Somerset.

Another new house which was named Ibcobo House (133) was built in 1898. In 1901 it was not known as Ibcoco House but simply listed as a being along Palmerston Road. Elizabeth Deacon a widow, her son John a brickyard labourer and daughter Jennie who was a dressmaker working from home, lived there. In 1891 John was a servant (confectioner) for John and Jane House who were confectioners at 41 Cowgate in Peterborough. In 1891 Elizabeth was living at 6 Percival Street in Peterborough with her husband George who was a carpenter born in Cherry Orton. George died during 1895 aged fifty nine.

Frederick Collison, a builder and contractor, lived at St Helier House with his wife Annie and their family. Thomas was twenty and worked as a bricklayer, Grace aged eighteen was a dressmaker working from home and Stanley aged ten attended school.

John Barrett was a widower by the time of the 1901 census as his wife Eliza died in June 1899 aged sixty two and was buried in the local cemetery. He had been living at 145 Palmerston Road since around the time of the 1891 census. Two of John's children, Herbert and Nellie, were living at home. Sarah Valentine, sister in law to John also lived with the family.

By the time of the 1901 census John's daughter Alice and her husband Ernest Willett were living at West Bridgford in Nottinghamshire where Ernest worked as a railway clerk. They had three children.

At 153 Palmerston Road lived John Pape, who was the grocery manager to the Co-op store, and his wife Julia. They had five children the oldest being Thomas aged fourteen who was an office boy. His brothers and sisters were Alfred aged twelve, Rose and Daisy aged nine and John aged three.

George Smith, a wheelwright, and his wife Maria lived at 157 with their son Samuel aged twenty three who worked as a carpenter. In 1881 the family lived at High Street in Yaxley.

The next house along Palmerston Road was called Casetta where Mary Vergette lived. Her husband Edward was born on 9th February 1842 his parents were Edward and Sarah Vergette. Edward (Senior) was a draper and in 1841 they lived at Market Street in Peterborough. Sarah died in 1879 aged 64.
Edward entered into partnership with Mr S.C.W. Buckle, the Solicitor, after serving his articles with Alderman Percival of the Minster Precincts in Peterborough. Mr Buckle died in 1872 and Edward Vergette was elected unanimously to the position of 'Clerk to the Guardians' previously held by Mr Buckle.
Edward was a solicitor and coroner during 1881 and they lived with their four children along North Street in Peterborough. In 1885 Edward was appointed as the Mayor for Peterborough. He died on 24th March 1895 aged 53 at his home in North Street Peterborough after being in poor health for many years. Edward (Senior) died three weeks later in April aged 86.
Vergette Street in Peterborough was named after the family.
Edward's widow Mary had two of her children living with her by the time of the 1901 census. Mary Gertrude was twenty four and was a governess at a daily school and her brother Edward Dudley was twenty three and a law student.
Sarah Day was a general domestic servant for the family.

Two houses named Fairmead were next to Casetta in one of them lived Arthur Hill, a chief clerk in the Peterborough Diocesan office, with his wife Emma and their three sons. Arthur was ten, George was eight and Ernest was two years old.

Martha Jinks from Dogsthorpe was their domestic servant. Arthur was the son of George and Annie Hill who lived at 3 The Woodlands Fletton during 1881.

The family living in the other Fairmead house was Daniel Collier, a corn mill manager and his wife Ethel. They had a one year old son named Gilbert. Florence Morris aged sixteen was their domestic servant she was born in Fletton.

John William Crawley, son of Charles and Adelaide from Woodstone, married Florence Elizabeth Vergette during March 1894 at St John's in Peterborough. Florence was the daughter of John and Eliza Vergette who lived at 5 Market Place Peterborough during 1881.

John and Florence had two children Charles John born in 1896 and Kathleen Mary in 1898 both in Woodstone. They lived in the house named Hazlehurst next to John's parents Charles and Adelaide. John was a whip manufacturer, like his father, and he employed Mary Ann Higgins from Lincolnshire as their general domestic servant.

Charles and Adelaide Crawley continued to live at Aboyne Lodge with three of their children. Evelyn aged twenty four, Charles aged twenty two who worked as a saddler's ironmonger, Percy aged nineteen was an architect's pupil. Annie Morgan from Spalding was their housemaid and Margaret Faulkner from Peterborough was their cook.

Charles and Adelaide's daughter Agnes married William Boyer on 13th September 1894 at St Augustine's church in Woodstone. At the time of the 1901 census they were living in the parish of St John's in Peterborough with their two young daughters Evelyn aged two and Vera under one year old.

Charles and Adelaide's other daughter Evelyn married Alexander Campbell Ferrier on 22nd July 1902 at St Augustine's church. Alexander was an accountant who lived in the parish of St Mark's in Peterborough.

Charles Crawley was born during 1843 at Eaton Socon, William his father was carrying on the whip making tradition of the family which was first mentioned in 1806. At the age of sixteen Charles helped his father in the business. His brother Thomas came to Peterborough in 1861 where he opened his business in Priestgate, two years later he moved to Somersham in the saddlers business. Mr Crawley Snr. then moved to Peterborough and founded Crawley and Sons. When Charles father died in 1869 he took over the business and then, in their turn, his sons John and Charles carried on the firm. Charles Edward Crawley served on the Peterborough town council for the South Ward continuously from 1886 to 1919 and was appointed Mayor for Peterborough in 1911. Photograph show Crawley & Sons premises along Priestgate in Peterborough and images of Charles and Adelaide Crawley.

PLATE VIII.

1.—**JOHN BETTS TEBBUTT** and **Mrs. TEBBUTT**, 1909. Taking the Civic Chair in a quiet year, he carried through the office with dignity and credit. He was landlord of the "Crown." Died April 12. 1921.

2.—**WILLIAM CLIFFE** and **Mrs. CLIFFE**, 1910. A general dealer, he was a rigid abstainer. He was 26 before he occupied the Civic Chair. Died December 10. 1916

3.—**CHARLES EDWARD CRAWLEY** and **Mrs. CRAWLEY**, 1911. Mayor and Mayoress in Coronation year. A whip-maker and a man of sound business habits. Resigned the Council in November, 1919. Died May 3, 1922.

John Alex Robertson was a medical practitioner born in Scotland his wife Agnes was also born in Scotland. At the time of the 1881 census they were living at Harthill cum Woodall in Yorkshire with their five children John aged nine, Alexander aged eight, Margaret three, Arthur one and Lily was a few months old..

Ten years later at the time of the 1891 census they were living along High Street in Stilton where John continued his profession as a registered general medical practitioner. Their oldest son at home was Alexander aged eighteen who was a medical student. Their other children were Margaret aged thirteen, Lilybell aged ten, and David aged seven all attended school. The youngest child was two year old Malcolm.

By 1901 John and Agnes had moved to Woodstone and lived along Palmerston Road with their family in one of the larger houses named Kelvingrove not far from Aboyne Lodge. Their sons Arthur aged twenty one and David aged seventeen were both cycle merchants. Lily aged twenty had no occupation and Malcolm aged twelve attended school.

Hannah Crisp from Cambridgeshire worked at the family home as their domestic servant.

Frederick Shepherd was a widower by the time of the 1901 census. His wife Susan died in November 1898 aged fifty six and was buried in the local cemetery. Frederick had moved from 192 Palmerston Road where they lived in 1891 to Greta House (206) just across the road from the Robertson family by 1901. He continued working as a railway engine driver and his son Arthur aged twenty three worked as a clerk in one of the Co-op stores. Ada aged twenty one was not shown as having an occupation so possibly looked after the home after her mother died.

Thomas Richard Hunting continued to live at Murton House (204) although his first wife Rose died in the December of 1894, aged thirty seven, and was buried in the local cemetery. Thomas married Ellen Searle from Stanground towards the end of the year in 1895. Ellen was the daughter of James and Mary Hill from Water End in Stanground she married William Searle during 1890 and in 1892 they had a daughter Hilda. William most possibly died hence the reason Ellen remarried.

There were seven children at home, Ernest aged eighteen worked as a railway clerk, Mabel aged seventeen was a milliner and

Norman Richard aged fifteen was a wood carving apprentice. Frank Bertram twelve Marcus Edward ten and Hilda nine all attended school. Nellie was born towards the end of the year in 1896 and Arthur was the youngest born in 1899. Ada Sutton from Peterborough worked for the Hunting family as a general domestic servant

Number 186 Palmerston Road was not occupied the census showed it as a 'House to Let'.

Mary Ann Wright lived at 182, her husband Charles died in 1885 aged fifty four. During 1881 they lived at 49 Ackland Street in Peterborough. Charles, born in Woodstone was the son of Charles and Elizabeth Wright, and the brother of Ellen who married George Piggott and also lived in Woodstone.
Mary had been living in the same house since the time of the 1891 census. Also living with Mary was her daughter Elizabeth and her husband Samuel Holmes. They had three children at home Laura aged twelve, Thomas aged ten and Albert aged two.

Thomas Eveleigh, a retired railway goods agent, and his wife Mary were still living at Linton House (178). Their oldest son James was living at home but supporting himself financially. In 1881 James worked as a clerk for G E Railway and was a boarder with Elizabeth Walker, who was a grocer, at Paxton Terrace in Kings Lynn.
Thomas and Mary's son Thomas married Florence Turner Dudley during 1897 in the district of Peterborough and by 1901 they were living in Ramsey where Thomas worked as a potato merchant's clerk. They had a two year old daughter Nora Winifred.

Alfred Humm married Lilian Marsden Willett during 1897 in the district of Stamford. Lilian was the daughter of Samuel and Emily who lived at 3 Station Cottages along Station Road in Fletton. Alfred, born in Fletton, was the son of Edward and Mahala Humm who lived along Elm Street in Fletton. By the time of the 1901 census Alfred and Lilian were living at Clarkson House (176) Palmerston Road with their three year old daughter Doris and their son Robert who was one year old.
Alfred died at the age of sixty three in February 1923 at the Peterborough Infirmary and was buried in the local cemetery. He

163

owned property which consisted of five cottages situated in Park Street, London Road in Peterborough. These he left to Lilian.

Mahala Humm, a widow aged seventy five lived two doors away at 172 with her daughter Jane Elizabeth aged forty one who worked at home as a dressmaker. Jane was sister to Alfred. Jane married Timothy Bull towards the end of the year in 1901 in the district of Peterborough. At the time of the 1881 census Timothy was a boarder with Martha Wallis, a dressmaker, who lived at 45 Ackland Street in Peterborough. This was two doors away from Mary Wright and by 1901 Mary was also living two doors away from them in Palmerston Road. In 1891 Timothy was lodging with Martha Wallis at 54 Gladstone Street in Peterborough. At the time of the 1901 census, before he married Jane, Timothy was living in the parish of St Johns in Peterborough.

Photograph of John and Sarah Garfield.

John Garfield and his wife Sarah had moved from 186 Palmerston Road where they were living in 1891 to 170 Palmerston Road by 1901. They had three children still at home John William was a railway engine stoker, Nellie was a dressmaker and Herbert attended school.

Their daughter Emma Gertrude married Herbert Neaverson towards the end of the year in 1898. Herbert was the son of William and Harriett who lived at the Railway Inn Peakirk during the 1881 census and was a farmer of 72 acres.

By the time of the 1891 census Herbert was a boarder with William and Emma Reynolds who lived at Bridge End in Fletton where Herbert was a grocer's apprentice.

James Garfield, brother of John, was still living at 162 with his wife Mary, their daughter Fanny was also living at home with them. Their son Alfred Henry married Eliza Hart during 1898 and by 1901 they were living at 128 Palmerston Road with their four month old daughter Elsie. Mary Hart, Eliza's sister was also living with them, she worked as a milliner.

Gilbert Gibbs was a baker and lived at 156 Palmerston Road with his wife Elizabeth (nee Shrapnell) they married in Islington London during 1897.

Next to the Gibbs family at 154 were Charles and Kate Sanderson and their daughter Laura Mary who was ten months old. Charles was a baker who possibly worked for Gilbert Gibbs.

Tom Goulding, a miller's foreman, and his wife Ann were still living at 150, only their seventeen year old daughter Evelyn, was still living at home.

Their daughter Alice married Charles Sydney Talbot during 1892. They lived in the parish of St John's in Peterborough in 1901. Charles was a saddler, the son of Thomas and Ellen, his father was a saddle and harness maker and who lived in Whittlesey during 1881. By the time of the 1891 census they had moved to Gunthorpe in Peterborough where Thomas continued to be a saddler.

Tom and Ann's other daughter Susan married John Alexander Macmillan during 1893. John was a railway engine driver and was born in Scotland. In 1901 they were also living in the parish of St John's in Peterborough.

The funeral of Mr Thomas Goulding was reported in the Peterborough Advertiser dated 30th March 1923:-

"Another of the Old Guard, in the person of Mr Thomas Goulding, of 150 Palmerston Road Woodstone, passed away on

Saturday in his 81st year. Mr Goulding was a native of March, and after being at Alwalton a short time came to Colman's Mill at Peterborough , where he was employed as a miller for half-a-century, until his retirement ten years ago, when he was presented by the firm with two divan chairs. He was one of the pioneers of the Co-operative movement in the City, being a tower of strength to the Society, both as a member of the Committee, and for some years as President."

Alfred and Mary Tomlin were still living at 146 Palmerston Road with eight of their children. John aged twenty six and Alfred aged twenty five were both railway stoker's. Sarah aged nineteen worked at home as a domestic, Lily aged seventeen was a dressmaker, William aged fifteen was an errand boy. Mabel aged thirteen, Horace aged eleven and Arthur aged four all attended school.

Their oldest son Frank married Alice Spridgeon during 1895 and by 1901 they were living at Hornsey in Middlesex where Frank was a tailor's cutter.

Another of their sons Ernest was living at Dudley in Worcestershire by 1901 where, at the age of twenty two, was a manager of a boot shop. In 1904 he married Mary Jane Smart in the Dudley district.

William Rimmington Culpin married Annie Adams during 1888 in the district of Peterborough. William was a gardener and lived at 136 Palmerston Road with Annie and their four children. William George aged ten, Sydney Rimmington aged seven, Cecil Edward aged five all attended school, the youngest child was Florence Annie aged three. William and Annie took in two boarders who were railway porters.

At the time of the 1881 census Annie Adams was working as a servant for Edward and Sarah Harrison who lived at 45 Bridge Street in Peterborough where Edward had a grocer's Shop

The Rimmington part of their name came from William Rimmington's Grandmother Elizabeth Rimmington. She married William Rimmington (senior) during 1861 in the Grantham district. Elizabeth died during 1875 in Peterborough aged thirty nine. William and his brothers Thomas and George were the sons of William and Elizabeth. After Elizabeth's death their father married Emily Neal during 1877 in the Peterborough district.

William and Emily lived in a farmhouse in Thorney during 1881 with the three boys and their young daughter Emily aged two.

Robert and Harriet Biggadike were still living at 132 Palmerston Road. He was shown on the census as being a master baker. Their daughters Mabel and Gertie still lived at home.

Albert Henry Garfield, a railway engine stoker, lived at 128 with Eliza his wife and their four month old daughter Elsie.

John Wright, a railway platelayer, and his wife Elizabeth lived at 126 Palmerston Road with their family. Albert aged sixteen was a railway engine cleaner, Ethel aged twelve, William aged eight and Gertrude aged six all attended school.
John was the son of William and Mary Ann Wright who had lived along Water End in Woodstone since the time of the 1841 census.
John and Elizabeth also took in two boarders, Frederick Bird from Norfolk was a boiler smiths' assistant and Edward Martin from Ely was a railway engine cleaner.

William and Elizabeth Bonfield had lived at 120 Palmerston Road since the 1891 census. Their children were Charles William aged fifteen who was an apprentice carpenter, Ives aged thirteen, Ethel aged seven and Rowell aged five all attended school. The youngest children were Elsie aged two and Arthur Robert who was seven months. Ann Rowell sister to Elizabeth lived with the family and worked as a dressmaker from home.

Living in the next cottage at 118 was Reuben Bingham, a fishmonger working from home, and his wife Sarah Ann. Reuben married Sarah Ann Joyce in the Stamford district during the winter of 1891. They had two children Alfred aged eight and Gertrude aged two.
In 1891 Sarah was a servant for Henry and Susan Markham who lived at 17 St Marys Street in Stamford, Henry was a butcher.
Reuben also lived in Stamford during 1891 at 1 Exeters Court along Broad Street where he worked as a moulder of iron. He lived there with his widowed mother Caroline and his brother Harry.

Elizabeth Fowler lived at 110 Palmerston Road, her husband Joseph died in 1896 aged seventy two. Elizabeth continued

working in their butchers' shop which was part of their home.
Rhoda Wade from Peterborough lived with Elizabeth, the census
showed her occupation as a cashier. Rhoda was the daughter of
Charles and Elizabeth Wade, shoemakers, who lived at 53 Westgate
Street Peterborough.

Albert Riddle married Fanny Starmore during 1894 in the
Peterborough district. They lived at 108 Palmerston Road with
their children. Nelly Gertrude aged six, Alfred Edward aged four
and Ernest Albert aged three.
Fanny was the daughter of John and Frances Starmore who were
living at 108 Palmerston Road during 1891. At the time of the
census their daughter Fanny was a servant for John and Sarah
Austin who lived at Wheepley Hill Latimer Hamlet in Chesham.
Also during 1891 Albert Riddle worked as a railway porter and was
lodging with John and Fanny Freeman who lived at 4 Duke Street
Warkworth in Banbury. Albert was the son of Edward and
Elizabeth Riddle from Tansor.

Photograph show Demontfort Terrace as it was in later years.

James Grice continued to live at 84 with his son Richard, a railway clerk, and his nephew John Yates a railway engine stoker. James died on 7th September 1904 and was buried with his late wife Mary in the local cemetery.

By 1901 Elizabeth Mary Yates, wife of John, was also a widow and continued to live with her father Henry Bigley and sister Catherine at 23 Grove Street in Fletton.

Her daughter Elizabeth Mary Rodwell Yates was a domestic cook living at Morpeth in Northumberland.

Photograph shows Elizabeth Mary Rodwell Yates when she married John Holland on 28th May 1911 at St Augustine's church.

Photographer was William Henry Major from Water End.

Stephen Bunyan, a shoemaker, lived at 72 with his wife Charlotte and their son Walter who at the age of fourteen was a greengrocer.

Oakey Robert Gowler married Amelia Dockrill during 1885 in the district of Peterborough. Oakey was a railway engine driver and by the time of the 1901 census they were living at 60 Palmerston Road. Oakey and Amelia had two children William Oakey aged fifteen who worked as an apprentice to a drapery and Ethel aged thirteen attended school.

Amelia was the daughter of James and Matilda Dockrill who lived at 14 Davis Terrace in Tower Street Fletton during 1881. James died in June 1893 and was buried in the local cemetery. Matilda lived at 4 Palmerston Road.

Oakey was the son of Pedley and Martha Gowler who lived at Mill Street in Houghton Huntingdonshire during 1881. By 1891 Pedley and Martha had moved to Eynesbury. Martha was shown as being in the household of her son George and his wife Amy Gowler who lived somewhere between Hemingford Grey and St Ives at the time of the census.

Sophie Dockrill married Samuel Wright, a carpenter and joiner, during 1895 in the district of Peterborough and by 1901 they were living at 58 Palmerston Road next door to Sophie's sister Amelia Gowler. Samuel and Sophie's' children were Gertrude aged four, Bertie three, Winifred two and Jack was three months old.

Ploughright and Clara Rolph moved further along from 38 Palmerston Road where they lived during 1891 to number 56 by the 1901 census.

Ada was their only daughter to be living at home she was eighteen and worked as a draper's assistant.

Their daughter Florence married Walter Jackson, a setter in the brickyards, on 24th October 1899 at St Augustine's church in Woodstone. At the time of the census they were living at 2 St James Cottage number (106) New Road.

Ploughright and Clara died within weeks of each other. Clara died on 14th November aged fifty four, and Ploughright on 29th December aged sixty, both in 1914

They were buried in the local cemetery alongside their late son Thomas William who passed away on 24th July 1891 aged ten. On their gravestone it states he was their only son.

John William Parkinson worked as a railway fireman in 1891. By the 1901 census he had changed his job to a railway engine stoker and with his wife Jane had moved from Woodstone Hill to 28 Palmerston Road. Their children were Ernest aged ten, Lucy aged eight, Thomas aged seven, John aged four and Frank aged three all attended school. The youngest was two year old Rose. All children were born in Woodstone apart from Ernest who was born in Huntingdon.

John's mother Ann Parkinson lived along Water End Woodstone with her son Charles.

Charles and Ellen Dockrill had moved from 4 Palmerston Road where they lived in 1891 to a few houses along at number 20 by 1901.

Matilda Dockrill was a widow and lived at 4 Palmerston Road where her occupation was shown on the census as 'Let Lodgings'. Her husband James died during June 1893 aged sixty one and buried in the local cemetery.

Her son Eliab was living in the urban district of Fletton with his five children William fifteen, James twelve, Charles nine, Kate seven and Bertie was four.

Details of Charles bravery which led to him being awarded with the Military Medal can be read further on in the book.

The Enumerator recording the census moved on from the beginning of Palmerston Road to half way down Cemetery Road and began opposite John Baines' shop. This part of the road was named New Road.

NEW ROAD

The first house was Fernleigh House (49) where William Eayrs, a butcher, and his wife Martha lived with their children. Charles aged six attended school, Beryl was four, Tom was three, Violet was two and Beatrice was fourteen months old. Fanny Grocock a widow and aunt to William also lived with the family. William was the son of John, a whitesmith, and Frances Eayrs who lived at 27 Brown Bridge Street in Peterborough during 1881 and had moved to 9 Broad Bridge Street by 1891..

The next group of cottages were built in 1897 and named Rutland Terrace with the initials 'W.E.' inscribed in the brickwork.
Charles Amos and Minnie Clay lived at 1 (51) with their one year old son Frederick. Charles married Minnie Woolley towards the end of the year in 1898 in the district of Peterborough. Charles was the son of Joseph and Susan Clay who lived at South Street in Stanground during 1881. By 1891 they were living at 4 Woodville Terrace along Love Lane in Fletton. Joseph was a miller's labourer and his son Charles was a baker. Charles sister Annie was a dressmaker and their brother Frederick was an apprentice painter. Joseph and Susan were living at 6 Rutland Terrace by 1901 a short distance away from their son

Robert William Abbott was the son of William and Harriet who lived at High Street in Yaxley during 1881. He married Lucy Baines towards the end of the year in 1895. Lucy was the daughter of John and Martha Baines who lived at Water End in Stanground during 1881 and were shown as living at Tenter Hill Stanground by 1891. At the time of the 1891 census Lucy was a domestic servant for William and Fanny Hare who lived at 9 Saxon Villas along London Road in Fletton, William Hare was a draper.
Robert, a brickyard labourer, and Lucy lived at 3 (55) with their three sons. Jesse aged ten and Oswald aged eight both attended school, the youngest child was Arthur aged three.
Robert was first married to Eliza Olive Askew during 1890 in the Peterborough district. They lived along Chapel Street in Yaxley

with their first born child Jesse aged one. Eliza died towards the year in 1894 aged twenty three.

Living at number 6 (61) was Joseph and Susan Clay parents to Charles at number 1. Joseph was a miller's labourer at the age of seventy. Their daughter Laura lived with them as did their son Frederick Robert who worked as a carpenter.

The last cottage in Rutland Terrace was number 9 (67) where William Hillson, a brickyard labourer, his wife Rosetta and their daughter Elizabeth aged four lived. William married Rosetta Jenkinson on 25th January 1897 at St Augustine's church Woodstone.
William was the son of George and Sarah Hillson who lived at 5 Papley Lodge in Warmington during 1881 although by 1891 they had moved to Jones Cottage along London Road in Woodstone.
Rosetta was the daughter of John and Rosetta Jenkinson who used to live in Yorkshire and Lincolnshire but by the 1891 census were living at The Rose and Crown Inn along Bridge Street in Peterborough where John was a licensed victualler. In 1901 they had moved to Water End in Woodstone possibly to be near to their children and grandchildren.

The building after William and Rosetta Hillson's home was the Primitive Methodist Chapel.

There were many gaps between the houses as the area was gradually being developed. The next group of three cottages were Providence Villas also built around 1897.
Harry and Kate Ellis lived at number 2 (91) with their two year old son Hubert and Harry's sister in law Rose who worked as a dressmaker.

Lander Haydon was a painter and decorator, he lived at 97 New Road with his wife Mary and their three children. Walter aged sixteen was a builders labourer, Gordon aged fourteen was a painters assistant and Lily aged twelve attended school.
During 1891 Lander and his family were living at 116 Marlborough Road in Islington London where Lander was a house painter.

.

Mary Ann Garner lived at 99 with her family although her husband David was not at home at the time of the census. Mary had four children, Sarah aged nineteen, Charles aged fifteen was an errand boy at a grocers shop, George aged six and Ruby aged four attended school. Harry Gray a bricklayer was a boarder with the family.

The census then shows another area where five houses were in the process of being built these would be from 101 through to 109. It then states another 'House and Shop building'.

In the next house along lived George Hailstone, an engine driver in the brickyards, with his wife Alice. Their nephew Thomas Smith aged seven was living with them. George was born in March and Alice in Holbeach. In 1891 George and Alice were living along the Turnpike Road in Surfleet.

Thomas and Bertha Downes from Yorkshire were visiting the Hailstone family.

Thomas worked as a clay digger and Bertha was a spoon and fork polisher who worked from home.

William Rimes, a brick setter, lived at 1 Sawtry Villas (115) with his wife Ethel Althea and their two young sons. William was one year and Justin was five months. They married during 1891 in the Peterborough district.

Ethel's mother Mary Cross was a widow and lived with the family.

William was the son of Martin and Kezia Rimes from Farcet where he was recorded as Walter William although he was baptised as William Walter.

Ethel was the daughter of William and Mary who in 1881 lived at the cottage and grocers shop in Upwood. William was a market gardener and Mary a grocer. At the time of the 1891 census Mary was a widow and lived at Bury with Ethel's sister Agnes. Ethel's father William died during 1883.

At 2 Sawtry Villas (117) lived John Busby, a brickyard labourer, and his wife Emma (nee Green) they married during 1889 in the Peterborough district. Alexander Green also lived with them he was five years old and nephew to John and Emma. Sarah Palmer, a tailoress, boarded with the family. William Jolly, a widower aged eighty eight, lodged with John and Emma.

In 1891 John and Emma were living at 17 Albert Place in Peterborough where John worked as a woodyard labourer.

William Swiffen married Eliza Read on 9th December 1872 in Peterborough. They lived at Jauncey's Yard in Peterborough during 1881 with their four children. William Edward was born in 1873, Mildred Elizabeth in 1876, James Henry in 1879 and Agnes Fanny in 1880. The family then moved to Fletton where they had two more children Rose Anna born in 1883 and Clara Eleanor in 1885.

By the time of the 1901 census they were living at 3 Sawtry Villas (119). Two of their daughters were also living at home, Agnes Fanny aged twenty one and Clara aged sixteen who were both dressmakers.

Arthur Brewster, a brickyard labourer, was a boarder with William and Eliza Swiffen. He was brother to Thomas William Brewster who lived further along New Road.

Charlotte Murdock's husband Richard died on 2nd February 1898 aged 58 and was buried in the local cemetery. In 1891 they lived along Oundle Road, by 1901 Charlotte had moved her family to 1 Brook Villa (127). Charlotte had eight children to support although three of them worked. Richard aged twenty seven William aged twenty four and Arthur aged twenty two all worked for the railways as firemen. Annie aged sixteen was not shown as having an occupation, Walter aged fifteen was an errand boy. Albert aged thirteen, Emma aged ten and James aged nine all attended school. All the children were born in Woodstone.

Charlotte died on 4th January 1907 aged sixty two and was buried with her late husband.

Brookhall Terrace was built in 1894.

Thomas Odell lived at 1 Brookhall Terrace (131) and worked as a general labourer. His wife Jane was in Irthlingborough at the time of the 1901 census where her occupation was shown as a monthly nurse. Thomas had five men lodging with him. George Rose born in Newport Pagnell was eighty years of age, William Julyan born in Alwalton aged sixty, Frederick Fletton born in Oundle aged twenty, Arthur Baker born in Old Fletton aged nineteen and John Harrison born in Paston aged twenty one were all general labourers.

New Cross Terrace was built in 1892.

James Risely, a brickyard labourer, and his wife Emily lived at 1 New Cross Terrace (139). Three of their sons worked for the brickyards they were William aged eighteen who worked as a foreman, Charles aged sixteen worked as a carter and Harry aged fourteen worked as a press boy. Arthur aged eleven and Frederick aged five attended school.

Living at 2 New Cross Terrace was Thomas William Brewster a brickyard labourer. He married Mildred Elizabeth Swiffen on 11ᵗʰ April 1898 at St Augustine's church in Woodstone. Thomas was the son of William and Emma Brewster who lived at Thorpe-By-Water in Rutland.

Mildred was the daughter of William and Eliza who lived at 119 New Road. Thomas and Mildred had two children Edith aged two and William Henry aged eleven months.

Rose Swiffen aged seventeen daughter of William and Eliza was visiting her sister.

Photograph of Thomas and Mildred Brewster, my husbands grandparents, taken at 115 New Road where they later lived

Charles Revis was shown on the census as the Royal President R S A. In 1881 he was on the vessel 'Crocodile' in the Royal Navy. Charles married Georgina Butterwick during 1886 in the district of Peterborough. Georgina was born at Orton Longueville. At the time of the 1881 census she was working for William and Eliza

Preston as their servant. William was a retired governor of a gaol and lived in the Longthorpe area of Peterborough.

At the time of the 1891 census Charles and Georgina were shown as living in Orton Longueville. By the time of the 1901 census they had moved to 3 New Cross Terrace (143) and had three children Elsie aged two, Jack aged one and Charlie aged two months. All were born in Woodstone.

William Swiffen, a brick burner and the son of William and Eliza, married Mary Jane Saunders on 17th May 1898. They lived at 4 New Cross Terrace (145) with their two year old son Edward William. Eventually they moved to 111 New Road where they set up a coal merchant's business.

The last two houses were named Diamond Jubilee Houses in one of them lived David and Sarah Ireland, David worked as a moulder. David married Sarah Woodcock in the Peterborough district during 1899. Sarah was the daughter of William and Ann Woodcock who lived at Great Stukeley where William was a shepherd

David was the son of Thomas and Sarah Ireland. He lived with his mother along Westwood Street in Peterborough during 1891. Thomas his father died in the Peterborough district during 1873 aged forty three.

Sarah was the daughter of John and Alice Upex who lived along the Peterborough Road in Warmington at the time of the 1861 census.

In the last house numbered 149 lived Charles Woodford, a blacksmith in the brickyards with his wife Emma and their four children. Beatrice aged twelve, Gertrude aged eleven, Dorothy aged nine and Charles aged two years. Charles, Emma, Beatrice and Gertrude were born in Leicester. Dorothy was born in Ramsey and Charles junior in Woodstone.

The last recorded building on the census was a 'Signal Box and the man on Duty being enumerated at home'.

Woodstone or Woodston – Over the centuries the spelling has been varied, an ancient spelling showed it as ending with 'tun'. At the end of the 19th and the beginning of the 20th century Ordnance survey maps showed it as Woodstone. The 'e' was used up to 1911 but from 1912 the village was shown as Woodston.

JOHN CATHLES HILL

Having found an impressive monument in memory of the Hill family in Woodston cemetery I was lucky to make contact with Paul a descendent of the family who lives in Australia. He sent me the following information:-.

"Robert Hill (Snr) was born in Auchterhouse Dundee Scotland. Elizabeth Cathles was Meigle Scotland to John Cathles and Joanna Campbell. Robert and Eliza had at least six children. John Cathles Hill was born in Auchterhouse on 12th December 1857. Much of the family information regards him as the founder of the London Brick Company or the London Development Company.

According to what I was able to find out John lost most of his fortune during the depression of around 1895. Both John and his younger brother Robert were 'Wrights' having been taught the trade by their father Robert (Snr).

The family estate in Auchterhouse was known as East Pond Park, and can be found in several Census records. I am guessing that after Robert (Snr) reached a point where he needed to retire from his business as a Master Wright that he and Eliza his wife moved to Peterborough to be near their son John."

Robert Cathles Hill (Snr) was Paul's great grandfather and John Cathles Hill was his great uncle. Mr John Cathles Hill was also famous for building in the streets of Harringay during the late 1890's. He also built a row of shops and the Salisbury Hotel.

The Fletton Brickyards as reported in the Peterborough Advertiser dated 3rd January 1930
In 1877 there was only an odd plastic brickyard or two which were owned by the late Mr Robert Gollings and Messrs.A.J.Rixom and Co. Later that year Mr James Craig bought the land known as 'Watts Lane' and began making plastic bricks for a while. By 1880 the land was sold to four different companies who by the next year were manufacturing plastic and semi-dry bricks. After many changes in ownership and the stipulation in the large London contracts that Fletton semi-dry bricks were specified, came the time when Fletton began to become prosperous. This enticed many more influential people into the industry, notably in the

year, that great long sighted, kind-hearted Scotsman, the late Mr J.C.Hill. He individually bought more land for brick-making purposes and more land for building workhouses for his work people than any other known man. Included in the purchase was the farm owned by Messrs.Thompson and for many years farmed by the late Mr. Thos. Richardson. This is now covered with streets of houses (except for the land which he sold to Messrs.Joseph Farrow and Co., who famed for peas, mustard, ketchup and sauces, built their large factory, which has been a great boon to the parish and the young people employed there).It was also one of the late Mr.J.C.Hills introductions.

Picture shows Belsize Avenue with Phorpres House in the distance.

BELSIZE AVENUE

The following reports were printed in the Peterborough Advertiser during 1913:-

Listed are details of various acts of felony by residents of Belsize Avenue:-

"The following persons were summoned by Superintendant Wilson for keeping dogs without licenses;

John Crowson – Butcher – Woodstone. One dog. February 4th 1913. Fined 5s 6d, 2s costs.

Edward Aspittle – Belsize Avenue. One dog. February 25th 1913. Fined 5s 6d, 2s costs. "

"George Potkins, Charles Elger, Percy Plowman and Harry Rollings, youths all of Fletton and Woodstone were summoned by Arthur Robert Nichols of Peterborough Postal Telegraph Engineer, for throwing stones at the insulators on the telegraph poles at Woodstone on February 9th 1913.Fined 4s each."

During June 1913 there was a great storm in Peterborough where four houses were struck by lightning around the town. One of them was in Woodstone and the report read as follows:-
"The lightning struck the chimney of Mr A F Hargraves house in Belsize Avenue in Woodston. Mrs Hargraves and the three children had fortunately just gone out of the house to see her mother who lives next door. If they had been in the front room they must have been injured, for the firegrate was torn from its setting and flung upon the hearth, the marble mantelpiece being also wrecked and scattered about the room."

"Ernest Ploughman and Percy Tibble, both of Belsize Avenue, were summoned by William Harman, Inspector of the G.N. Railway Police, for trespassing on the Great Northern Railway at Woodstone on September 19th 1913. Penalty 2s 6d each.
Emma Wakefield, married woman of Woodstone was also summoned by William Harman on the Great Northern Railway on September 19th. Penalty 2s 6d."
Ernest was the son of William and Jane Plowman who lived at 155 Belsize Avenue.
Percy Tibble married Rachel Webster during 1911 in the Peterborough district.

"Benjamin Bollard of Belsize Avenue was summoned by Felix Bower School Attendance Officer for not sending his children George Bollard and Charles Bollard to school on 10th and 29th October 1913. Penalty 3s 6d each case."
Benjamin, his Canadian wife Sarah Jane and their daughter Ethel May were all buried in New Road cemetery. Private Benjamin Bollard was killed in action in Burma on 22nd February 1945 aged thirty five. Ethel died in 1960 aged sixty two and Sarah in 1962 aged ninety.

DIPHTHERIA IN WOODSTON

A report in the Peterborough Advertiser dated 28th November 1930 stated

"The sympathy of a wide district went out to Mr and Mrs E.C.Henson of Belsize Avenue, Woodston, Peterborough, in the terrible bereavement they sustained by the death of three children of Mrs Henson. The deaths occurred on successive days last week, diphtheria in a violent form being the cause. The children's names were:-

Lucy Emma Harrison, who would have been 12 early next month and who died on Tuesday.

Bertha Frances Pywell aged 14 years who died on Wednesday.

Josephine Daphne Rose Harrison aged 6 years who died on Thursday.

The eldest of the deceased girls, Bertha, left school last August, and had recently started work at Farrows' mill".

THE GREAT WAR

The following details were taken from reports printed in the Peterborough Advertiser commencing 8th August 1914:

"War was declared upon Russia by Germany on 1st August 1914. Also Great Britain declared war with Germany as from 11.00am on 4th August 1914.

The government had control over railroads in Great Britain for the purpose of ensuring that the railways locomotives, rolling stock and staff shall be used as one complete unit in the best interests of the State for the movement of troops, stores and food supplies. Nearly twenty million men as far as it is possible to calculate are under arms in Europe, Great Britain sending approximately 750.000 men but the figure does not include Navy men.

Work on the Great North Road and the Soke of Peterborough was brought to a standstill by the war.

Enquiries at the London Brick Company's office were met by the reassuring statement that at present there seems no reason to fear any slump in trade, and beyond the slackening of work in one of the yards due to withdrawal of twenty men who have to go to service as Territorial's or Reservists, no immediate change in working arrangements is anticipated.

Scenes at Peterborough station - All day long on the Tuesday, Wednesday and Thursday every train contained soldiers and sailors travelling to their stations. All contingents which left were given a cheer by the crowd on the platforms as the trains steamed out. There were pathetic scenes too, where husbands and fathers were bidding adieu before facing the unknown. The women were very brave, concealed their faces and swallowed their tears. The children did not know what it was all about and rather enjoyed the excitement. They proudly carried their fathers coat while mother turned her face away.

It was decided that the Peterborough & District Association of Bell Ringers should not ring a peal in the towers of St Johns, St Marys and Woodston as had been arranged.

The War Office has a number of representatives in the district engaged in collecting horses for the purposes of the Peterborough Battery and the Northants. The method of purchase is that every officer examines practically every horse he sees and if it is suitable he asks the proprietor what he wants for it. The price is generally agreed but if it is not the Government purchaser takes the animal at his own valuation and gives the seller an order on the Government for the amount. Various businesses supplied horses two of which were from Oundle Road, Mr W. Tebbs – 16 and Mr W. Tebbutt – 4. Practically every responsible trader in the town and every farmer in the neighbourhood had surrended animals to the service of the country. This will create an enormous demand for hand labour on the countryside this harvest".

Lord Sandwich sent letters to District Councils recommending they appoint a County Committee to relieve the distress which might occur during the war. Mr J.E Bains and Mr A.Adams from Woodston were appointed alongside Mr E.Dickenson and Mr W.Hawkins for Fletton and

Rev. E.G.Swain and Mr Lomas for Stanground

Every week during the war the Peterborough Advertiser filled a whole page with details from the war. This included a gallery of local war portraits who were missing, wounded or had been killed.

Listed below are some of the Woodston men who received the award '1914 Star and Riband':-

Pte.C.Vincent - Royal Warwicks-2 Orton Avenue enlisted 1913 killed 17th May 1915 (France)

Pte.G.Bee - 5th Northants-149 New Road Woodston enlisted October 1912 (France) August 1914 twice wounded, still serving in France.

Corpl.James Bryan - Kings Own Royal Lancs - Gladstone Cottages Water End Woodston enlisted 1908 France August 1914 discharged 1917

Pte.E.Plowman - Hunts Cycles attached Royal Warwicks - eldest son of Mr and Mrs W Plowman of Belsize Avenue Woodston aged 29 who was reported missing from April 23rd 1917 is now officially reported killed from that date.

Pte.F Raement –Australians - Woodston killed.

Sgt.F.A.Roope - 2nd Bedfords -Tower Street New Fletton enlisted 1910

Pte.Reginald Eyles-Northants -19 Palmerston Road enlisted August 1910 killed March 1915 Neuve Chappelle.

Pte.Frank Baker -1st Northants Regiment-Woodston killed January 6th 1915

The 'Star and Riband' decoration is for all officers and men of the British Indian Forces and doctors, nurses and others who served under Field Marshall Sir John French during the first phase of the war up to midnight November 22nd and 23rd 1914.

Other reports regarding local men:

Lieut.C.J.Crawley M.C.- Monmouthshire Regiment att. M.G.C.- only son of Mr and Mrs J.W.Crawley and grandson of Councillor C.E. and Mrs Crawley Peterborough has been wounded in the shoulder and had a marvellous escape from death as his machine gun Corps., was firing at point blank range at the oncoming German masses until almost overwhelmed.

Pte.C.Sharpe-Hussars- eldest son of Mrs J Sharpe Orton Avenue Woodston has been wounded by gunshot in the hand. He returned to France from leave on February 26th and was wounded March 26th. This is the third occasion on which Pte.Sharpe has been wounded.

Pte.J.B.Woodward – Missing.

Pte. Owen Wright - Belsize Avenue – killed.

Pte.J.W.Dunkley - Coldstreams-was killed.

Pte.J.C.Papworth - 2/4th London R.F.-only son of Mrs Papworth Belsize Avenue Woodston was reported wounded and missing March 22nd 1918. He was in the Hunts Cycles before going to France. Any information would be greatly appreciated by his mother as above.

Pte.H.D.Hughes - R.N.D.- Woodston missing.

RIN H.R.S Morris - Rifle Brigade - Woodston missing.

<u>Rifleman Sharp</u> - Royal Irish - Oundle Road missing.

<u>Sergeant E.Nash</u> – Lincs.Regiment - Woodston wounded.

<u>Pte.E.C.Crowson</u> - Northants Regiment - Woodston killed.

<u>Pte.F.R.Lewis</u> - K.R.R.- Belsize Avenue Woodston missing March 21ˢᵗ.1918.

<u>Lance Corpl. Frank Lewis</u> – Royal Warwicks - son of Mr and Mrs J.Lewis Belsize Avenue was killed in action on August 9ᵗʰ 1918 in Italy.

<u>Pte.J.W.Dunham</u>-Coldstreams- Woodston killed.

<u>Pte.C.Pollard</u>-Lancs.Fusiliers- Fletton shellshock.

<u>Pte.W.Hall</u> – Australians – Woodston killed.

<u>Pte.C.F.Parker</u> – East Yorks' – Woodstone accidently killed.

<u>Pte.W.Darkin</u> – Middlesex – husband of Mrs W.Darkin New Road Woodston has been wounded for a second time losing his left eye but is going on well in a London hospital.

<u>Pte George Baker</u> – London Regiment – youngest son of Mr and Mrs Charles Baker of Woodston Hill was wounded in his left leg on September 18ᵗʰ 1918.

<u>Pte.T.Woods</u> – Royal Fusiliers – Belsize Avenue Woodston wounded in right leg.

<u>Second Lt. G.Franklin</u> – Northants- youngest son of Mr and Mrs R.Franklin, was killed in action on October 19ᵗʰ 1918.

<u>Woodston Sergeants Long Service</u> – report dated 26ᵗʰ January 1918

Reg.Sergt.Major F.L.Hemment son of Mr and Mrs Hemment 98 Water End is in Leamington hospital suffering from rheumatism. He enlisted in the R.A. in 1900 as a Gunner and received the rank of Sergeant in April 1908 whilst in India. On the outbreak of war he was promoted to Battery Quarter Master-Sergeant and mobilised the 4ᵗʰ Division Ammunition Column at Woolwich and proceeded to France with that unit on August 19ᵗʰ 1914. He was transferred to the 7ᵗʰ Division on November 19ᵗʰ 1914 after they fought the 1ˢᵗ Battle of Ypres. He was appointed Acting Regimental Sergeant Major on September 17ᵗʰ 1916 which appointment he still holds and was invalided home with rheumatism on December 4ᵗʰ 1917 having served three years three months and four days in France. He will complete his eighteen years service in June of this year and has extended to complete twenty one years with the Colours for pension.

Well known Racing Cyclist – report dated 13th April 1918

Pte.Albert Sidney Rimes, Northants Regiment, third son of Mr and Mrs W.Rimes Bread Street New Fletton was killed in action on March 25th in trying to bring in a wounded comrade. Pte.Rimes who served his apprenticeship as a linotype operator at the office of our contemporary joined up soon after the outbreak of war and was wounded at the Battle of Leos in September 1915 and again at Menin Road in July of last year. He was home on leave on March 15th and the last letter received from him was dated March 21st the opening day of the German offensive. He was a well known Racing cyclist and very popular amongst a large circle of friends.

A report in the Peterborough Advertiser dated 22nd June 1918 stated:-

Leading Seaman C. Dockrill R.N.D. a native of Water End Woodstone, formerly a call-boy on the G.E.R., and brother of Mr J Dockrill, Palmerston Road Peterborough, has been publicly presented at Doncaster with the Military Medal. This was gained in April last year for gallantly bringing up ammunition for several hours under heavy shell fire. In December he was severely wounded by shrapnel, having to have his right leg amputated. Since then he has had a very rough time, having undergone no fewer than 16 operations.

The Mayor, before presenting the medal to Seaman Dockrill, read the official report of the action which gained him the reward, this stating that "on the 17th April, 1917, he was engaged in an attack at Arras when unfortunately the ammunition ran out. Volunteers were called for to bring a further supply of ammunition. Along with others Dockerill immediately offered his services and it was necessary for them to go through a barrage. On arrival, however, no ammunition was found, so the party emptied sandbags and collected ammunition from their dead comrades. These operations lasted until the ammunition wagons arrived some three hours later".

A report in the Peterborough Advertiser dated Friday 5th July 1918 stated:

"The Great Joint Red Cross Effort" – Under the presidency of Councillor F.E.Hunting, an enthusiastic and businesslike committee got to work on Wednesday in the South Ward, at the Church Hall. An attractive programme was drawn up, and the various committees appointed. The event takes place in the Oundle Road Recreation Ground on Thursday July 25th, 5 to 10pm.

The attractions foreshadowed include:- Bowling competition (arranged by the South Ward Bowling Club); Tennis competition (Mr R.Purdie); Croquet competition (Mr H.Whittome 'Shortacre'; Open-air Whist Drive (Messrs Exton, Haynes and Williams); Tug-of war (Messrs Bonfield, Grice and Gollings); Pound Stall (Mrs Dunn, Miss Biggadike and Miss Yates); Blindford competition for Ham (Messrs Gollings, Warren, Scotchbrook, Warrington and Grice); in addition to music and dancing, skittles, bowling boards, hoop-la, guessing competitions and draws for War savings certificates and other valuable prizes. It is hoped to arrange concerts, maypole dances and gymnastic displays. The refreshment catering is in the hands of Mrs C.E.Crawley and a strong committee of ladies.

Any offers of help will be gladly welcomed by the joint hon. Secretaries, Mr A.S.Dickens and Mr A.W.Tillett. The Executive Committee for the effort is; Messrs. F.E.Hunting (Chairman), H.B.Hartley, J.Brawn, J.Crawley, T.R.Hunting, R.Purdie, H.Whittome, R.Hill and J.Fletcher.

A report in the Peterborough Advertiser dated 16th November 1918 stated:-

"The Prime Minister announced at 10.20 on Monday morning 11th November that war had ended, the Armistice was signed between the Allied and German Armies and hostilities are to cease on all fronts at 11.00am today"

A report in the Peterborough Advertiser stated:-

The proposed War Memorial for the parish of Woodston took definite shape at a public meeting in the Church Hall, Palmerston Road when the Rector (The Rev.N.J.Rapier) presided over a largely attended gathering of parishioners and residents, and no less a sum than £121.10 shillings towards the proposed cost of a Lych-Gate - £250- was promised before or at the close of the meeting. During the meeting the Rev.N.J.Rapier said "In every respect a Lych-Gate met the various considerations, which should be taken into account when attempting to come to a conclusion as to a fitting monument to those who had given their all for the sake of those at home. The site was central; it was outside in the open, clear to all who passed by; it was striking, inasmuch as Lych-Gates were not common hereabouts; it would be artistic, and a real addition to the beauties of the parish we could enumerate; it was congruous, or in harmony with the fundamental idea of a memorial, for the names of the fallen would be inscribed on the inside walls, and thus they would be associated with the memorials already existing in that "Gods acre" of the "forefathers of the hamlet," whose bodies slept there. Altogether the proposal was likely to satisfy in full degree, the desire of everyone that due honour should be rendered to our gallant heroes, and also prove a pride and delight to the present and succeeding generations of parishioners."

Picture shows the Lych-gate opening ceremony.

UNVEILING WAR MEMORIAL LYCH GATE, WOODSTON. 1920

'**Woodston Lych Gate is to be dedicated on Saturday 10th April 1920**'.

"The new Memorial Lych Gate at Woodston Church, to the sailors and soldiers of the parish who gave their lives to the Great War, was dedicated by the Rev. N.J. Raper on Saturday afternoon. The Gate is designed by Mr H.F. Traylen, architect of Stamford, and the work has been carried out by Messrs Thompson & Co of Peterborough. The special features of the erection are the figures of the Good Shepherd facing the roadway, one of St George with the slain dragon facing the church, together with two bronze tablets facing the roadway, one on either side of the entrance, with the statement of the raison d'être of the Lych Gate and the names of the fallen heroes of the parish".

In December 1934 the Lych Gate was taken down and rebuilt nearer the church due to the widening of Oundle Road.

Picture shows commencement of the above work.

ERIC HEATH

Eric Heath grew up in Belsize Avenue and wrote <u>Klondike to Belsize</u> which is about the memories of his childhood. Eric gave me permission to quote the following literature from his writings of the Klondike.

"Locally given the name of 'Klondike' (after the Yukon Goldrush) Belsize Avenue accommodated mostly the influx of brickyards, the nearest brickyard workers.

To the south-west of Belsize the railway ran parallel the full length, linking the LMS lines to the LNER and serving the sugar factory and the brickworks. From Belsize there was an un-gated crossing over the railway where at seasonal times trains could be as frequent as every 15 minutes, access was opposite the 'Woodston Hotel'.

The Woodston Hotel was owned by Ted Walker. Walter Sprawson was a later landlord.

At the Northern end of Belsize there was a track known as Baker's Lane (since adopted and developed), it ran through to Oundle Road. A family named Baker lived at the Oundle Road/Peterborough side of the lane and were thought to own a pit close by which was used as a local dump – old wheels, bike frames, mangles, pots and pans. Absolutely anything unwanted found its way there. The waste ground at the Belsize end was developed with a 'Cold Store' around the beginning of the war and further commercial units followed, with EMAP and others two decades later.

Woodston Junior School in Belsize Avenue was opened in the early 1930's and I was one of the early in-take – a brand new school, a keen young pupil and exceptional teachers, Miss Muriel Braybrook, Miss Stanyon and headmistress Miss Bessie Chapman come to mind. What a start in life!

Shortacres, Westbrook Park Road and parts of London Road were developed by Cosy Homesteads and it was thought that the houses cost around £400 each, this being just pre-war.

Before the war, milk was delivered by horse and cart and dispensed from churns. If skimmed milk was required, the cream was scooped from the top and the measuring jug was dipped into the skimmed area. Waste was collected by dustmen most of it unwrapped, some in newspaper, but no plastic bags. Our particular kitchen waste was taken across the road where Tommy Barrett kept his pigs (his garden backed onto the railway). Everyone thought Tommy was doing us a favour but he knew he was getting his pigs fattened for free!

Before the World War 2 every house used coal, which was delivered by horse and cart or later by lorry. Most front gardens were bounded by dwarf walls with iron railings at the top and iron gates at the entrance: these were removed for recycling for the war effort, many being replaced with brick walls and wooden gates after the war."

Picture of the Mission Hall.

GEORGE BOTT

George Bott from Wharf Road told me the following details:-
"Sidney Bott married Emma Bradley in the Stamford district during 1913 after Sidney came out of the army. During 1918 Emma Bott, wife of Sidney, purchased two newly built houses for £90 each. These houses were 122 and 124 Belsize Avenue. They lived at 122 and 'Let Out' 124. George Bott was born in 1921 at 122 Belsize Avenue and remembers many details of when he was growing up.

Sidney kept chickens within some chicken wire in the back garden when George was about two years old. George happened to scratch his knee on this wire and developed blood poisoning. He remembers having to go into hospital which was along Priestgate in Peterborough (now the Museum) where he had an operation on his knee.

When George was around six years old he remembers open topped buses which were the first form of public transport into town. When it rained there was a tarpaulin cover in every seat although it was only suitable for children to shelter under.

David Scott, the landlord of the Woodston public house would get the children to line up on a Sunday morning ready for a race. They ran down Orton Avenue turned right and went along New Road to London Road for a short distance then they turned up Celta Road and back along Belsize Avenue to the 'Woodston'. David gave the first child back six pennies. This was a regular event for many years. David was a tiny man about five feet high.

It was safe for the children to play football in the street. At the time George used to play he only remembers one car in the street which belonged to Mr Brand who lived along Orton Avenue.

The children who went to the Wharf Road School were given a nick name of 'Wharf Road Water Rats'.

George enlisted in the Navy from 1940 to 1946. First he was sent to Skegness to HMS Royal Arthur which was temporarily set up on the Butlins holiday camp. Here the new recruits were assessed and kitted out before being sent on to their respective posts. After the war the site was changed back to the holiday camp. HMS Arthur was relocated to Wiltshire.

During George's time in the Navy he travelled on the Russian, Canadian and Malta Convoys. When the war ended he was sent to Burma for just over two years.

Picture of Peterborough Infirmary in Priestgat.

THE CLAYTON FAMILY

Maurice Clayton was the son of Walter and Winifred Clayton who lived at 133 Belsize Avenue. They ran a corner shop where they sold groceries. Maurice and his friend Alan Laxton reminisced to me of their days in Woodston as young children. They went to the Woodston School from the age of four until they were eleven. From there they both went to the Fletton secondary school until the age of fifteen. Any children who did not pass their scholarship exam would instead go to the Board school along Fletton High Street just before the railway bridge. The head teacher Miss B. Chapman tended to select those children who she believed would get through the exam then gave them extra tuition. Most of the children who lived in Belsize Avenue and Celta Road went to Miss Chapman's school.

Maurice's grandparents were Edmund and Ann Potkins who lived at Stanground during 1901. His mother Winifred was their daughter. The family came from Arlesey in Bedfordshire where Edmund worked in the Brickyards before moving to Stanground. Later they moved to 137 Belsize Avenue not far from Walter and Winifred Clayton.

Maurice's Uncle George also worked on the railways as a fireman. He was in the First World War and got wounded in Ypres when the German's were firing at the Cathedral. Some masonry fell and knocked George out, he was brought home and taken to a hospital in Scotland. George managed to bring home an old German sword and a Lugar pistol which were put away when he arrived back home in Woodston. Maurice remembers these were kept in a cubby hole at the top of the stairs in his grandmother's house. One day his grandmother took them out of the cupboard went out of the house and walked to Basil Green pond near the allotments where she then threw both the gun and sword into the pond.

During 1941 George was at the front of the train when the blackout curtain over the tender blew up. George stood up to pull it back down but hit his head on a bridge at Etton and was killed instantly. He was buried in New Road cemetery in the grave next to his parents. Maurice remembers the following inscription on a grave near to his uncle's which read:-

"Kiss of the Sun for pardon
A song of the birds for mirth
One is nearer Gods heart in the Garden
Than anywhere else on earth"

Both Maurice and Alan would often find a stick and an old car tyre which they would beat along the road. They once managed to reach Yaxley and often went miles with their hoops (tyres) trying to get lost but they never succeeded. Photographs of Maurice with sword and Clayton's shop.

When the snow came they would take their sledges to the top of the bank near to the bridge at Hotpoint and then slide down the embankment. Further along from Hotpoint was the cold storage unit and on the surrounding land it was possible to make a large slope which they could also use their sledges on. There was a fence at the bottom that would stop them when they travelled down at top speed.

Maurice and Alan would walk across the fields at Basil Green and catch around a hundred cabbage white butterflies which they put in their jam jars, They would then take these butterflies to the council offices at Fletton and were paid between 4d and 6d, (it would vary on the amount they were paid). The reason the council encouraged this task was to try and cut down the butterflies from eating the local cabbages.

After the war when ice-cream had come back into circulation if they went to the Savoy and wanted an ice-cream they had to take a dish and spoon with them.

A brief history of the Potkins family from 1871 to 1901 goes as follows:-Robert and Emma Potkins lived at Primrose Lane, Arlesey in Bedfordshire during 1871. Their five children were Charles, Clara, Edmund, Harry and Ellen. Ten years later they were living at Wilton cottage still in Arlesey where Robert worked as a brick burner. Charles had married and Clara was not at home at the time of the census. Other children at home were Edmund working as a brick dresser, Harry was a general labourer, Ellen aged twelve and Frederick aged four attended school. Moving on to the 1891 census Robert was living along High

Street in Arlesey, his wife Emma died during 1888. Living with their father were Clara aged thirty, Frederick aged fifteen who worked as a baker's assistant and Ellen who married Walter Brooks although he was not shown as living with the family at that time. Also shown was Robert's granddaughter Maria aged three months.

Edmund (recorded as Robert Edmund) married Martha Ann Papworth during 1882. By the time of the 1891 census they were living along Asylum Road in Arlesey where he worked as a general labourer. They had three children Albert, Florence and Emma. In 1901 they had moved to Tenter Hill in Stanground where Edmund worked as a brickyard labourer as did their son Albert, Florence known as Florry was a general domestic servant, Emma, Winifred and George attended school.

Anglers at the Boys Head.

Walter Clayton and special constables.

Woodstone Boy scouts.

Minnie Weston 1895.

Edmunds father continued to live in Arlesey in 1901 and shared his home with his daughter Clara, shown as Clary. Cuthbert Clayton aged twenty was a boarder with Edmund and worked as a station clerk for G.N.R. He was born at Hornsey in London.

Photographs show Edmund Potkins and family and Maurice Clayton and Alan Laxton on bicycles.

Edmund, Martha Ann and their sons Albert and George were all buried in the cemetery along New Road in Woodston.

GEORGE PICKERING

George and Ivy Pickering told me about George's family. His parents were Henry and Alice (nee Glover). Henry was born in Woodstone in 1895 and was the son of Joseph and Maria Pickering who lived at 142 Belsize Avenue from 1881 through to at least 1901. Joseph passed away on 28th March 1938 aged eighty two and Maria passed away on 14th February 1946 aged eighty two and both were buried in New Road cemetery. At the time of their death Joseph and Maria were living at 58 Belsize Avenue. Henry married Alice Glover on 26th December 1919 at St Augustine's church in Woodstone. Alice was the daughter of John Thomas Glover who worked as a Horse keeper.

Henry was a fireman for the Great Eastern Railways prior to that he cleaned the locomotives. To help the men get to work on time 'call boys' were employed who would ride around the streets on bicycle's then tap on the workers cottage windows with a rod and called out their name to wake them up. This would be around 4:00am.

Around the 1940's Henry was shown as living at 7 Gordon Avenue just off Orton Avenue.

George was born in 1921 at Star Road in Peterborough. During the year in 1924 George and his family moved into one of the new houses in Gordon Avenue just off Orton Avenue.

He remembered when someone died a candle would be lit and kept alight in the home until the body had been removed, only then would the candle be snuffed out.

George used to run errands for many of the local families in payment of 1d. This he would save up until he could buy 'one and one' (fish and chips) for 3d.

He remembers opposite the Co-op on Huntly Road corner was the Church Army. Members of the boy scouts, cubs, girl guides and brownies would march to Woodston church once a fortnight on a Sunday morning.

As a child he would take his granddad George's jug to the jug and bottle entrance of the Woodston Hotel for 1 pint of mild beer, which would cost 6d a jugful, and half an ounce of tobacco.

Another of his memories was when the town bridge replaced the Iron Bridge in the 1930's. The soil was dredged out then taken to Wright's gravel pits behind the cemetery in New Road to help build them up.

THE GOWLER FAMILY

Samuel and Florence Gowler married during 1912 and rented rooms at 146 Belsize Avenue. Samuel received compensation for a bad leg injury and decided to use it to buy 153 Belsize Avenue. They had four sons and three daughters George, Frederick, Kathleen, Margery, Charles Alfred, May and Ronald.

Samuel, born in 1889, was the son of Fred and Naomi Gowler from Little Whyte near Ramsey. At the time of the 1881 census before Samuel was born his parents and family lived at Water End in Stanground. Ten years later when Samuel was two years old his parents had moved with their children back to Little Whyte where Fred continued working as an agricultural labourer. Samuel's siblings were Emma, Job, Ann, Absalom, Arthur and Freddy.

The following has been told to me by Sheila the wife of Terry Gowler. Terry is the grandson of Samuel and the son of Charles Alfred (Alf) and Phyllis Gowler.

"George Gowler, son of Samuel and Florence, was born in Woodston and grew up in Belsize Avenue. George left school when he was fourteen and went to work at the London Brick Company. He also enjoyed entertaining and presented a magician's act at various clubs and parties in Peterborough. George took on a part time job at the Empire Theatre as a scene shifter which led to him joining up with a touring show until he went off to war in 1939.

After the war he opened a fish and chip shop in Lancaster. With his interest in food George later became qualified as a chef and went to work at the Savoy in London.

After travelling on the tube to work for about six and a half years George and his wife Evelyn decided to go back to live in the country. Time went by and one day George was sent an appointment by an agency to visit Agatha Christie at her Chelsea home for an interview for the job as a butler. (At this time George had no experience in this area.)

Two weeks later Agatha informed George both he and his wife had been accepted to work for her, George as their butler and Evelyn as their cook. While waiting at Paddington station George saw a book titled 'How to be a Butler', he bought the book and read it all on the way to Devon where they would be working.

He found it to be a very elegant lifestyle. Depending how he felt George would either wear black trousers, bow tie and a white coat or tie and tails. When he sounded the gong at 7.40pm for 8o'clock dinner someone would pop into the hall to see what George was wearing. The white coat meant they could remain casual but the tails indicated they had twenty minutes to dress for dinner.

George carried out this lifestyle for about seven years.

Throughout his entertaining work he had fond memories of working with some famous people; David Nixon, Tommy Cooper, Charlie Chester and Arthur Askey to mention a few. When George and Evelyn decided it was time to retire a great friend of Evelyn's gave them a house in West Bay Bridport. When Evelyn was younger she worked as a nanny for this family and the house was given as a thank you for all her help."

A report in the Peterborough Advertiser dated 24th February 1939 stated:-

Mr George Gowler, the well known Peterborough entertainer, whose home is at 153 Belsize Avenue Woodston, who for the past two years has been with Ernest Binns Arcadian Follies and has toured the leading theatres up and down the country has been released to fill variety parts. This week he is featuring his yodelling ventriloquist act."

ler saw

CHRISTIE FAN: The thriller writer's butler, George Gowler

THE WHITE/VINCENT FAMILY

James Vincent was the son of William and Annie Vincent who lived at Great Gonerby in Lincolnshire during the time of the 1901 census. James married Ivy White on 4th August 1919 at St Augustine's church in Woodstone. At the time of their wedding James was living at 2 Orton Avenue and Ivy at 214 Belsize Avenue. Ivy was the daughter of Arthur and Catherine White who in 1901 were living at 112 Belsize Avenue.

James and Ivy's daughter Catherine told me the following;

"James was in the 1st World War, he belonged to a cycling unit where he progressed to the rank of Sergeant. He was shot in the arm whilst in France and was told he would never use it again. James could not accept this and on leaving the army his wife Ivy massaged the arm regularly and eventually James got the use back.

Catherine was born in the family home at 178 Belsize Avenue. Her father James began his working life at Newells in Peterborough where he trained as an engineer. From there he moved to Hotpoint which was then known as BTH (British Thompson Hewston). In 1944 he left BTH and at some stage was involved with the Air Ministry where he was involved with AVRO – servicing Lancaster Bombers. James enlisted in the Army in 1945 and joined the Royal Engineers Regiment. He left in 1947 and found new employment at R Hoe & Co in London where he worked as a millwright engineer. As time went by and lots of hard work James passed the Marine Engineers exam in 1952. He then joined the United Africa Company and worked for the Forestry mainly in Nigeria. He stayed with this company until 1979 and then returned to Old Fletton to enjoy his retirement.

As a young girl Catherine belonged to the Mavis Neal School of Dance which was held in the building known as the Wooden Box in Palmerston Road. They mainly learnt tap dancing although some did ballet also. The group would often put on shows locally at garden fetes and various other charity events. They would practice about twice a week.

THE ABBOTT FAMILY

Robert Abbott married Eliza Olive Askew during 1890 in the Peterborough district. At the time of the 1891 census they were living along Chapel Street in Yaxley where Robert worked as a labourer in a maltings. They had two children Jesse Nathaniel and Oswald both born in Yaxley. Eliza died during 1894 aged twenty three leaving Robert with two young children to bring up.

Robert Abbott married Lucy Baines during 1895. They had a child in 1897 who they named Arthur Thomas.

During 1891 Lucy Baines was a domestic servant working for William Hare, a draper, and his son and four daughters at 9 Saxon Villa along London Road in Fletton. Lucy was the daughter of John and Martha Baines who in 1881 lived at the Houses-in-the-Hill in Stanground.

At the time of the 1901 census Robert, his wife Lucy and their sons Jesse, Oswald and Arthur were living in one of the Rutland Terrace houses along New Road Woodstone. Robert worked in the brickyards as a labourer. By 1925 he had changed his occupation to a joiner and lived with his family at 206 Belsize Avenue.

Jesse Nathaniel Abbott married Rose Elsom during 1914. During 1925 Jesse was a joiner and lived with his wife and family at 126 Belsize Avenue.

Ron Abbott, son of Jesse told me the following:-

"Robert William saved his gold sovereigns so he could buy two houses along Belsize Avenue, numbered 204 and 206 he lived in the latter.

They remember a terrible storm in Woodston which was so bad the sheep in the field, opposite where the British Sugar site now stands, were struck by lightening and killed.

Jesse worked for the Peterborough City Council before the 2nd World War. After the war Jesse drove the Eastwoods Brickyard Locomotive Engine that pulled the clay up to the kilns and presses ready to be made into bricks. Photograph of Locomotive with Jesse in driving seat.

His grandfather enjoyed showing his collection of Canaries and became President of the Peterborough and District Bird Society. He also took part in the judging. Ron's uncle Oswald won a Rose Bowl for showing his birds.

Oswald and his wife and family moved from rooms they were renting in Belsize Avenue to live along Woodston Hill in the houses along the lane from the Cross Keys Inn".

Picture shows Mr and Mrs J. Abbott.

WOODSTON HOTEL

Gwen Sprawson wife of the late Walter Sprawson told me they were once tenants at the Woodston Hotel. "They took over from Mr Walker on 9th May 1950 and stayed there for twenty seven and a half years. Gwen remembers one of their customers, Mrs Street, would enjoy playing their piano.. After many local people had finished working on their allotments they would come for a drink at the 'Woodston' and some would even take their wheelbarrows into the bar. At one time the cost of a Spirit drink was 11d (pre decimalisation).

Some of the families Gwen remembers are Mr and Mrs Abbott who had two sons and one daughter. Mr and Mrs Griggs and their family who lived over the butchers shop which was opposite the Woodston hotel also Mr and Mrs Clay, Mr and Mrs Hounsham and Mr and Mrs Chamberlain including all their families."

WOODSTON JUNIOR SCHOOL

Woodston Junior County Council School was opened on 5th January 1931 by the most Honourable Marquis of Huntly on 6th January 125 children were admitted to the school.

The members of staff were:- Miss Bessie Chapman – Headmistress; Miss M Stanyon; Miss M Green; Mrs D Whitewell; Miss L Cox; Miss M Smith; Miss M Gale; Miss M Braybrook; Miss M Davison; Miss M Edwards; Mr S E Lane; Miss R Burton; Miss D M Crick; Miss P L B Rudd; Miss J Yarrow; Miss R Speechley; Miss a H Earl; Miss B E Hall; Mrs Barron; Mrs A L Halliwell; Miss H R H Steep; Mr G A Martin; Mrs E G Coxell; Miss V C Robinson.

There were 120 in the morning session and 5 in the afternoon session.

The school was forced to close for one day on 28th June in1937 for disinfection due to an outbreak of diphtheria. During the month of July in 1938 there was an epidemic of whooping cough and mumps.

Milk was supplied to the children by the Co-operative Society and cost one halfpenny for a third of a pint including the straw.

The school piano was tuned by Messrs Claypole & Son and the school clock was overhauled by Mr Newell both local firms in Woodston.

In the September of 1939 the school did not re-open due to the reception in this district of evacuated school children from London at the outbreak of the war. The re-opening was postponed until four air raid shelters had been constructed. There would be two in the boys and two in the girl's playground.

Sylvia Coulson, widow of Henry (known as Harry) told me about her memories of Woodston Junior School in Belsize Avenue. Harry was demobbed in 1946 from the RAF and went into Teacher training. He taught in various schools in the Cambridgeshire authority. They came to Peterborough and Harry took over the post of headmaster at Woodston School in 1964.
Gwen mentioned various ladies who Harry had worked with at his time in the school.
Grace Devine and Margaret Mitchell were both teachers. Pauline Turner did all the fundraising. Violet Tilley had lived in Belsize for forty years, her husband John was born in Celta Road.

Violet was the caretaker at Woodston School her husband helped for around twelve years before he moved to Hotpoint. Violet did all the cleaning and helped with other tasks. It was one of the happiest jobs she had done. The teacher's would involve her in all activities. When they were collecting funds to build a swimming pool Violet would go round the local streets on the back of John Taylor's lorry and ring a bell. This would be a signal for the residents to come out with any items they no longer needed. They would put the items on the lorry so the school could sell them and add the takings toward the pool funds.
Violet Tilley remembers the Coldstore which was along the dirt track (now Bakers Lane). Army trucks would come to collect tins of corned beef. Not far from the coldstore along the lane near to Oundle Road was a garage which she believes only sold VW cars.
At the time of the sugar beet campaign Irishmen would come to do the seasonal work. Violet would wash their work and day clothes to earn a bit extra money.
Violet also remembers a man called 'Linnet' who sold newspapers and ice-creams under the bridge at Hotpoint.
Like many people Violet remembered a Mr Mould, he owned a donkey who he called Jenny.

STAN FOREMAN

Stan Foreman was the son of William Beaumont Foreman and Elizabeth Ann. William was the son of Edward and Harriet Foreman who lived in Woolwich during 1891. When William was fifteen years old his parents died. They were buried in the local cemetery on 6th August 1949. Harriet passed away at the beginning of 1899 and Edward at the end of the same year. By the time of the 1901 census when William was seventeen he worked as an electrician and lived in Woolwich with his relations Herbert and Rebecca Foreman. Picture shows Stan with his siblings.

Stan talked to me about some of his memories of Woodston. He was born during 1915 and grew up in Belsize Avenue. Eventually they moved to The Crescent, a cul-de-sac just off Orton Avenue.

"The butcher's shop was run by Mr Crowson and the slaughter house was along the side on Orton Avenue. Slaughtering was done on a Monday although if there were more sheep than were needed these would be taken down to the field at the Grammar School on London Road where they kept the grass short.

Stan remembers some of the people who lived along New Road in Woodston. Firstly his very good friend George Hockney, Joe Ward a cobbler who lived at 103, Harry Landin a carpenter who also made coffins and lived at 101, Ron Jakes who lived opposite the off licence, Mrs Harold who lived next door to the Franklin family, Mr and Mrs Elger, Gwen Waite, Walter Sulch, Ken

Church to name a few.

At the bottom of Water End was Woodston Staunch where there used to be lock gates. Down by the river were the swimming baths that were run by a Mrs Jackson who was very strict. Stan remembers going there in the 1930's the ground was covered by coconut matting and the small children's area would be boarded in to stop them falling in the river. Swimmers would dive off barrels. Stan was a keen boy scout.

DEREK CLAY

Frederick Charles Clay was the son of Charles and Minnie Clay who lived at 1 Rutland Terrace along New Road in 1901. His grandparents were Joseph and Susan Clay who lived at 6 Rutland Terrace. Frederick married Olive Burgess during 1924 and they moved into a brand new house along Huntly Road in Woodston just off Orton Avenue. Their son Derek told me about some of his memories whilst growing up in Woodston.

"It was a dead end at the bottom of Huntly Road which backed onto land belonging to Mr Baker who lived in the large detached house (296) on Oundle Road. During the 2nd World War a cold storage unit was built on the land that until then was a gravel pit. There were many shops along Belsize Avenue; the Pick family ran a general store in the front room of their home.

Mr Chamberlain ran the butchers on the corner of Belsize Avenue and Orton Avenue.

Johnny Braines ran a barber shop in his front room opposite the Woodston Hotel.

Mr Tolliday ran a post office from his home.

Further down to around the lower numbered houses was Mr Burton who ran a cobblers business.

Mr Jauncey had a workshop at the back of his home where he had a grinder and sharpened scissors and knives. During the war he would often be seen riding everywhere on his motorcycle although he only had one leg.

Not far from Mr Jauncey was Mr Apthorpe who had a workshop where he repaired bicycles.

At the end of Belsize Avenue was BTH (Hotpoint) where items such as guns and tanks were made. Diggers used on the site left huge mounds of earth which pleased Derek and his friend Peter Lee as they would love to ride their bikes up and over the mounds. Derek broke his mother's bike once, on arrival back home he put it back in the shed and hoped she would not realise. Unfortunately she caught him and sent him off to get it repaired.

Derek and Peter loved going off on their bicycles and would often ride to Conington during the war to watch as planes caught fire and came crashing down.

BOB SOWMAN

<u>A report in the Peterborough Advertiser dated 6th April 1918 stated:</u>

"Pte.J.R.Sowman, Wilts Regiment, late of Princes Road Old Fletton, is safe in Switzerland. He was taken prisoner at Mons in September 1914 and after imprisonment in Germany for over three years was transferred to Switzerland on Christmas Day 1917 and is now doing well there."

The story of James son, Douglas Sowman, was told to me by his brother Robert (Bob) Sowman,

James Robert Sowman married Lydia May Mendham the daughter of Thomas and Isabella from Fletton. After James and Lydia's marriage during 1919 they lived at 22 Orton Avenue in Woodston. As a young man James joined the army and took part in the 1914 war.

James and Lydia had four children Douglas, Joan, Robert and Blanche.

When Douglas left school he went to work at London Brick Company in the Transport Department and later joined the Suffolk Regiment in 1940. Later he was transferred to the Signals and then became a para-troop commando.

Eventually Douglas became Randolph Churchill's Batman. Picture of Douglas and Randolph.

Douglas travelled alongside Randolph right up to the day of his death. On 16th July 1944 after a delay of having to

wait for an aircraft they took off for Yugoslavia. They thought the descent was going well until they hit the ground. Bob told me Randolph was injured but able to escape from the aircraft. He was distraught as he could not find Corporal Douglas Sowman and attempted to return to the burning plane in the hope of finding him. Douglas had burnt to death in the crash. Randolph was apparently in tears as his servant had been killed.

Douglas's body was laid to rest in the Belgrade War Cemetery in Yugoslavia. A memorial stone was laid on his father's grave in New Road cemetery Woodston.

A letter of sympathy was sent to Douglas's widow from Clementine Churchill.

A copy of a scroll was given to me by Bob, it reads:-

"This scroll commemorates Private D.J. Sowman Special Air Service Regiment held in honour as one who served King and Country in the world war of 1939-1945 and gave his life to save mankind from tyranny. May his sacrifice help to bring the peace and freedom for which he died"

This scroll commemorates

Private D. J. Sowman
Special Air Service Regiment

held in honour as one who served King and Country in the world war of 1939-1945 and gave his life to save mankind from tyranny. May his sacrifice help to bring the peace and freedom for which he died.

A report in the Peterborough Advertiser dated 4th August 1944 stated:-
" Reported killed in 'plane crash' in Yugoslavia. Paratrooper Douglas John Sowman the beloved husband of Joan youngest daughter of Mr and Mrs D. Watson 33 Tower Street, and eldest son of Mrs Sowman and the late Robert Sowman, 22 Orton Avenue Woodston."
Another report in the Peterborough Advertiser dated 11 August 1944 stated:-
Memorial Service will be held on Sunday 13th August at St Augustine's church.

PARKINS FAMILY

James Parkins married Annie Elizabeth Grammer during the spring of 1902. Annie was the daughter of William and Mary Grammer who lived in Sawtry during 1891. By the time of the 1901 census they had moved to Alwalton where William worked as a Horse keeper on a farm.
James was the son of Peter and Mary Parkins from Oriel Terrace along Oundle Road. James and Annie lived at 50 Orton Avenue in Woodston with their children William (Bill) Peter Edmund (Ted) Violet, Ruby, Edith (Edy) Ernest Robert (Bob) and Laura.

A report in the Peterborough Advertiser dated 27th September 1913 stated;
"Walter Setchfield (14), Harold Sapey (15) and Reginald Platt (15) all of Woodston was summoned by James Parkins of Cottage Gardens Woodston Hill for stealing apples from the orchard of Mr J B Tebbutt at Woodston Hill on 15th September. Mr W B Buckle prosecuted – Defendants were ordered to pay 2 shillings costs each."

The following information was told to me by Gwen and Eileen who are two of the daughters of Walter and Violet Brookbanks.
"Annie was a qualified nurse for Dr Simpson whose surgery was along London Road Fletton. Annie would wear her navy coat and a nurse's hat. She rode her bicycle (a sit up and beg type) to her various families who needed her assistance. Annie delivered all of her grandchildren as well as many more babies in the area.
Violet married Walter Brookbanks on 5th April 1926 at St Augustine's church. Violet lived at 52 Orton Avenue and Walter

lived next door at 50 Orton Avenue. Walter was the son of Christopher and Harriett Elizabeth Brookbanks. Picture shows Christopher and Harriett sitting with Ernest back row far left, Emma Elizabeth back row far right Alice Ann and Gertrude between the two. Walter is sitting at his parent's feet.

Violet used to have in her charge a key to the cemetery which was opposite their home. She would unlock the gates in the morning and lock them at the end of each day. For this Violet was paid 37 shillings and 6 pence a year.

The organ in St Augustine's church was worked by bellows which Violet did when she was old enough. The Parkins family seat was in the area where the St Augustine's altar now stands. Bill, Ted and Bob were in the choir.

James played the organ at the mission hall while Annie was out nursing and the rest of the family were at church. When Annie arrived at the church James would play a certain piece of music which the children recognised as meaning 'Mother was in church'. Annie was very well known in the area.

James worked for Baker Perkins and in 1926 he went to Glasgow to help with installing the bread ovens in the Queen Mary liner.

Around 1935 there was a diphtheria and scarlet fever epidemic. Any children suffering with this would be wrapped in a red blanket, carried out to an ambulance which would take them to the Isolation Hospital.

There was a lane alongside the cemetery where people would walk along from the mission hall to pray for rain.

Picture shows James and Annie Elizabeth Parkins with their family.

Back row left to right William, James, Ruby, Violet, Annie and Peter Edmund (Ted). Front row Edith and Ernest Robert (Bob) sitting on mother's lap. Laura was born after photograph was taken.

Bob (Ernest Robert) Parkins wrote a poem titled:-

OUR FAMILY

Seven of us kids with a Mam and Dad,
Happy days I remember, but some must have been sad,
Our BILL then TED were the first to arrive,
That was in the days of hard work and a struggle to survive
Followed by VIOLET, RUBY and EDIE then, and the world was
still ruled by men
My name is BOB the next to come,
Then after the 1914 war our LAURA to join the fun.

Our home was a kitchen with two up and two down,
Nowhere to get if DAD gave you a frown,
Nine of us together in a room of that size
To get near the fire made you crafty and wise.
A pew in the church on a Sunday we would fill
TED was in the choir and the organ pumped by BILL

A photograph was taken of us all standing in a row
With our pinafores and big boots all on show
You ought to have heard us when we were young and small
When MAM played the piano we would sing and ball
Nobody could stop us making such a din,
When DAD played at her side on his old Mandolin.

Last of all our old dog called Gyp,
If he got out after the horse and cart he would rip
He was so lucky to grow so old,
Never once in his life did he do as he was told
Isn't it lovely to stop and look back,
Then delve into the Bottom of LIFE'S BIG SACK."

NEWSPAPER REPORTS OF WOODSTON RESIDENTS

CHILD FOUND

A report in the Peterborough Advertiser on 25th November 1921
stated:-

"A baby girl, apparently about nine months old, was found
abandoned at Peterborough on Wednesday evening and is now in
Peterborough Workhouse. At about 7.30pm Mrs Moxon of 14
Jubilee Street Woodston was sitting in her house when she

suddenly heard an infant crying most vigorously outside. On going into the passage adjoining her residence she found an infant lying on the floor. An examination revealed that though fairly well clothed the child was very cold and Mrs Moxon immediately took it into the house and gave the necessary attention, afterwards informing the police by whom it was removed to the workhouse".

The child was described as having fair hair, hazel eyes and pale complexion. She was dressed in a cream fleecy coat with a small cape collar, a new white woollen tam-o-shanter with a pom-pom on top, home made woollen undervest, calico petticoat, a white cotton dress and an old white linen napkin made out of old underclothing.

WOODSTON'S BONNY FOUNDLING.

THE BONNY BABY GIRL of nine months which was found abandoned in a passage in Jubilee Street, Woodston, last week, and is now in the Nursery of Thorpe Road House, well cared for and the picture of health. There have been two applications to the Peterborough Guardians to adopt the child. Writing from Nottingham, a lady says: "If no conclusive evidence is forthcoming as to its identity, we are prepared to adopt and bring up this child as our own, so that it may help to fill up a vacant place in our home and in our hearts, owing to the loss by death of our only daughter in November, 1916." Another latter from North Kensington states: "Having no children of our own, we would be very pleased if you will give us consideration for its adoption if you intended to pursue that course. In making this offer we do so for the love of the child, and not for any monetary consideration whatever."

A report in the Peterborough Advertiser dated 9th December 1921 stated:-

"At the weekly meeting of the Peterborough Board of Guardians on Saturday the clerk reported that he had four or five applications to adopt the abandoned child, and the Master told him he had also received several letters from all parts of England. He would suggest they be referred to the House committee."

'GRUESOME NEWS FROM APRIL 3RD 1909'

"A gap accident befell Oswald Ford, a Great Eastern Railway fireman, of New Road, Woodstone, at Ely, on Saturday. It appears that Ford, who is only 25 years of age, was changing the headlights in front of his engine at Ely in the early hours of Saturday morning, when he slipped and fell on the line. The engine was moving slowly at the time, and one of the front wheels passed over both the man's legs, crushing them badly. The members of the station ambulance corps at once removed the injured man to the waiting room, and Dr Beckett was summoned.

The doctor who was at the station, within half an hour ordered the injured man's removal to Addenbrooke's Hospital, Cambridge. A special train was hurriedly prepared, and Cambridge was reached by 7.15, Dr Beckett taking charge on the journey. It was found necessary to amputate one foot of one leg and to sever the other leg completely".

Oswald was the son of William and Sarah Ford, William was born in Woodston and Sarah in Benefield. At the time of the 1901 census they were living at 6 St Leonard's Terrace (74) Rose Lane (New Road) with Oswald, a railway engine cleaner and his sister Agnes.

Sarah passed away during 1907 aged sixty two and William in 1916 aged eighty two. Both were buried in New Road cemetery.

THE CURRINGTON/BLOODWORTH FAMILY

Bertha Currington, daughter of John and Mary Ann Currington from 36 New Road Woodston, married Herbert James Bloodworth during 1909. Herbert was the son of Jonathan and Martha who came from Dogsthorpe Road in Peterborough.

During 1881 Jonathan and Martha were living at 12 Alma Road Peterborough where Jonathan was an unemployed bricklayer. They had three children at that time Ernest, George and May.

By the time of the 1891 census Jonathan Bloodworth, his son Ernest David and his nephew George William Bloodworth were boarders with Charles and Julia Hadson who lived at Well Street Langham in Rutland. Both Jonathan and George worked as masons and Ernest worked as a mason's labourer. Ernest's age was wrongly recorded on the census as it showed him as being seven when he was really seventeen.

At the time of the 1891 census Jonathan's wife Martha was living at 1 Portland Place, St Martins Street in the parish of St Pauls in Peterborough with four of their children. George aged thirteen, Mary aged eleven, Herbert aged six and Lillie aged three.

George William Bloodworth was the son of James and Rebecca Bloodworth who in 1891 lived at 16 Henry Street Peterborough. James was a mason and local Methodist preacher. Jonathan and James Bloodworth were brothers.

Ten years later when the 1901 census was recorded Jonathan, Martha and their children lived at 43 St Martin Street Peterborough in the parish of All Saints. Jonathan and Ernest were bricklayers and Herbert worked for as a messenger for the G.N.R. May was a tailoress and their youngest child Lillie was thirteen years old.

In 1901 John and Mary Currington continued to live at 36 New Road in one of the Rutland Villas. Bertha worked as a milliner.

The following information has been told to me by Herbert's son Alec Bloodworth.

"As a lad living with my parents in Orchard Street in the 1920's there was no such thing as supermarkets. The long established family shops in the town supplied all our household needs, but what we required for our daily living was supplied by tradesman calling at the door or by the small shops at the corner of the streets. Our milk was delivered daily by Jack North who lived in High Street Old Fletton near the church. He came with a pony and trap with two milk churns which in hot weather were covered with sheets to keep the milk cool. He had a pail or bucket with an outer rim from which hung two mugs one for a pint measure and the other half a pint. The milk was delivered to the door and emptied into a jug or basin with an extra dip for good measure.

Boot Repairer – There were two of these, an old man called 'Gray' who had a workshop (which is still there) next to the library in Orchard Street, and Will Freear, uncle to the Freear girls in Long Eaton. He came regularly, more times than necessary collecting the boots or shoes for mending and returning them a few days later. He had a shop in Milton Street Peterborough (now under the Queensgate shopping centre).

Mrs Taylor – Her shop was at the corner of Orchard Street and Silver Street and sold mainly dry groceries, but she also owned the adjoining bake-house which she let. Mrs Taylor also sold the bread and cakes from the bake-house. The baker, besides delivering bread and cakes would for 2d cook the Saturday cake in the heat of the oven or if wanted would roast a joint.

D.V. (Divi) Dykes – This shop was at the corner of Queens Walk and Palmerston Road. The owner was a dapper little fellow with black plastered hair with a centre parting and pencil thin black moustache. He always wore a clean white starched apron down to his highly polished black boots. He sold groceries, cooked meats, hardware items and paraffin. This is the shop that supplied our lamp oil when we had oil lamps for lighting before we had electricity installed.

Grice's – Another small front room shop in Palmerston Road selling mainly groceries and sweets. It was also an off-license. This shop was situated at the entrance to the walkway from Palmerston Road to Woodston church.

Butcher – Most of our meat came from "Fogey" Fowler who had a shop at the corner of Bread Street and Tower Street. The shop had a wooden floor and was always covered in sawdust to soak up the blood spills. The meat used to hang from hooks on rails or lay on tables in the shop and on which all manner of flies and insects would settle and have a feed and lay their eggs. Hot or cold it didn't matter. No hygiene in those days and none the worst for it. Nellie Fowler became Cyril Ingleby's step-mother. She was the one who, at the weekend used to sit at the cash desk and collect the money and in cold weather would be wrapped in a coat, hat and shawl and her feet standing on a wrapped hot brick.

Baker – Our baker was "Smith's" in Oundle Road. They had a shop and bake house at 234 Oundle Road. There was an old gent who I didn't see very often and two sons George and Alf who used to come round delivering daily. Both of the sons had been in the First World War, and if Dad was at home would like to stop awhile and have a chat. They first came round with a horse and trap but later had a motor van which did not have a windscreen. Many a time they took me for a ride to the end of the road and I had to find my way back. On the other side of the road opposite Smith's the bakers lived the Bodger family who ran a sweet shop in their front room.

Grocer – Our weekly groceries were supplied by C.J. Robinson & Son who had a shop at the corner of Harris Street and Windmill Street. Why we had a grocer in New England was something to do with Mr Robinson who once worked for a grocer in the town and when he left and set up business on his own Mother transferred her allegiance to him. At Christmas time they always gave their customers a quarter of a pound of tea or half a pound of sugar. It was Mr Robinson who sold my Mother chocolate bars, cakes and biscuits at cost price for her to sell retail, the profit going to the

Baptist Church building fund in Oundle Road. This church was built and opened in 1936. Mum was able to raise over £100 for this cause, a lot of money in those days, considering the profit could only have been a few coppers.

Between Nightingale's shop at 69a New Road and the then Methodist Church was a path which went down to the Great Eastern Sports Field which included six tennis courts and a cricket pitch." Photograph of John and Mary Currington in back garden at 36 New Road.

DICK PRESTON'S MEMORIES

Dick Preston told me of some of his memories of growing up in Woodston:-

"My parents lived at 41 New Road from the late thirties until the late 1970's when the house was renovated and they moved for a short time nearer the Oundle Road end of New Road. In the war years my mother and four children shared the three-bed roomed house with a procession of evacuee families and girls who worked on munitions at BTH (Hotpoint). Memories of living in the front room, sleeping in a Morrison shelter, are still vivid. Life for my mum wasn't too easy during the war but neighbours rallied round and everybody kept surprisingly cheerful.

I have many memories of Michael Brewster's parents and grandparents who lived at 49 New Road and of many hours spent playing in 'Brewster's Field' where the school now exists. I can still recall many of the names of the families who lived in the area from Nightingale's shop to Oundle Road junction.

I believe Mr Brewster senior was known as Jerry. I remember Mrs Brewster as a very pleasant lady who would always smile and stop for a brief word if I was playing in the front garden.

Speaking of playing, the area in front of the garages between numbers 41 and 49 was the 'sports ground' for most of the local children. football, cricket, rounders, granny's footsteps and many other games were played there in season. I still don't understand how the 'seasons' for such games were determined but each year was the same.

One other memory I have relating to 'seasons' is of the enormous queues of lorries bringing sugar beet to the factory in Oundle Road. These stretched from the factory and down New Road, back to the junction with London Road.

My two sisters, brother and I attended St Augustine's Infants and Junior School in Wharf Road.

Saturday afternoons were spent at the Savoy Cinema in Palmerston Road, where for 6d we could see three films – a cartoon, a feature film and a 'serial'.

I spent many hours helping out in Mr Baines shop, being paid in pop and ice-cream!"

THE WASPE FAMILY

John William and Sarah Waspe lived at 48 New Road all their married life. John liked to be known as William. He worked for the railways as a blacksmith.

One of John and Sarah's children was Sidney who married Florence Harriet Ladds during 1930 in the Peterborough district. Their daughter Margaret told me her granddad was a keen Quoits player. The following details of Williams' competitions were found in the local papers.

A report in the Peterborough Advertiser dated Saturday 25th January 1913 stated:-

"At a smoking concert at the Carpenters Arms (Stanground) on Friday, the quoits championship cup was presented to Mr W. Waspe, and medals to Messrs H. Beeby, A. Afford and W. Cobb."

A report in the Peterborough Advertiser dated 20th September 1913 stated;
"The final quoits match for the 'Lampson Cup' in the northern area of North Hunts Quoits Competition was played at the 'Carpenters Arms' Stanground on Saturday last before a good company. Mr W. Waspe 41 being the winner by 22 points.
Mr W. Waspe won this trophy now two years in succession. Should he be fortunate enough to win it next week it becomes his property".

Another report in the Peterborough Advertiser dated 27th September 1913 stated:
"The final Quoits match for the cup given by Mr O. Locker Lampson was played at the Ferry Boat Inn Stanground on Saturday last. There was a moderate attendance, the football matches somewhat lessening the interest in quoits. A fine game was witnessed between the finalists
A. Afford being repeatedly outplayed by W. Waspe who beat his opponent on the 'pin' continuously, and won by 41 points to 23. Final score W. Waspe 41 A. Afford 23".

Nearly eight years later Mr W Waspe was still playing Quoits to a high standard.
A report in the Peterborough Advertiser dated 29th July 1921 stated;
"The match WASPE (Pe) v SCHOLES (Lincs) in the all England Cup was played on Saturday and resulted in a win for WASPE by 9 points. It was rather windy but both players proved they could play a good game despite unfavourable conditions. Scholes is quite a young player and when he gets more experience will make the best of them travel. We had a fine game and one of the most orderly crowds ever seen at a game in Peterborough. For the first time a lady witnessed a game of quoits and she quite enjoyed herself. And why not! They patronise all other sports and this one is one of the most skilful games played.
The score at the interval was Waspe 31 Scholes 29. Final score Waspe 61 Scholes 52."

A report in the Peterborough Advertiser dated 9th September 1921 stated;

"A Quoits Match to be played on Saturday at the 'New Inn' Oundle Road between J. Kirby (Champion of England and International) and W. Waspe (Champion of Eastern Counties). Mr Waspe is a Peterborough player and recently by splendid play reached the semi final of the News of the World 18 yards championship."

WAR HOSPITAL QUOITS at Peterborough.

THIS COMPOSITE PICTURE of the Quoit Contest for the New Peterborough War Memorial Hospital, played at Fletton on Saturday, shows **J. KIRBY**, the champion of England, throwing (to the left), who won. The other with the Quoit (to the right) is **W. WASPE**, champion of Peterborough and District. Kirby won by 61 to 58, in one of the best games ever seen in this district. In the circle is seen the champion's lighter up, **ALF. BROOKS**, a star turn, ready for the final Quoit.

The Peterborough Quoits League headquarters were at the Boat Inn along Bridge Street in Peterborough and were established in 1921. During the 1920's William Waspe from New Road was their Chairman, A.R.Ayres from the New Inn also at Woodston was the Vice Chairman.

THE STRICKSON FAMILY

The following memories have been told to me by Jean, the daughter of George and Phoebe Strickson who lived at 54 New Road, and the granddaughter of John and Mary who in 1881 lived at 6 Davies Terrace Fletton. By 1891 they had moved to 79 Oundle Road, known as 1 Kisby Villa and they were still there at the time of the 1901 census.

"When Jean's father was of school age he worked on Saturdays for Piggott's where he helped to make chips with the large slicing machine. George also worked as a delivery boy for a butcher along Oundle Road.

I was born at number 54 and lived there until my marriage. I have many memories of Woodston and New Road in particular. Being a very curious child I knew just about everybody in that vicinity. I went to the cemetery along New Road every week with my grandmother to take flowers from the graves, throw them in the trash and fill the pots with new ones. I remember all the people in our row of terrace houses and most of the ones on each side.

Quite a tragedy happened during the war. The Baines daughter, Mrs Holdich, lived in London with her husband and three children, Stanley, Elizabeth and Margaret. They came to live in Peterborough during the war but went back to London when the bombing tapered off. Shortly afterwards their house received a direct hit. Mrs Holdich, Stanley and Elizabeth were killed. After this occurrence the Baines moved and the 'Trayfords' took over the house.

In the early 50's the row of houses was sold by Mr Quincey and bought by Mr Taylor (my brother-in-laws father), who in turn sold each one privately to tenants desiring to buy. This included my parents.

Of course everyone knew Bert Baines when he owned the shop. When I was a child Mr Baines mother lived with them. On the other side of the shop lived Mrs Jakes and I believe next door was

Mrs Sulch (sic) Mr Baines sister. Florence was the daughter of John and Emily Baines and she married John Sulch during 1916. Across the street a little further along on the other side towards the cemetery was a small shop owned by Mr and Mrs Nightingale and their daughter Florence. In the 30's there were three shops in New Road; the other one was Franklins. When my mother sent me there to buy ham it was quite a performance. Mr Franklin would take a beautiful cooked ham from the meat safe, sharpen his knife and delicately cut it paper thin. It was quite a piece de resistance and fascinating to watch. Mr Franklin also sold face powder (Phulnana) in little boxes. When the Franklins had gone their daughter Myra and her husband Tom ran the shop. They all seemed to specialise in something a little different. Mrs Nightingale sold some fresh fruit and small stacks of wood for starting the fire (two pence). Mr Franklin had the cold meats and Mr Baines had the off-licence. My father would go in every Sunday for a quarter of a pound of palm toffee".

THE BAINES FAMILY

<u>Peterborough Military Funeral as reported in the Peterborough Advertiser dated 11th May 1918</u>

Private Walter Edmund Bains, Northants Regiment, eldest son of Mr J.E.Bains of Woodston, who died in hospital from wounds was buried with full military honours at Peterborough on Monday afternoon. He was the husband of Mrs Kate Bains of Cromwell Road Peterborough, and son-in-law of Mr and Mrs Few, of Westgate. Private. Bains, who was 28 years of age, joined the Army about three years ago, and had been in France about eighteen months. He was wounded by shrapnel on the 21st March, and brought over to the Canadian General Hospital, Taplow, where he passed away on Tuesday. Before joining the army Private Bains was employed as a clerk in the Midland Railway Goods Office at Peterborough. The service at the cemetery was of a most impressive character. The firing party was provided by the kindness of Captain Coleman of the R.D.C. The 'Last Post' was perfectly sounded by Staff Sergeant Holman. The coffin, upon which were placed the deceased's hat, belt and bayonet was covered with a Union Jack.

<u>A report in the Peterborough Advertiser dated 6th June 1930 stated:-</u>

"Mrs Baines and Miss Lily Baines both sustained injuries to the legs on Sunday evening by a motor car driven by Mr Arthur Woods of Bedford as it came out of Oundle Road. He collided with them as they were walking across the road at the junction of London Road and Oundle Road. They were admitted to Peterborough Memorial Hospital and Miss Baines was detained."

Photograph shows the Baines family.
The Baines family at the back of the shop at Australian House in New Road around 1906.
Back row standing from left to right Walter Edmund, Christopher, and John William.
Middle row sitting Florrie (Ellen), John Edmund with Alice Mary on his lap, Emily with Bert on her lap and Reginald.
Front row sitting Charlie and Dora.

THE BENTLEY/PACEY FAMILIES

John and Harriet Bentley married in the Rugby district during 1885. At the time of the 1891 census they were living at 12 King Street in Rugby with their three children John, Nellie and Mary. At this time John was a locomotive fireman. Living at 13 King Street was John's parents Thomas and Mary with their other children May, William, Samuel and Harry. By the time of the 1901 census John had progressed to a locomotive engine driver and with his wife Harriet and their children Nellie, Mary, Sarah, Minnie, George and Kate were still living next to John's parent's in Rugby. John and Harriet's son John Thomas was working for a family in Bromsgrove as a pantry boy. John senior moved to Peterborough with his family in 1908. They lived next door to the Garfield family at 98 New Road. When their son George was fourteen he moved back to Rugby where he was born to serve an Apprenticeship.

Mary Bentley daughter of John and Harriet married Alfred Dowse at St Augustine's church. Details of their wedding was in the Peterborough Advertiser dated Saturday 29th March 1913 it read as follows:-
"Holiday weddings – Several pretty weddings were solemnised in St Augustine's Church on Monday. The first was between Mr Alf Dowse, third son of Mr and Mrs J T Dowse of 92 New Road Woodston, and Miss Mary Bentley, the second daughter of Mr and Mrs J Bentley, 98 New Road Woodston. The bride, given away by her father, looked very pretty in a dress of silk Medras with true-lovers knot trimming and cream insertion. She wore a wreath and veil, also a spray of lilies of valley, and carried an ivory prayer book. The bride was attended by four bridesmaids – Miss Nellie Bentley (sister), Miss Florrie Dowse (sister of the bridegroom) Miss Sarah Bentley and Miss Minnie Bentley (sisters of the bride)."
Mary was only married for twenty one months as she passed away at the end of December 1914 aged twenty three. At the time of her death Mary and Alfred were living at 10 Elm Street in Fletton.

Sarah Bentley, daughter of John and Harriet, married Bertie Edwin Pacey during 1919. Bertie and Sarah made their home at 29 Orton Avenue Woodston Bertie was the son of Richard and Annie Pacey who lived at Garton End Road. Before Bertie married he sailed to Fremantle in Australia on 22nd July 1910 where he went to work as a labourer.

Cecil Pacey, son of Richard and Annie, married Hilda Hurrell, daughter of Henry and Jessie Hurrell who lived in the parish of St Johns in Peterborough. Cecil and Hilda made their home at 94 New Road Woodston.

Richard Pacey was born in Woolsthorpe in Lincolnshire. He was the brother of William Pacey who in 1871 was a gardeners apprentice for John Bruce who lived along Woodston Hill.

William married Betsy Ann Johnson during 1877 in the Peterborough district and by 1881 they were living in the St Johns parish of Peterborough.

In 1891 William had changed his occupation from a gardener to a railway servant although by the time of the 1901 census he was back to working as a gardener. He lived with his wife Betsy and children in a cottage along Dogsthorpe Road. Their son John worked as a sheet repairer, Elizabeth aged sixteen was not shown as having an occupation and they had another son Richard aged nine. By 1925 they had moved to 122 Palmerston Road and at the time of Betsy's death in 1937 they had moved again to 117 Palmerston Road. William died during 1945 aged ninety one.

THE WAITE FAMILY

Frederick married Ellen Gertrude Ellington in the Northampton district during 1913. During the mid 1920's Frederick and Ellen lived at 2 Nene View, Station Road Peterborough. Frederick was the son of George Henry and Annie Waite who lived at Sibson where Frederick was born. George and Annie moved to Woodston at some stage as at the time of their deaths in the 1940's they were living at 26 Palmerston Road and were buried in New Road cemetery. Frederick's sister Eleanor never married, at the time of her death she was living at 24 Palmerston Road.

The following information was told to me by Joan White, daughter of Frederick and Ellen who lived at 109 New Road.

"The Nightingale family used to own 109 New Road where they ran a grocers shop in the front room during the early 1920's. Down the side of the house along the fence was a hinge which allowed the fence to move round slightly. The fence closed off about seven feet which enabled Mr Nightingale to bring his cart down and leave it at the back near his outhouse. He kept chickens and during the war he also had a pig at the bottom of the garden. Later Mr Nightingale moved to a newly built shop near the Methodist Chapel, he sold 109 New Road to Frederick and Ellen Waite.

Frederick Waite worked for the railways. He was a passenger guard on the London Midland Scottish which he travelled on from Peterborough to Leicester and Peterborough to Northampton. During the late 1950's Frederick was one of the founder members of the 'Over 60's Club. Initially the meetings were held in the Church Hall along Palmerston Road, it then was held in the Baptist Chapel Hall along George Street and later at the Grove Centre. Frederick's daughter Joan was Secretary for the club during the later years, it closed down in the 1990's".

Picture shows Frederick Waite, third from the left, who worked for the railways.

The following photograph shows Joan and her friends of Class 1 Orchard Street School during 1933. Starting from the <u>back</u> row from the left are:-

Mr Tillett; Freda Beaumont; Beryl Hawkins; Olive Beales; Winnie Foreman;

Maureen Simmonds; Kathleen Walker; Joan Quincey; Phyllis Curtis; Unknown; Vera Carter; Dorothy Smith.

<u>Middle Two Rows </u>include – May Wright; Marjorie Harrison; Winnie Pollin; Olive Richings; Rhoda Robinson; Lily Bee; Gladys Wright; Joan Waite; Phyllis Roope; Winnie Curtis;

Muriel Sharp; Noreen Quincey; Joan Watson; Joyce Coles; Muriel Capp; Vera Bent;

Doreen Hawkins; Mary Berridge.

<u>First Row Seated </u>– Gladys Hull; Mary Palmer; Edna Nelson; Betty Crowson; Barbara Blake; Mary Banham; Phyllis Smith; Ivy Tokins; Joan Phillips; Florrie London.

<u>Front Row </u> - May Wright; Kitty Adams; May France.

Joan remembers there were fifty seven girls who would congregate on the all-girls side of the school and the boys probably did the same on their side of the school. Girls and boys rarely met at school in those days."

THE PICKIN FAMILY

Thomas Pickin, his wife Hannah and their family were shown on the 1901 census as living at
3 Limetree Cottages otherwise known as 112 New Road. Their youngest child Hannah Maud was born in 1899 at 108 New Road Woodstone and shown in picture.

They moved to Woodstone from Montague Street in Eynesbury after the 1891 census where all the family except Hannah were born. Hannah was born in Eaton Socon. The children at home in 1891 were Lizzie aged eight, William aged seven, Alfred aged five, Thomas aged four, Sarah Rose three and Violet Lily aged one. Photograph is of Thomas and Hannah Pickin.

The following information was told to me by Rosemary Cross the granddaughter of Alfred Pickin.

"Thomas initially got a job at the brickyards but then later worked at Brotherhoods in Peterborough. Alfred was a harness maker he did his apprenticeship at 'Days' in Peterborough and then (except for a short spell in his own business) he worked at Crawley & Sons until he retired at the age of seventy. There was a report in a local paper as he had been the last remaining traditional harness maker in Peterborough. I remember as a young girl going to see him at work, he sat on a small stool amongst the straw, and did the horse collar by hand–stitching himself, and pushing the straw in until it was very hard. He had a lady working with him, cutting out the plaid material which lined the horse collar. Alfred married Winifred Mitchelson during 1910. (Winifred was the daughter of John and Hannah Mitchelson who lived at 8 Oriel Terrace along Oundle Road during 1891). Winifred, her mother and family (her father died in 1898) lived at 110 Oundle Road Woodston, and that was how they met. She worked as a nursemaid in Crawley but my grandfather waited for her. Following their marriage and the short spell in business in Irthlingborough they and my mother Mary Winifred born 1911 moved back to Woodstone – to 294 Oundle Road where they stayed. Picture shows Mary Winifred Pickin and her sister Edith taken around 1916.

They had two more daughters Edith Jean born 1913 and Joyce Elsie born in 1916. Sadly their mother Winifred died young in 1926. My mother went to live with her grandparents Thomas and Hannah Pickin in New Road. Edith and Joyce stayed with their father. He did eventually marry again to Florence Coddrington in 1935 – and to me she was always 'Grandma'. Also the highlight of my childhood each year was coming to stay with my grandparents at 294 Oundle Road. I can even vaguely remember Hannah Pickin who died in 1947.

Alfred died on 6th August 1970 just before his eighty fifth birthday. The Pickin family were Baptists, and most attended Woodstone Baptist Church, except Uncle Will and family (William married

Emily Florence Gray during 1911) who attended the Baptist church in Peterborough. My mother Mary Winifred was the second bride to marry in the new Woodstone Baptist church on 2nd October 1937.

I also mentioned my grandmother Winifred Pickin (nee Mitchelson) lived at 199 Oundle Road. Two of her sisters continued to live in Woodstone. Jane (known as Jean) married Sydney Leach, a cabinet maker they had a daughter Jean who lives in the USA. The other sister Marjorie married Gilbert Crick. Later she lived at 198 Oundle Road. Her sister Jean moved in with her after she was widowed and I understand during that time she did an Altar Cloth for Woodstone parish church". Photograph shows Winifred Pickin on her bicycle.

THE HOCKNEY FAMILY

George Hockney married Lillie Violet Pickin during 1913. Lillie was the daughter of Thomas and Hannah who lived at Limetree Cottages (112) in 1901. George was the son of George and Mary Hockney from Wittering. George and Lillie made their home next door at 110. They had one son George, who was born during 1919, he told me the following details. George and Rosemary Cross are cousins. Photograph of George and Violet Hockney with their son George.

An extremely long report in the Peterborough Advertiser of Friday 30th March 1928 gave a very detailed account that was headed **An Awful Head-On Crash** which took place on the Great North Road nearly opposite the entrance gates at the Burghley Park Stamford.

George was travelling as a pillion rider on the back of his friend's motor cycle. In the report various suggestions were made as to the speed the car was travelling that hit them. George received a great many fractures and it was believed he died from shock of his injuries. His friend Thomas Wayman died from a fractured skull. Thomas was a baker aged eighteen who lived at 32 Grove Street New Fletton. Thomas Blackman identified the deceased as his nephew. He told them Thomas had owned the motor cycle for about a year but did not take it out during the winter months, and had only recently recommenced using it.

Prior to his death George worked for Barford & Perkins Limited of Peterborough as a turner.

After her husbands death Lillie, who had worked as a Seamstress for many years, started up her business in the front room of her home which she named Hockney's Drapers. Lillie bought any

goods she needed from St Paul's in London. The photographs show George (junior) outside his family home and view from bedroom window of 108 New Road.

PRIMITIVE METHODIST CHAPEL

<u>A report in the Peterborough Advertiser dated Saturday 1st March 1913 stated;</u>

" Mr Herbert Wootton, J.P., has promised to give a donation of £5 towards the new Primitive Methodist Church at Woodston, and will lay a stone at the stone laying ceremony there next month.

The iron building which has served the New Road (Woodston) Primitive Methodists for so long for the dual purpose of Sunday school and place of worship, will soon have to give place to a more commodious building of brick. It is proposed to have the present building removed further back from the road in order to make room for the future Church. This work will be commenced in the course of a few days. The members of the church are doing their utmost to get funds together and are arranging shortly two events which they hope will be well supported."

<u>A report in the Peterborough Advertiser dated Saturday 5th April 1913 stated;</u>

"Another step forward in the progress of religious work in the city, was recorded on Thursday, when the foundation stones of the

Primitive Methodist Chapel were laid at New Road, Woodston, the Mayor and Mayoress of Peterborough, Councillor and Mrs J.G. Barford, gracing the ceremony by their presence".

A report in the Peterborough Advertiser dated Saturday 26th April 1913 stated;
"The New Chapel – The contractors Messrs Hawkins & Son are making rapid progress in the erection of the new Primitive Methodist Chapel. The walls are up and next week the roof will begin to grow, so that the place will be ready for opening in June."

A report in the Peterborough Advertiser dated Saturday 21st June 1913 stated;
" A grain of Mustard Seed' The new Primitive Methodist Church at Woodston – the building particulars of which were published in these columns at the foundation stone laying two months ago – was opened on Thursday afternoon by Mrs J Farrow. Following the hymn 'Come let us raise our cheerful songs' and prayer, the Chairman Mr Jos. Farrow gave an address reminiscent of the progress of Primitive Methodism in the city, comparing it to the parable of the grain of mustard seed. In 1856 the chapel had a membership of 242 and one hundred Sunday school scholars. Later on in the ceremony the architect Mr W Wills, then handed Mrs Farrow a golden key which she unlocked the door of the new Chapel."

Towards the end of the year in 1919 the Chapel was registered for solemnizing Marriages.

The following details have been taken from the Primitive Methodist Chapel's Minute Book of the Trustees meetings which can be viewed at the Northamptonshire Record Office.
14th December 1921 - 'A tablet placed in the Chapel in memory of Messrs.F.Bye and G.Wilkinson who lost their lives in the war 1914 – 1918.
Thanks were given to Mr Smith and Mr Vinter for work done in renovating exterior of Chapel and Schoolroom.'
13th December 1922 – 'Letter of thanks to Mr and Mrs Parkins for 25 Hymnals given for use for visitors.'

4th January 1932 – 'Discussed, the question of Electric Lighting and a resolution was passed that Messrs.Tyres and Smith obtain estimate.

11th January 1932 – 'Electric light in chapel, estimated £13.10s.0d. – School £6.10s.0d.

The Trustees agreed to employ the 'Co-operative Society' to do the above work in chapel only.'

17th January 1944 – 'The Trustees put in a request for a wall in front and at the side of the school be erected.'

15th October 1944 – 'The Secretary reported the wall had been finished.'

13th January 1958 – 'The Secretary said he was very perturbed at the very poor attendances at our church and collections were very poor, and said he could see nothing in the future but to close if things did not improve and said he would like to try for another year to see if any improvements were made.'

The Chapel closed in the 1960's the remaining members joined the Methodist Church on London Road. The Primitive Chapel was sold to the Ukrainian Mission who took over in 1964 for their use in prayer.

Margaret Bates (nee Garfield) told me she remembered there being a building at the back of the Methodist Chapel along New Road which was known as an Iron Building where the Sunday school was held.

AUSTRALIAN HOUSE

Mr John Anker, a general dealer, lived with his wife Elizabeth and their family at Australian House along Cemetery Road at the time of the 1891 census. Their five children were Albert, Agnes, Horace, Ernest and Mary. William Julyan was an agricultural labourer who was a boarder with the Anker family. Edith Daynes aged fifteen was their general servant.

By 1901 John had changed his occupation to a sand and gravel merchant and had moved a short distance to the end of Australian Terrace. They had four children still living at home, Agnes was a general servant, and Mary a dressmaker, Ernest was a milk boy and their youngest son Leonard who was born after the previous census.

Elizabeth died on 21ˢᵗ July 1911 aged sixty three.

Two years later there was a report in the Peterborough Advertiser which stated;
"A SAD END – John Anker, sand and gravel merchant of Woodston, was found hanging in a shed in his garden on Monday morning. He had suffered from insomnia for the past twelve months but had no other worry or anxiety."
John died on 1ˢᵗ July 1913 quite near to the anniversary of his wife's death.
A report in the Peterborough Advertiser dated 4ᵗʰ October 1913 stated;
"Valuable Freehold Dwelling Houses – Fox and Vergette have received instructions from the executor of the late Mr John Anker to sell by auction at the Angel Hotel Peterborough on Wednesday 22ⁿᵈ October 1913 at seven o'clock in the evening. Brick and slated dwelling houses no's 68 – 74 – also six similar dwelling houses adjoining no's 76 – 86."

John and Elizabeth's son Albert married Ada Newling during the summer of 1913. Ada was the daughter of Frederick and Agnes Newling who lived a few houses away from Albert's family in Australian Terrace. In 1925 Albert was a Nurseryman and lived along New Road. Ada's mother Agnes Newling died in January 1912

PALMERSTON ROAD

SCOTNEY/ODELL FAMILY

John and Maria Scotney married in 1888 and by the time of the 1891 census they were living along Palmerston Road at number 85 with Gertrude their one year old daughter. In 1881 Maria was a general servant for William Smith, a retired farmer, living at Stilton. Also at that time John Scotney was a farm labourer for Frances Saxton who farmed 130 acres at Leaves Lake in Pinchbeck Lincolnshire.

Marian Odell (nee Scotney) told me the following:-

"Her grandparents were John and Maria Scotney who lived at 33 George Street. John was a Life Deacon at the Baptist Chapel which was situated on Oundle Road. Marion remembered the

Co-operative Society took over the piece of land opposite the Baptist Chapel. There were four cottages on the site so all four families had to be re-housed before their homes were demolished.

Some of the children Marian went to school with were Margaret Bates (nee Garfield) George Hockney and Stan Foreman.

George Hockney taught Marian to ride a bicycle. Her father said he would not let her have a bicycle until she learnt to ride one. While out playing Marian saw George riding his bike so she told him what her father had said. George decided he would teach her. Even though George's bicycle had a cross-bar it did not deter Marian from trying to ride it. They would go up and down George Street until at last Marian conquered it. She then went home to her Dad and told him to come outside where she then showed him what she had achieved. Shortly after this he bought Marian a bicycle of her own.

Marian married Roger O'Dell in the new Baptist chapel. Marian belonged to the Girls Brigade and was a Captain when she was about twelve years old. Roger was also a Captain in the Boys Brigade. Marian loved it when they went to camp and enjoyed taking part in the sports especially the high jump.

Roger trained as a Welfare Officer and would visit houses and schools to check the children were well cared for and not ill treated. He belonged to the Territorial Army and would go for regular training before the war. Roger was called up at the time of the 2nd World War and joined the Royal Corporation of Signals

THE KINGERLEY FAMILY

The following information was told to me by Janice the great granddaughter of Joseph and Elizabeth Kingerley. Grace Kingerley, daughter of Joseph and Elizabeth, was Janice's grandmother who married Percy Smith at St Augustine's church in Woodstone on 5th July 1904.

"Joseph Kingerley and his brother Henry George lived in various houses on Palmerston Road. I have a rental agreement for one of the houses '19 Palmerston Road' – Rent charged 5/- weekly. My father Walter Kingerley Smith was born at 111 Palmerston Road during 1913 at the home of his grandparents Joseph and Elizabeth Kingerley.

Joseph, the eldest son of Joseph and Elizabeth, lived at 16 Tower Street Fletton he was employed by the Railways.

Grace Kingerley when first married to Percy Smith (a soldier) lived at Silver Street before being posted to the Isle of Wight."

Another of their daughters Ethel Kate married Arthur Pyle Gunton on 3rd July 1909 at St Augustine's church. At that time Arthur was living at 110 Palmerston Road just over the road from Ethel and her family.

Joseph Kingerley (junior) married Susan Apthorpe (baptised Maria Susan) during the beginning of the year in 1901 prior to the census. They began their married life in Fletton.

Photograph of Percy Smith and Grace Kingerley.

Key from left to right

Back row – daughter of Walter Kingerley, ?, Joseph Kingerley junior, ?, Joseph Kingerley senior.

Middle row – Millicent Maude Kingerley daughter of Joseph senior and Elizabeth, Walter Kingerley (son of Joseph and Elizabeth), the Bridegroom Sergeant Percy Smith,?, Grace Kingerley, ?, Elizabeth Kingerley, wife of Joseph, ?.

Front row - Susan Apthorpe Kingerley wife of Joseph junior, Vene' daughter of Joseph junior, Millicent daughter of Joseph junior, Daughter of Walter Kingerley.

Joseph Kingerley (senior) died during September 1908 aged 74. His wife Elizabeth died during August 1913 aged 71 and was buried with Joseph.

Henry George, brother of Joseph, died 20th June 1906 aged 69. On 2nd August 1909 Henry's wife Mary died aged 68 and was buried alongside Henry.

Maria Susan Kingerley, wife of Joseph, died towards the end of the year in 1909 aged 29. Joseph died on 22nd January 1929 aged 60.

Joseph and Susan's daughter Millicent never married and died 4th September 1938 aged 62.

Her sister Letitia Elizabeth married James Smith in the Stamford district during 1917.

Letitia passed away on 6th February 1946 aged 74 and was buried with her sister Millicent.

George died on 11th February 1930 and his wife Mabel Alice died 26th April 1942 and was buried with her husband.

Walter Kingerley died 30th July 1931 aged 58.

All the above Kingerley family members were buried in New Road cemetery."

A report in the Peterborough Advertiser dated 21st February 1930 stated;

"P.C. George Kingerley was a most esteemed member of the Peterborough City Police Force who died the previous Tuesday at the age of fifty. Police Officers who attended in memory of a popular comrade included representatives of the Peterborough City Police Force, the Norman Cross Division of Hunts., the Liberty of Peterborough Police, the L.N.E.R. Police and many Police Pensioners."

Another report mentioned – "P.C. G Kingerley was laid to rest at Woodston Cemetery around a gathering of colleagues, responsible citizens and surrounding constabulary which was testimony to a golden opinion of a constable such as in a long experience we have seldom seen so unaffectedly offered."

George was the son of Henry and Mary who in 1901 lived along Jubilee Street. At that time when George was twenty one he worked as a Policeman. Henry and Joseph Kingerley were brothers and the sons of George and Letitia Kingerley who came from Parson Drove.

THE ROBERTSON FAMILY

The Robertson family lived at Kelvingrove (165) along Palmerston Road in 1901 having moved from Stilton where they were living at the time of the 1891 census.

The following information was taken from the BBC's website on 'A Sporting Nation' 'Edwardian Heroes 1900 – 1913 Athletics'

"Arthur John Robertson, son of John Alex and Agnes Robertson was educated at Kelvinside Acadamy in Glasgow and later at the King's school in Peterborough. The first recorded athletic achievement was winning the 'One Mile Race' in a record time whilst a pupil at the King's school.

In 1905 when he was twenty five Arthur began to compete seriously after being injured in a cycle race.

In 1906 Arthur moved from Peterborough Athletic Club to join the Birchfield Harriers in Birmingham. The following year he won the Midland Counties Ten Mile Title and came second and fourth a couple of times in various races. Arthur also won the International Championship in Paris. He was runner up in the 1908 AAA four miles championships and won two medals at the 1908 Olympics at London's White City Stadium. He also won gold in the three miles team race and silver in the 3,200m steeplechase.

Arthur's brother David was a member of the Great Britain Cycling team at the same Olympics.

Arthur continued to compete in various places and was constantly creating new records in the races he competed in. He also travelled across the North Sea where he took part in a running tour of Scandinavia where he was running every day and continued to win more races.

Due to the intensity of his racing schedule Arthur could hardly walk for quite a time as he had excruciating soreness and bruising to his ankles and feet.

Arthur was runner up in the individual race at the 1909 English National Cross Country Championships at Haydock Park Racecourse and he led the Birchfield Harriers to their tenth National Team title. He won two more silver medals in the same afternoon for his one and four mile events in his last year. He retired from racing in 1909.

Arthur then returned to cycling when he was thirty years old and later became Director of the Peterborough Town Football Club after playing for the club during his sporting career."

The Robertson's Allsports trade name was registered in 1896 and traded along Broad Bridge Street in Peterborough. After Arthur's success in the Olympics they renamed their business to 'Robertson's All Sports'. Later they moved into the premises along Cowgate. During 1925 Arthur James Robertson also ran a 'Cycle Factor & Sports Outfitters' at 88 London Road.

A report in the Peterborough Advertiser dated 9th December 1927 stated;

"Funeral of Mrs A.C.Robertson of Woodston and Stilton – Mother of Famous Athletes

It is with regret we record the death on Monday, at the age of 75 years, of Mrs Agnes Cairns Robertson, widow of Dr. John Alexander Robertson, who, for many years, was a popular and well known medical practitioner at Woodston and Stilton. Twenty seven years ago the late Dr. and Mrs Robertson came to reside at "Kelvingrove" Palmerston Road Woodston, where Dr Robertson passed away about seven years ago. Mrs Robertson was the mother of a family of seven (five boys and two girls) among whom were three famous athletes.

They were Mr. Jack Robertson, who was popular over the whole of Europe as a great racing cyclist; Mr.A.J.Robertson, the well known sports-outfitter, of Bridge Street and London Road Peterborough, who gained fame as a cross-country runner; and Mr.D.C.("Dubs") Robertson of Lutton, the Champion of English cycle racing in 1908. Other children were; Dr. Alec Robertson, who up to a few years ago was in practice at Peterborough and Whittlesey, now of Weston-super-Mare; Mrs Maggie Brown (deceased), and Mrs Lily Paterson, wife of the esteemed Dr.A.Paterson, of London Road, Peterborough Medical Officer to the Old Fletton Urban District Council, and Infant Welfare Consultant; and Mr Malcolm Robertson who resides in Canada.

In 1962 Mr Upson took over the business but it was agreed he would keep the Robertson's name as it was a well established firm. Picture shows Robertson's shop when it was along Bridge Street in Peterborough.

HEAT-WAVE FIRES

A report in the Peterborough Advertiser dated 15th July 1921 stated
"Eight at Peterborough in one day – The heat has been more intense than ever this week,
ninety-one degrees being registered in the shade at Peterborough.
A lady residing in Palmerston Road, Peterborough, was reclining in the shade in her garden on Sunday afternoon when she noticed a savoury odour as of jam-making, but investigation showed it was raspberries on the canes sizzling in the heat of the sun (Ugh!)."

OUNDLE ROAD/WOODSTON HILL

THE EATHERLEY FAMILY

The Eatherley family originated from Peakirk as far back as 1787. William and Louisa Eatherley were living at 42 Narrow Bridge Street in Peterborough at the time of the 1891 census where William was an ironmonger. They had two sons and a daughter, Edward and Charles were both ironmongers like their father and Elizabeth attended school. William was the son of Joseph and Hannah Eatherley from Peakirk. . In 1901 William and Louisa were living at Mount View 169 Oundle Road, they also had two young men lodging with them. Duncan Smith was a foreman to a timber merchants and Percy Knight was a clerk in a tailors shop.

Their son Edward married Esther Jane Lightfoot during 1896 and two years later they had a daughter who they named Eveline. Edward died during the winter of 1898 when Eveline was only a few months old.

The following details were obtained from some family papers. These were originally purchased by a lady who bought a job lot of items at an auction. I was able to buy these papers and eventually found someone living in Canada who was a descendant of the Eatherley family. She was happy for me to copy and use anything relevant for the book. After which the papers were forwarded on to their new home in Canada.

"On Wednesday 7th March 1923 an auction took place at the Angel Hotel Salesroom in Peterborough at 7 o'clock in the evening by Fox and Vergette Auctioneers.

Details of the property:-

'On Oundle Road - Lot 3 – The double-fronted Freehold Residence, no. 167 situated on the North side of the road, known as "PRESTON VILLA" now in the occupation of Mrs Gillings, the owner.

The house contains: Minton tiled Vestibule and Hall, Dining and Drawing Rooms with Bay Windows, Pantry, Kitchen, Scullery, Coalplace and W.C. Good staircase and Landing.

Two Front Bedrooms with Bay Windows, Two Other Bedrooms, Dressing Room and Bathroom.

There is a small garden in front. Side entrance and garden in the rear with a boarded and corrugated coalplace and an open Shed.

This is a conveniently arranged residence, within easy distance of the city, pleasantly situated on the Hill overlooking the Nene Valley, and in excellent state of repair and decoration.'

Photograph shows a gentleman outside Preston Villa, believed to be Mr Eatherley.

Mr George Henry Eatherley, nephew of William Eatherley, purchased the property named Preston Villa in March 1923. Before moving to Woodston he was living at Goodmayes in Essex with his wife Emma. They paid £875 for the property.

Amongst the papers was an invoice, dated 20th May 1923, for a new suite that George and Emma ordered. They purchased it from Barrett & Co Ltd. Pollard Row, Bethnal Green, in London.

It was a Rossmore suite in Moquette (brown) Stuffed black fibre at a cost of £29 – 10s -0d

George died during 1934 aged seventy two and was buried in Peakirk churchyard.

As a result of the war Emma experienced some damage to the home. An invoice showing this was also amongst the papers and was sent to Mrs E Eatherley on 19th March 1943 from George Brummitt Oundle Road Woodston. The cost of repairs came to £28 - 3s - 3d

Emma passed away during 1952 at the age of eighty six and was buried with her late husband in Peakirk churchyard.

THE BRIDGEFOOT FAMILY

Fanny Diana Bridgefoot was the daughter of James and Helena they lived at Parson Drove in Lincolnshire during 1881 where Fanny was born during 1875. By the time of the 1891 census James and his family were living at 'Violet House' (83) Oundle Road. Miss Fanny Bridgefoot was still living in the family home during 1925.

By 1940 Miss Fanny Bridgefoot was living at the Manor House (174 Oundle Road), There was an alley-way to one side of the

Manor House where the horse's pulled the coach's up to the coach house. Fanny's sister Nellie was living a short distance away at Manor Farm along Oundle Road with her husband Frank Edwin Hunting. Another of their sisters Angelina lived with her husband George Brummitt at 45 Oundle Road. George was a Plumber when they married and later extended his business to a painter and decorating service. Picture of Brummitt family outside their home.

Fanny died during 1964 aged eighty nine and was buried with her late sister Ada who died in 1934 aged fifty seven. Another sister Angelina died during 1933 aged sixty six.

The Claypole family were piano repairers who ran their business in a barn next to the coach house.

THE HANKINS FAMILY

William Dawson Hankins married Maria Jane Kelly Mawby during 1897 in the Thrapston district. They made their home at 288 Oundle Road. Maria died in 1914 and was buried in New Road cemetery. William then married Florence Hales during 1915 in the Peterborough district. Florence was the daughter of William and Ellen Hales from Peterborough.

Leonard Hankins told me the following. He was the son of William and Florence Hankins who lived at 288 Oundle Road. William worked for the LMS as a foreman at Crescent Wharf. Leonard believes the school teacher George Edward Hankins was related to him through his grandfather. (George lived at 19 Jubilee Street around 1925 and had moved to 255 Oundle Road by 1940. Although when his wife Daisy died in 1960 they were living at 266 Oundle Road. George died during 1963). Len remembers the 'New Road' sign being put up to replace the original name of Rose Lane at the junction with Oundle Road. Another of his memories was of local talk regarding Oliver Cromwell who, it was said, attempted to knock the Cathedral down with the use of a Canon from Battlefields Road. This road was down the east side of British Sugar offices almost opposite to where Len lived. At one time there were a row of cottages along Oundle Road between the Cross Keys Inn and where British Sugar now stands. Another row of cottages backed onto the railway line just past the Cross Keys Inn.

On the corner at 296 Oundle Road lived Charles Baker and his family. Behind their home was a gravel pit. Charlie was known as Pasher Baker and owned a steam engine which was used to cut up wood. They took in whole tree trunks that were then cut into logs and stacked up until needed. The children loved to play on these logs but were often taken off guard when members of the Baker family came outside and shouted at them.

During later years Mr Baker was approached by Diesel Perkins who asked as to whether they could build a gradient. This was along the dirt track alongside Mr Baker's house. They laid tarmac and the area was then used to test the company's road rollers.

Harry Wright Smith was the local baker at 234 Oundle Road. He also sold chicken corn which was kept in large bins and sold by the scoopful. As children, they would often dip their hands in and rootle about but were never corrected for this.

Harry Whitehead lived at 213 Oundle Road where he ran his Gentleman's Hairdressing business in his front room.

Mr A E Armstrong was the choirmaster at St Augustine's church. Len remembers practising for approximately two hours every Friday night. The senior boy was allowed to bring along a Harmonium purely for practice purposes. During the 1930's Woodston choir consisted of thirteen boys and eleven men".

Photograph of Woodstone choir.

CHRISTINE BRIGGS MEMORIES

Christine Briggs, daughter of Charles Stanley Ward and granddaughter of Ann Ward, told me of her memories of Woodston life.

"Christine grew up at 49 Grove Street which was once a private school for girls. She remembers it had big windows which went to floor level and faced the recreation ground.

Women worked on the railways as carriage cleaners. They wore navy overalls and had their hair tied up. Their day began at 5.00am they would walk down the footpath by the side of the Cherry Tree Inn, past the East/West line and past the river on the bridge by the end where the electricity station now stands. This is where the carriages were left overnight for cleaning in the mornings.

There once were cottages on the land which later became the Co-op car park. In one of these lived the 'Brummitt' family who ran a plumbing business in the general hardware shop. Mrs Brummitt was also in business and ran a wool shop.

Further along Oundle Road was Piggott's fish shop. Nellie Lock had two shops, one along Oundle Road and the other in Palmerston Road. Her shops were crammed full of children's, men's and ladies clothing which included underwear, knitting wool and lots of various haberdashery.

On the corner of Tower Street, Orchard Street and Bread Street opposite Swiss Cottage Inn was Mrs Phillip's shop. Here she sold ice lollies and drinks. Further along in a double fronted shop was Miss Stapleton's sweet shop. She would open on Sunday afternoon's when most other shops stayed closed.

Another shop that seemed to be open all day and night was 'Lee's who had fruit, vegetable flowers and plants displayed at the front of the shop.

Ann Ward, Christine's great grandmother, ran a fish and chip shop along Grove Street. Her husband worked for the railways and often went to Yarmouth where he bought the fish or knew people who would buy it for him. Christine's father Charles remembers people would come to their shop from all over Peterborough as Ann was renowned for selling good fish and chips.

Christine's Uncle Baker Ward lived next door but one to the school on Oundle Road where he ran his business as a sign-writer, decorator and furniture restorer'.

NELLIE LOCK'S SHOP

Nellie Lock's shop seemed to make a lasting memory as most people I talked to mentioned her. Various descriptions of goods sold were wool for knitting, sewing and embroidery items, underwear, blouses, scarves, to name a few. Apparently it often smelt of moth-balls.

I was very lucky when Doreen Foster found out an Elastic card which was bought in Nellie's shop at 76 Oundle Road Woodston.

250

SCHOOL ON OUNDLE ROAD

There was once a school along Oundle Road known as the British School which was built in 1850 and enlarged during 1889. Mr A.W. Tillett was the Master of the school.

Mr French kindly let me have a copy of a photograph which is believed to be taken at the school.

WHARF ROAD / OUNDLE ROAD

Nell Creamer (nee Wilson) was born in Grove Street. During the war Nell's sister got her a job working for the railways as a carriage cleaner although this was usually a man's job. Nell remembers the coal yard at the bottom of Wharf Road owned by Mr Garnham, also the 'Boat' otherwise known as the Ferry Boat Inn. As children they would swim across the river to the opposite bank.

When Nell was first married she moved into the pre-fab houses along Wharf Road with her husband. During the early 1970's these houses were knocked down to be replaced with brick built homes. Many of the families were able to move back in to the new homes which stood in the exact place as their pre-fab homes had once been.

There was a lane at the side of the Cherry Tree Inn which they called the black pad at the bottom of this lane was a large old house where the railway police worked from. At one time Nell cleaned these offices for Inspector Martin.

Nell remembers there was a school situated between 25 and 37 Oundle Road before the decision was made to move to Orchard Street.

Photograph of the Pre-fabs.

BATHING PLACE ATTENDANT 1913

George Watson, the bathing place attendant at Woodston Staunch, was well known for saving peoples lives. One evening in August of 1913 three boys ran to Mr Watson telling him a young boy named Hodson had fallen into the Staunch. The boy had sunk to the bottom of the river among the weeds and had been there for a good ten minutes. Mr Watson immediately plunged into the river and brought the boy back up to the land, he was helped by a fisherman to get the boy to safety. The boy was lifeless but Mr Watson began artificial respiration using the Schultzer's system. After fifteen minutes the boy began to show signs of recovering but it was not until after twenty five minutes before Mr Watson decided it was safe to stop working on the boy. The boy was the son of Mr George Hodson of Gladstone Street.

Mr Watson then left the boy in the safe hands of two good Samaritans from Water End.

It was reported that this brave man had saved sixteen lives at the Bathing Sheds and three at Woodston Staunch.

Wharf road cottage.

Wharf road flooded.

Wharf road school.

Wharf road infants 1908.

A report in the Peterborough Advertiser dated 25th August 1939 stated:-

GEORGE WATSON, Peterborough Bathing Place Attendant, who was presented by the Mayor of Peterborough at the City Council on Friday with the honorary parchment of the Royal Humane Society. It will be remembered in August Mr. Watson rescued a lad, named Hodson, from the river, near Woodston Stanch, and, although he was apparently extinct, by continued respiratory exercises, he brought him round. Mr. Watson had previously saved eighteen lives, sixteen at the Bathing Sheds and two at Woodston Stanch.

"The peril which attends children who bathe in the Nene in Peterborough was once more demonstrated on Thursday when a fifteen year old boy was rescued from drowning by a boy two years his junior, Desmond Farrow, of Belsize Avenue Woodston. A number of boys, only one of whom could swim had been enjoying themselves in the river at the rear of the sugar Beet Factory. The river was shallow at the edge, but a little way out there was a sudden shelving into deeper water, where the bed of the river had been dredged. The boy who, with the others, had been pretending they were drowning, went over the edge of the shelf out of his depth into over 8 feet of water. The other boys did not see when this happened, and when he cried for help took no notice. Naturally thinking he was still playing the game of drowning.

Suddenly, the lad's brother realised the fact and told the other boys that his brother was drowning. Without hesitation, Desmond Farrow, the only swimmer amongst them, dived in and brought the boy to the bank just as he was going down for the last time.

Artificial respiration was applied by the boys, most of who were 12 to 13 years old, and proved effective.

It was fortunate for the rescued boy that Desmond Farrow happened to be among the bathing party, for only that day his mother had bought him a ticket for Peterborough swimming pool. The boy soon recovered from his experience, which should be a warning to others."

THE CROWSON FAMILY

The Crowson family lived in Nassington from at least the time of the 1841 census.

William Crowson, a timber merchant, his wife Eliza and their family lived at 11 Grove Street Fletton during 1891. They were shown on the 1901 census as living in Fletton Urban which was later named New Fletton where Grove Street was situated. William and Eliza's family included John William aged fourteen whose occupation was a tailors assistant and Bertie aged thirteen as a joiner's assistant. Ernest Alfred aged twelve, Percy aged eight, Eva aged six and Annie Adelaide aged five all attended school.

From at least 1911 to 1925 William was living at 255 Oundle Road where he was also a district councillor.

William and Eliza's son John William Crowson married Annie Christmas during the beginning of the year in 1912. Annie was the daughter of Mark and Emma Christmas. In 1881 before Annie was born they lived at 3 Palmerston Road. Annie was born in 1890 and by the time of the 1891 census they had moved to 3 Acorn Cottages along Water End.

John and Annie lived along Oundle Road and had a son Kenneth. On 4th April 1921 when Kenneth was eight years old he was tragically killed by a motor car whilst playing with his dog. There was a large congregation of sympathisers at his funeral which also included the children of Class 1 from Woodston School where Kenneth was a member.

Another of the brothers was Henry who in 1891 lived at 61 Tower Street Fletton with his wife Francis and their five children. Eliza aged twenty six, Elijah aged seventeen who was a dentist's apprentice, Herbert aged fifteen was an errand boy, Willie aged eleven and Fanny aged seven attended school.

By 1901 Henry was a hurdle maker, Herbert was a brickburner, Willie was a wagon lifter and Fanny stayed at home. Eliza married William Hillyard during 1893 they were living in Nottinghamshire with their daughter Francis aged two.

Henry and Francis' son Elijah married Hannah Sergeant during 1895, by the time of the 1901 census they were living at 288 Oundle Road.

William's brother Alfred was living at 17 Tower Street Fletton during 1891. Like his brother William he was shown as living in Fletton Urban at the time of the 1901 census Alfred and his wife Sarah had five children. Alfred (later known as Albert) aged ten, Arthur aged eight (he died during 1902) Gertrude aged six, Hilda aged five and Elsie May who was a few months old.
Alfred and Sarah had three more children after the 1901 census. Maud was born in 1903, Gladys in 1905 and Mabel in 1907.
Alfred and Sarah later moved to 240 Oundle Road. Their daughter Gladys died during 1932 aged thirty eight, Sarah passed away during 1942 and Alfred died during 1947 aged eighty two. They were all buried in the same grave in New Road cemetery - Reunited.
Mabel married Wilfred Arthur Robinson and they made their home also at 240 Oundle Road
Wilfred and Mabel's son Neville told me the following:
"Wilfred was a machine planer in the engineering department at the London Brick Company. During his time there he complained that there was not a safety guard on the machine but the workers still had to use it. Unfortunately one day Wilfred got his overalls caught in the machine which then dragged him along before finally ending up with his leg caught in the machine. Wilfred was rushed to hospital where many people offered to give blood to save his life. Sadly Wilfred did not survive this dreadful accident and died on 22nd January 1941 aged thirty. He was buried in New Road cemetery.
With the help of the Union Wilfred's brother Albert took the London Brick Company to court for negligence. The outcome of the case was the family were awarded compensation.
Before Wilfred worked for the brickyards he helped install the boilers at the British Sugar factory on Oundle Road."

Various male members of the Crowson family came up with the amazing idea of a safety ladder. The company was founded in 1900 by William Crowson. The Directors were Bertie and Percy Crowson. They named their assignment The Patent Safety Ladder Company Limited.

I have copies of two of their catalogues which were produced in the 1920's and 1940's. A paragraph in both states:-

'You cannot have QUALITY, "either in merchandise or men", at the price of <u>ordinary</u> material. For <u>24 YEARS</u> (1920's) <u>38 YEARS</u> (1940's) our object has been <u>QUALITY</u>.'

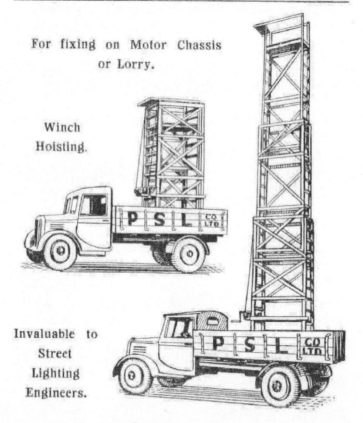

TOWER

FOR

Street Lamp Maintenance

For fixing on Motor Chassis or Lorry.

Winch Hoisting.

Invaluable to Street Lighting Engineers.

The Tower illustrated is in three sections.

Platform height 29 feet from ground level.   Reachable height 35 feet

These can be made in varying heights and in 2, 3 or more sections.

Prices on application.

THE

PATENT SAFETY

EXTENSION

ROADSTER

TOWER

CLOSED.

THE PATENT SAFETY EXTENSION ROADSTER TOWER can be made in either two or more sections. The illustration shows one in three sections. It is mounted on good strong wheels, well shod.

We consider this the simplest and most efficient Tower made. No extension or adjusting pieces are required to raise it. To bring the travelling wheels into action, simply press down the handles and insert pin.

Prices quoted on receipt of height required.

EXTENDED.

All Towers are made of the Finest Selected Timber

Another paragraph reads "At the Civic Luncheon given by the Mayor and Corporation at the opening of Peterborough's New Managing Director of The English Electric Co., Ltd., said "that just as Peterborough in the past had been famous as a place where the Best Ladders were made, so in the future it must become famous as a great industrial centre" This was an article printed in the Peterborough Advertise dated September 7th 1923.

THE PATENT

SAFETY

EXTENSION

LAMP CLEANERS'

LADDER.

FOR SUBURBAN WORK

FOR TOWN WORK

IN USE

Christine Briggs told me her ancestor Charles Stanley Ward was one of the brains who helped to work on this project with Edgar Crowson and his family.

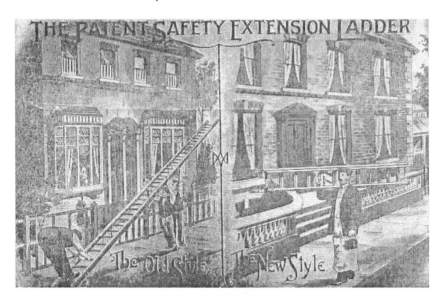

THE POLLARD FAMILY

Here is an insight to the lives of the Pollard family from Rugby in Warwickshire before they moved to Peterborough.

James Rowland Pollard was born in the Market Harborough district during 1859. In 1881 he worked as a railway fireman and was lodging with George and Hannah Peskett who lived at Newbold upon Avon in Warwickshire.

In 1883 James married Sarah Ann Barratt in the Rugby district. Sarah died during 1885 aged twenty one.

At the time of the 1891 census James was shown as a widower living with Thomas Mewis, a railway engine driver, his wife Ann and their four children. The children were Thomas, Ann Elizabeth, Charles and James. They all lived at Vicarage Hill which was in Clifton on Dunsmore in Warwickshire.

The 1881 census showed Thomas Mewis as 'Phineas Mewis' also their child Thomas was also recorded as Phineas. This was possibly an error by the enumerator.

During the late summer of 1891 James Pollard married Ann Elizabeth Mewis in the Rugby district. Her father Phineas died during 1893 aged fifty.

By the time of the 1901 census James, a Railway Engine Driver, and Ann were living in Warwickshire with their children Dora aged eight, Phineas aged seven and Marjorie aged one. Ann's widowed mother was recorded immediately after them in the census in Warwickshire. Ann Mewis also had two of her sons Charles and James living with her. They were both railway engine stokers.

The following has been told to me by Rowland Pollard son of Phineas:

"Phineas Pollard married Edith Smith in the winter months of 1918. Edith was the daughter of Harry and Eliza Smith who were living at 234 Oundle Road where Harry owned a bakers shop. At the time of the 1901 census Harry and Eliza were shown as living at 3 Henry Street in Peterborough where they ran a bakers shop. They later moved to Silver Street where they ran their bakery business before moving to 234 Oundle Road.

They used a horse and cart to deliver their produce but in 1930 Harry Wright Smith was the first person to own a delivery vehicle in Peterborough.

Harry was born in North Luffenham and in his youth went to London with his brother Bill who was a policeman. Harry wanted to be like Bill and go into the police force but it did not happen. He began his bakery career working for Fowlers the bakers in Peterborough.

Harry and Eliza had four children, Gertrude (Gert), Edith, George

and Alfred (Alf). When Harry retired Alf took over the business along Oundle Road.

Marjorie Pollard, sister of Phineas, went to the County School along Lincoln Road in Peterborough. She enjoyed playing in the school hockey team and eventually became Captain of the England hockey team. In 1921 they played the German team and beat them 8 – 0, Marjorie scored all eight goals. She later was presented with an OBE.

Rowland (Rolls) Pollard first went to the school down Wharf Road before moving up to the Fletton Grammar School. When he left school Rolls worked at Rowan's nursery and smallholding which was situated where British Sugar now stands opposite to where he lived. Rolls remembers going along Oundle Road on Saturday mornings in the horse and cart selling tomatoes, cucumbers and various vegetables. He was paid 4shillings a day. They also grew daffodils but would not be cut until they were in bloom. During the war they had to grow vegetables and were not allowed to grow flowers.

Rolls enjoyed the time he spent in the Woodston Scouts that used to meet along in the

Wonderful Goal-Getter.

MISS MARJORIE POLLARD, the English Amateur International Hockey Forward, Captain of Peterborough Ladies' Hockey Team and Captain of St. Peter's College, Peterborough. Just now Miss Pollard is playing with the Northants. team in the Midland Counties Ladies' Hockey Tournament, and is increasing her fame as a dashing, tricky forward and marvellously accurate goal-scorer. In the first three matches Northants. played against Shropshire (won 7-0), Notts (won 4-5, and Bedfordshire (won 5-2) Miss Pollard put up a wonderful performance and had the honour of netting all the goals against Beds. Her work in the team is being watched with more than a little of local interest, and the leading sporting newspapers have spoken in high praise of her work.

("Advertiser" Photo).

Church Hall in Palmerston Road. He was enlisted to the army in 1948 and joined the Royal Electrical Mechanical Engineers based at Lanark in Scotland.

Rolls' sister wanted to start up a business but could not do it on her own so Rolls decided to go in with her. They bought the shop along Oundle Road from Mr Ellis, (cycle shop) in an auction and Pollards shop began. Rolls sister sold carpets in the shop. There was a small warehouse at the back where they sold florist sundries. As time went by they decided to move their shop to Queen Street in Peterborough. Apart from selling flowers they also made Pin Holders which were later replaced with oasis. Another of their products was the Pet Abode, plastic houses, for Hamsters. From Queen Street they moved to Broadway in Peterborough where they owned a very large business. Rolls and his staff entered many exhibitions all over the country and won a vast amount of awards.

Rolls enjoyed rowing and became chairman of the Peterborough Rowing Club. He first began rowing in 1952 when the club was based at the Peterborough embankment where the boathouse was a wooden hut.

MR ACKROYD

Thomas Ackroyd was the son of John William and Alice Ackroyd. John's family originally came from Keighley in Yorkshire. He decided to move to Peterborough to work for the railways which is where he met Alice. Her parents were George and Sarah who lived at Bamber Street in Peterborough during the 1901 census. John and Alice married during 1909 and made their home at Queens Drive West and later at Millfield along Lincoln Road.

Thomas Ackroyd was born in 1917 he attended Lincoln Road school and later was a pupil at Deacon's school in Peterborough.

Thomas married Doris during the 1940's and they lived at 298 Oundle Road. After the war Thomas worked for Marshalls along Bridge Street in Peterborough. He began his business at 338 Oundle Road in 1951.

The small Nissan shaped hut at the top of the picture was the first building of his business. Later more buildings were erected. The small concrete area at the very top behind the hut was a gunning placement in the war which went underground. There was a tank trap (concrete dyke) along Shrewsbury Avenue which in later years was a play area for local children.

Thomas took in cars that had been involved in accidents or that were in need of body work repair.

Photograph shows the business in the 1950's.

THE VALENTINE FAMILY AT THE CROSS KEYS INN

Jean Frith, the granddaughter of Tom and Flora Valentine told me of her childhood memories:-

"Tom and Flora were landlord and landlady of the Cross Keys Inn. Jean remembers just beyond the Cross Keys was a house and not far from this house was a row of cottages. Prior to being a landlord Tom was a guard for the railways. Tom and Flora regularly took in commercial travellers as lodgers up until the Second World War. Jean remembers when there was an air raid during the war she would go with her parents, brother and sister across the road to her grandparent's pub. They would sleep down in the cellars where it was safe and thought it fun as they had all they wanted in crisps and lemonade. During this time Jean lived with her family at 308 Oundle Road.

After the war when Tom and Flora retired they moved across the road to 308 named Bionea. Jean and her family later lived at 324 Oundle Road in a bungalow named 'Val-dor-hil.' At one time Jean's mother Hilda bought a private school in Fletton."

I came across a report in the Peterborough Advertiser dated 7th March 1930 with regards to Hilda's sister Doris's wedding:-

'Considerable interest was taken in the wedding which took place at Woodston church on Saturday, when the Rev.J.S.Powell officiated, of Miss Doris Irene Valentine, younger daughter of Mr. and Mrs.T.S.Valentine, of the "Cross Keys," Oundle Road Peterborough and Mr. John Thomas Callender Robinson, only son of Mr. and Mrs. T.K.Robinson of Dogsthorpe Road Peterborough. The bridegroom until recently was a popular master at St Marks School, Peterborough and three months ago took over the headmastership of Great Wilbraham School near Cambridge. The bride was for some time engaged on the teaching staff of Lincoln Road Girls School, Peterborough and is now also a member of the staff at Great Wilbraham School. The bride, who was given away by her father, was charmingly gowned in ivory georgette, trimmed with diamante, and wore a veil and orange blossom.

HAROLD EVANS

Doreen, the daughter of the late Harold Evans, was born at 407 Oundle Road. Doreen talked to me about some of her memories of Woodston. Their home was on the other side of the Woodston boundary and used to be classed as being in the country. Doreen went to the Woodston school and remembers walking down the lane, now Bakers Lane, to get to school. Her father Harold lived at 1 Grove Street when he was a child. At the age of ten he worked for Hunting's the butchers, as an errand boy, they were situated along Oundle Road. He continued working there all his life. Harold would deliver the meat using Kit his horse and a cart. When Harold stopped to have his break Kit would move on to the next house where Harold's next customer lived in readiness for when Harold continued after his break. Picture was taken along New Road in Woodston.

Doreen and her friend Edna went tap dancing every week at Mavis Neal's classes which were held in the Wooden Box along Palmerston Road. During the war it would be the black-out when they made their way home. The sirens would go off and Doreen and Edna would hurry home as it was very frightening for them.

THE FEW FAMILY DETAILS.

Fred Few a descendant of the Few family told me some details of life in Woodston.

"The Few family moved from Garton End Road in Peterborough to Woodston about 1935. I remember starting kindergarten at a school, north side of Oundle Road opposite Grove Street.

When attending Orchard Street school the Principal was Mr Tillot. When he retired the new Principal was Mr Peters who was an ardent cricketer.

My parents were Frank and Louise Few whose offspring were (eldest first)

Ron lived in Barnet London and worked as a mechanic restoring antique cars, he died in 2001.

Nancy was a war bride who resides in Washington USA.

Stan was a regular in the Royal Engineers he fought in Korea and Malaya where he was a warrant officer. Stan collapsed on parade in the UK and died of a brain tumour in the late 1970's.

Elizabeth was a reporter for a London paper owned by Lord Beaverbrook.

Fred went to Canada in 1952 and worked for Mutual of Omaha (Life Division) as a supervisor of Accounting and Computer Systems for 17 years. He then left them to work for the Western Life Insurance Company as an Accountant. Fred retired as the Vice President of Systems in 1992.

Details of other families who lived locally;

Mr Ruff lived along Palmerston Road and worked on the railroad. During a bombing raid he went to help a fellow worker when a bomb blew over a water tower which killed Mr Ruff.

The Chalmers family were London evacuees and lived with us for a while at 163 Palmerston Road. Later they either rented or purchased a house nearby.

32nd Guides, Scouts etc:

The troop was made up of guides, brownies, rovers (senior scouts) scouts and cubs. We all used the scout hall on Palmerston Road and had our own camping ground I believe west of Oundle Road at Orton.

I started in the cubs as soon as I reached the joining age and ended up as a senior scout.

The guides, scouts etc took turns using it, mostly used by the senior scouts and scouts if no others wanted it on the week-end. As we were attached to the church at times usually monthly, after church the 32nd guides, scouts etc led by the band would assemble at the church. We would parade along Oundle Road down New Road, up Palmerston Road and back to the church.

The rovers, senior scouts and scouts would take a vacation annually for a week to Southend or Felixtowe. Eventually the band members were all rovers and senior scouts (over 16). Our band was at times asked to play at functions in other nearby towns. As my father had a covered truck my brother Stan would drive us to the function. If we were to return the same day we sometimes would take our girl friends along.

On St Georges Day all the guide and scout troops would assemble at the back of the Town Hall and our band would lead a parade through the city centre.

Buglers - Rolls Pollard - Gordon White (Whitey) - Jim Pollard - Brian Barnet - Peter Wells
Drums - Fred Few - Stan Few - Keith Johnson - Derek Noble - ? Palmer - Ray Dobson –
Ken Pacey
Scout Master Jack Brummitt (Owner of Plumbing Store)

THE GARFIELD FAMILY

John was born in Wansford but grew up in Sibson with his parents William and Ann Garfield.

The following details were told to me by John and Sarah Garfield's granddaughter Margaret Bates and great granddaughter Betty Chambers.

"John was employed by the Midland Railway as an engine driver and reported by his grandson to have walked from Palmerston Road to his work at New England. He was a staunch member of the Salvation Army and reportedly never used bad language, his favourite swear word was juggering. Sarah was a Baptist and celebrated her 90th birthday at a party held at the Baptist Chapel at the corner of Oundle Road and George Street. Sarah died two years later in 1940.

Their children were William (Will) who never married, Albert Henry, Emma Gertrude, Ethel Rebecca, Ruth Elizabeth Nellie and Herbert. Photograph of Sarah Garfield sitting.

Ethel married Alfred Rowlatt and they lived at 107 Palmerston Road. They had five children, Cyril who was a chef at Neaverson's, Phyllis who looked after the sweet shop on the corner of Oundle Road. Vernon became a window cleaner, Herbert who was burned as a baby when coal fell out of the fire while he was lying on the hearthrug and finally Alec was born.

Albert Henry was born in Peterborough during 1875 and followed his father on to the railways. He was employed by the Great Eastern Railway and was a fireman in 1901 (designated as railway engine stoker in the census of that year) and later became a driver. He married Eliza (Betty) Hart from South Shields in 1898 they lived in Palmerston Road and had four children. They were Elsie, Winifred, Herbert John Richard and Molly. Eliza died in 1910 aged thirty four. Albert later married Florence Maud Allcock. There children were Constance (Con), Florence, Kenneth (Kennie), Leslie Albert Charles, Betty, Margaret and Kathleen Ethel.

Albert, Florence and family moved from Palmerston Road to 96 New Road before Florence was born. The house was small for their large family so sleeping accommodation was limited with beds having to be shared by a number of children. Albert was a good gardener and supplied the family with fresh vegetables and Florence was a skilful cook so the family were fed properly. There was no leaving food however, and anything not eaten at one meal was presented at the next cold. Con learned to eat parsnips under this regime, she disliked cold parsnips more than she did when they were hot. Con attended Woodston C.E School from three years of age at which time her brother Bert often carried her there. She broke her arm at a very young age by falling off the kerb along Oundle Road. She was being chased by a boy called Teddy Easy. Florence was unable to take her to the Infirmary, which had been established in the former town house of the Fitzwilliam family and which later became the Peterborough Museum. Mrs Booth, a young neighbour took her instead and pushed Con in a wooden pushchair with a seat made of carpet material and the broken arm was jolted painfully. Con said that a Chinaman with a pigtail x-rayed her arm in a darkened room and she was very frightened. (She also said the Chinese man later died from the effects of the x-rays but the museum staff were unable to corroborate his existence). The arm was put in a sling and later the doctors wanted to reset the bone but Albert refused, he said it was causing no problems and the arm has never done so but it has remained slightly bent. Florence always sent Con to school wearing an apron to keep her clothes clean but Con hated it and took it off and hung it under her coat before going into school.

Con and her friend Ethel Hawes acted as baby sitters for her younger siblings from time to time and they regularly pushed the clock forward so that they could put the children to bed as soon as possible and then enjoy themselves! They liked to cook and often used unusual ingredients such as dolly mixtures sweets. Photograph of the Garfield family.

A report in the Peterborough Advertiser dated 21st November 1921 stated

" Frightened by the smoke, children in bed gave the alarm of a fire at M.Garfield's residence in New Road Woodston on Thursday evening. The conflagration broke out in a clothes cupboard, some of the articles being accidently set alight by a member of the family. The Fletton Fire Brigade was called but the flames were extinguished before there arrival."

DETAILS OF JOHN COCKERILL A LONELY GARDENER

The following story has been taken from a report in the Peterborough Advertiser dated 1st June 1918.

"In January of this year the old man of 83, who recently had lived in a two-roomed tenement in Parkinsons Lane Whittlesey, was found dead. He was lying on his back and had apparently lighted the fire in the grate before he fell. All his furniture was packed as if on the eve of removal. When Cockerill's private papers were examined within the corded box in the tiny home Inspector Jacobs discovered a bank book, savings bank book and investment vouchers representing a sum of no less than £800! The poor old man died without a will - at least, it appeared so – and therefore the 'estate' reverted to the Crown. So it was believed.

The publication of the facts led the Peterborough solicitor to look up the firm's records. His father Mr W.A. Norris had made a will for Cockerill in 1904. Another lawyer in South Lincolnshire had drafted a more recent one which nullified the Peterborough one and altered the dispositions entirely. But it turned out that it had not been completed up to the time of Cockerills' death, and it was null and void. The Peterborough Will therefore became operative.

Details of the will were included in the newspaper report. – Jeremiah Brewster, baker and William Bland, carpenter, both of Oundle Road were appointed Executors and Trustees of the will. John Cockerill left sums of money to various people, some of whom were, Martha Burnham, niece of his late wife, Clara Burnham niece of his late wife, to Elizabeth Taylor of Park Road, Peterborough and Mary Burnham of Cemetery Road, Woodston both sisters of his late wife and to his cousin Mary Spinks of West Street Stockwell Street Colchester, and to the wife of John Butterwick of Orton Longueville.

The Old Man's Life – John was the only child of Harry and Mary Cockerill, born in Cinder Lane, Orton and afterwards went to live in Red Tile Row, now used as a wash-house by old Mrs Butterwick. His father worked for Mr Henry Hetley, and his mother was employed in the Hall gardens. John married Mr Hetley's housemaid, who had saved a cosy sum of money, and John received a nice little sum saved by his parents, his wife was eleven years older than himself. They went to Oxfordshire, he as a cowman and his wife to attend to the poultry, and her earnings were at times as much as her husband's. Thus they kept on saving for several years until age crept on and their thoughts turned once more to Orton. He then bought a plot of land on the Oundle Road, Woodston, and built a double-fronted cottage (called 'The Nook'), and for some years lived in peace and comfort, with all they needed. John found work with the late Mrs Terrot, where he was for some years, and was looked upon as a quiet and good neighbour. In 1900 came a tragic ending to their happy life, for on his return from work he found some difficulty in forcing the door. When he did get in his wife lay a corpse, and a very nice stone in Orton Churchyard marks the place where she was laid. For some time he lived alone, then he took in a housekeeper (who inherits the bulk of the estate). He afterwards sold his cottage and left Woodston and altered his will. However, he returned a sadder and wiser man, bought his cottage back again, and lived alone some time. Eventually he broke up his home again, sold his cottage, and went to reside at Werrington and then Whittlesey to the end.

THE ALLCOCK/PAGE/STARMORE/VINTER FAMILY

Sandra Vinter, daughter of Ernest Edward and Gwendoline Iris Vinter, told me the family details which I have intermingled with the census years.

The 1901 census shows that Ernest Rupert Vinter aged eighteen was an apprentice wheelwright living at Orton Waterville. Ernest enjoyed playing the Cornet and was a member of the Cherry Orton Brass Band. He married Gertrude Annie Alcock on 5th August 1911 at the Methodist church in Cobden Street Peterborough. Photograph of wedding party taken at 253 Oundle Road.

They made their home at 88 New Road Woodston. Ernest Rupert was a carpenter he died at the Peterborough Infirmary in 1926 aged forty three. Gertrude died at 253 Oundle Road during 1931 aged forty seven.

Their son Ernest Edward's Guardian was his grandfather William Alcock after both his parents had died.

Around 1932 Ernest did his apprenticeship with Barford Perkins in Peterborough. He also belonged to the Perkins Fire Brigade where he progressed up to be chief of the fire brigade there. When Ernest was in his teens he belonged to the Boys brigade. Ernest became a Deacon of the Oundle Road Baptist church in 1942 and continued this until he died.

Gertrude was the daughter of William and Annie Alcock who lived at 70 Dudley Road Somerby near Grantham during 1891.

By the time of the 1901 census William and Annie had moved to 6 St Leonards Terrace along Rose Lane in Woodston. By 1925 William was a signalman, district councillor and a Justice of the Peace and had moved with his family to 253 Oundle Road. They named the house 'Muston' which is also a place in Nottinghamshire where the Alcock family originated from.

Ernest's parents were Robert and Rebecca from Hardingstone. After Roberts' death Rebecca and children were living at Blisworth where Rebecca was housekeeper for William Twistlton and his family. Ernest Rupert was shown as Rupert.

Minnie Gertrude Starmore, born during 1882 in Woodston, was the daughter of John and Frances who lived at 108 Palmerston Road during 1891. John was a sawyer. By the time of the 1901 census Minnie's father had passed away and the family had moved to 37 Palmerston Road. On 26th December 1905 Minnie married Thomas Frederick Page.

Thomas was the son of Thomas and Elizabeth Page who lived at Great Bowden near Market Harborough. Thomas senior was a foreman in a coal yard but his sons did not follow their father's occupation. During 1901 Thomas Frederick aged nineteen was a 'marker out in a corset factory', his brother's George and Frank were 'hosiery hand footer's' and their younger brother Sidney was an errand boy in the corset factory. Thomas, known as Frederick, worked at Symington's factory in Market Harborough and came to the Peterborough branch in Orchard Street New Fletton to be their under manager.

Minnie Starmore was a machinist at the factory which is where they both met. After their marriage Frederick and Minnie moved in with her parents at 280 Oundle Road.

Frederick was a conductor for the city military band he died aged fifty of a brain tumour.

Gwendoline Iris Page daughter of Frederick and Minnie Page married Ernest Edward Vinter son of Ernest Rupert and Gertrude Vinter during 1937. Gwendoline was born at 280 Oundle Road and Ernest was born at 253 Oundle Road. They lived at 256 Oundle Road known as The Nook.

Gwendoline learnt shorthand and typing at Mrs Beans in Cathedral Square Peterborough which enabled her to get a secretarial job at Symington's. Later she was secretary to Archie Peters the Headmaster at Orchard Street School which was then a secondary modern school.

Photograph shows the stone laying ceremony for the Baptist church.

These families were all members of the Baptist church. The church began its' life during 1858 on the site where the Peterborough Co-operative (later Select and Save) car park stands, between houses 72 and 78 Oundle Road. This was in New Fletton. In 1901 a new Baptist church was erected in George Street. As the years passed by it was decided a more modern Baptist church was needed. The new church was built on the corner of George Street and Oundle Road and opened in 1937.

The building at the back was then used as a church hall but later demolished. The congregation of the Baptist church are preparing for the celebration of the church's 150th year in 2008.

SYMINGTON'S

The Peterborough factory was built in 1903 and as the business grew it became necessary to extend the factory both in 1912 and again during 1939 when they employed over 600 people. In 1905 the corset makers in Germany became a threat to the factory due to their mass produced imports. Frederick Cox, a board member of Symington's travelled to Germany where he purchased cheap cloth and returned it to the Peterborough factory. The cloth was then made into corsets of a German design and sold at a cheaper cost.

At one time John Williams, the manager at Symington's corset factory lived in a large double fronted house (166 Oundle Road) not far from Manor House.

Many of the ladies I spoke to, whilst collecting memories for this book, worked at the factory. One of these ladies was Babs Setchell who as a child lived at 8 Bread Street New Fletton. Her grandparents were William and Emma Allen.

At the age of seven Babs attended Orchard Street School until she was about four or five when she moved to the infant school in

New Fletton. Mr Williams was a governor of Orchard Street school. Babs remembers he was a stern man with blue eyes. At that time he was also the manager of Symington's corset factory and Maud Picken was his secretary.

(On checking Kelly's Directory for 1925 it showed John Williams – Manager of Symington's- living at 166 Oundle Road as did Reginald John Williams who was a Schoolmaster).

Babs left school when she was fourteen and went to work at Symington's.

Items needed to carry out the machinist job were two white overalls, decent pair of scissors, pen and a book to write in the description of your job and what had to be done. This was a record to decide what wages you were paid.

Strapping – Where the bones of corset went.

Fell binding – this required a two needle machine which was used to stitch the Bias binding around the edge of the corset.

Busking, Embroidery and Seamsevern (Long seams) – these were completed in a different department to which Babs worked in.

They worked a 48 hour week over five week days and Saturday mornings up to 12midday.

In the 2nd World War they helped to make Parachutes. These took up two machine spaces the hems were stitched along the bottoms and some had to have an interlining and stiff webbing. The smaller parachutes were used for the flares and were not so big to handle.

Some parachutes were made in different colours, yellow, and red and blue that would be used for dropping various items out of the planes.

At Symington's they also made under garments for the forces. The WRENS would have better quality clothing than the ARMY or RAF.

There were approximately 600 girls working at the corset factory and they would often have a sing-a long. Babs remembers Fran Davis used to start the singing then they would all join in. When the war was on they would put the radio on so they could listen to music as they worked.

Babs was a machinist at Symington's for twenty eight years. She remembers that as fashions changed and the large stores, Marks and Spencer, British Home Stores, and Littlewoods started trading there was not as much call for the Symington's range of underwear."

There was a report in the Peterborough Advertiser on Friday 31st March 1939 which read;

"Members of the 'Keep Fit Class' of Messrs Symington's Corset Factory at Peterborough gave a display at the Grand Hotel on Tuesday. Miss Willson of Park Road is their instructor."

THE WESTON FAMILY

George Canner Weston and his wife Annie were living along Oundle Road in 1901. Their daughter Annie Florence married Walter Setchfield, a tailor's cutter, on 27th October 1901 in St Augustine's church in Woodston. The following has been told to me by Roy, the grandson of Walter and Annie Setchfield.

"To the best of my knowledge, the Weston family have lived in Woodston (Woodstone) as far back as the early 19th century, most probably earlier as Richard Weston was born in Woodstone in 1811. The last Weston, Annie Setchfield, granddaughter of Richard, left Woodston in 1961. Richard Weston married Lucy Canner, a Rutland girl in the late 1830's hence appending Canner to their son's name. As far as I have been able to ascertain, Richard and Lucy had only one son, George Canner Weston. George was born in March, Cambridgeshire, but came back to live in Woodston where he remained for the rest of his life. As a family they originally lived at 4 Water Lane which was later named Wharf Road. Later they moved to 231 Oundle Road.

George married a Ramsey girl, Annie Whyman on the 10th of December 1860. Twelve of their children survived infancy (plus one, James who reached 10 years at least).

It is said in the family that there were 21 children in all. The youngest, my grandmother Annie, once told me that there were others who died in infancy, some were buried in Woodston cemetery.

Photograph show the Weston family having a party at Alwalton Lynch in 1910.

Key to family from left to right;

Back row - ?, Horace, Annie Florence wife of Walter Setchfield, Clara, Kate, Fred Elmer, Francis wife of Dick, Dick (son), Walter Setchfield.

Middle row – Annie Weston (mother) sitting, George Canner Weston (father)

Front row - Minnie (daughter), Fred Weston (son of Horace), Jack Setchfield, Florrie Setchfield, Doris Weston (daughter of Horace), Lillian (wife of Horace). At the front is Dick's gun dog.

George Canner Weston was an apprenticed carpenter, most likely with John Cracknell, an old established builder in Peterborough, a firm that George worked for over 40 years. He latterly became an undertaker and made many of the coffins that lie in the ground in Woodston cemetery.

There is a family myth reported to me by the son of Minnie Weston, (3rd child) that George's grandfather, also called George, and was at one time the royal coachman to William IV.

I lived at 220 Oundle Road from 1931 until 1954 when I married a Woodston girl and remained in Peterborough until 1965. I was a pupil at Wharf Road School 1934-1944. I was an Acolyte and Server at St. Augustine's church from 1938 at 7 years old, until 1945 when the Reverend J A J Atkinson was Rector. My time keeping for Saturday services was reprehensible but the kindly Rector never once took me to task. Just a disapproving look as I took my place at the altar after the service was underway each Saturday morning. Every Christmas and Easter a gentleman whose name I am sorry I cannot recall, came into the vestry after the service and gave every choirboy and young server a sixpence, a kind gesture. When I was not required to undertake my serving duties on a Sunday, I would be given the job of pumping the organ for Mr Armstrong, the Rectors father-in-law. My diligence was once again put to the test. Pumping was always shared by another boy, and in my case this was always Billy Green. I'm afraid the devil was always on duty when we were. We would dare each other as to how far we would allow the air indicator to go to zero before we would frantically start pumping again. I don't need to spell it out how on a number of occasions the organ ran out of puff before we could remedy the situation.

Photograph shows Roy Taylor when he served at the church.

One interesting story is of a Woodston family named Church, the mother was a widow I believe, and granny lived with them. As I remember as a child, granny only had one tooth. They lived in

New Road, somewhere around number 20, I know the house. The youngest daughter, Winnie, took me to school each day when I was only four. She tragically died of diphtheria when she was probably only seven (c.1936). Her elder brother Ken died of cholera in a Japanese prisoner of war camp and she had an elder sister Joan who worked at one time in Jack Sharpe's newsagents on Oundle Road and she later married an Irish RAF Officer and went to live in Ireland. I think the Church family had some very hard times.

I ramble on, but, one regrets that more meat cannot be added to the stories as memory gets lost in the mists of time. One story is of my great grandmother Annie Weston who went to either the church or school on the occasion of the distribution of Maundy money. On reaching her place at the head of the queue she was admonished by the Rector with the words:-

"Surely you have not come here for Maundy money Mrs Weston you're a tradesman's wife" Even in those days there was a kind of means testing. Bringing up a large family even a tradesman's earnings were not a consideration.

ALEC SETCHFIELD

Alec Setchfield was the son of Walter Setchfield and Annie Florence (nee Weston) and grandson of George Canner Weston. Alec served in the Royal Navy from 1936 to 1945 and saw service in the Mediterranean and on convoys to Russia.

The Russian Run written by Alec Setchfield
"On 11th November 1941, I, with the rest of the ship's company commissioned the HMS Marne at Wallsend near Newscastle. She was a Fleet Destroyer of about 2000 tons, her main armament twin 4.7inch HA/LA turrets, there were also quadruple torpedo tubes. We did our working up period at Lamlash and Loch Long. After a period we were considered ready to take our place at Scapa Flow, about to go over in the Russian Convoys, which was a very terrible task, what with U-boats, aircraft and surface ships. Coupled with bad weather and other adversities was the freezing spray which kept coming over the bows and was turned into ice before reaching the superstructure. If you were unlucky enough to get damage to the ship, the life expectancy was about 30 seconds.

We used to go either to Murmansk or Archangel or to the River Obi in Siberia.

One of the terrible scenes was when the HMS King George V cut

17

An amazing drawing of Alec Setchfield.

the tribal class destroyer Punjabi in half, making a gash of about 25ft just above the waterline. We were detailed to escort the King George V back to Gladstone Dock, Liverpool. Prior to this we were ordered to make an emergency run to Archangel. We were ordered on the return journey to escort USS Tuscalusa back to the UK. On this trip we encountered a German minelayer, Ulm, and sunk it with combined gun and torpedo attacks. We were one of the first convoys to get through to Malta. The reception we received was terrific. Later on that year, we were detailed to escort the depot ship HMS Hecla up the west coast of Africa, when she was hit by torpedoes from a U-boat, and we had about 40ft of our stern blown out. We were very lucky that we remained afloat. We had to wait until we were taken in tow by a tug – I believe it was called Immanent – and towed to Gibraltar to await temporary repairs. When this was accomplished we were towed home to the UK."

In January 1985 Alec received the North Russia Club commemorative medal awarded to those who served in the Russian Convoy during WW2.

On the right is another picture of George Alec Setchfield, this was taken in New York during 1940.

THE LANDIN FAMILY

James Landin, a railway engine fireman, and his wife Mary had eight children who were Rose Priscilla, Sarah Jane, John Henry, George William, James, Joseph, Alfred and Albert. At the times of the 1891 and 1901 census they were living at 244 Oundle Road. Clara Thurley from Stanground was visiting on the day of the 1901 census.

Rose Priscilla married Henry Frederick Thurley during 1897 in Peterborough. By the time of the 1901 census Henry and Rose had moved to Hampshire where Henry was a police sergeant. They had a young son who they named Frederick.

Sarah Jane married George Baxter, a corn merchant's clerk, during 1894. They were living in the next house to her parents along Oundle Road by the time of the 1901 census with their five year old son George.

John Henry married Ethel Harrold during 1898 in Market Harborough. Ethel was the daughter of George and Elizabeth Harrold who were living at Waterfield Place in Market Harborough during 1891. By the time of the 1901 census John, a carpenter and joiner, and Ethel were living a few houses away from John's parents with their son George aged one. They later moved round the corner where they made their home at 101 New Road, John extended his skills and became an undertaker.

George William married Florence Joyce from Millfield during 1898. By the time of the 1901 census they were living at Fletton with there three young daughters

James married Beatrice Linnell during 1899 and made their home in Fletton where their daughter Kathleen was born. By the time of the 1901 census they were living at Wisbech St Peter where James was a police officer.

Joseph married Rose Jessop during 1912. Rose was the daughter of Robert, a hay trusser, and Mary Ann Jessop who lived at Colne near Somersham.

Joan Garner, (nee Landin), was the daughter of Joseph and Rose Landin who once lived at 136 Belsize Avenue in Woodston. On the 1901 census when Joseph was twenty he was a soldier in the Coldstream Guards, Joan mentioned he later joined the army and went to South Africa during the 1st World War. Joan remembers her grandparents, James and Mary Landin, living at 244 Oundle Road. James, a railway fireman, died in 1917 aged seventy two Mary died aged eighty nine in 1930. Mary had been living at 101 New Road with her grandson Harry after James passed away.

Joan was born at 190 Belsize Avenue in 1914 and after she married Albert Garner in 1934 they made their home at 134 New Road in Woodston.

Joan went to the school in Wharf Road two of the teachers were Miss Walden and Miss Biggadike. When she was fourteen Joan worked at the silk factory. One of her tasks was to turn the silk round and round checking for faults, discolouration and any other discrepancies in the silk. There were not many opportunities in Woodston for work so many of the young people went to work for the Chivers company in Huntingdon where they canned fruit. Joan's last job before she retired was working at Marks and Spencers but she had to get up at 4.00am ready for an early start.

Joan remembers mixing up feed for their chickens which consisted of cooked potatoes or any available vegetables mixed with chicken meal bought from Beavers corn merchants in Long Causeway Peterborough.

Joan told me her sister Phyllis did not like throwing things away. When she died Joan was clearing out the house and came across a box full of fossils, bones and broken pieces of pottery. Phyllis had been very interested in archaeology and loved digging up interesting items. Joan had thrown out various bits and pieces but felt these should be kept so tried offering them to the museum. Unfortunately they could not accept any more items so Joan decided to make a rockery in her garden using Phyllis's collection. Many years later Joan invited a friend round to her house. This friend also brought along her Labrador dog it went out to the garden had a sniff around then began to dig until it had unearthed the bones. Not satisfied with finding them the dog then ate the bones!"

THE SECOND WORLD WAR

<u>The following details were taken from reports printed in the Peterborough Advertiser during September 1939</u>:-

"A week of hectic activity in the Town Hall and throughout the City has followed the declaration of war, and while all public preparations against air raids have been completed, every citizen has been besieging shops for black-out material and making what provision he can for the safety of individual householders. Many have been making their own dug-outs, reinforcing rooms and providing anti-gas shelters.

The Air Raid Precaution organisation in the city included six first-aid posts, the nearest to Woodston was at the Ex-Serviceman's Club in Fletton. The decontamination depot locally was at the Savoy Cinema in Bread Street Woodston. A public Air Raid shelter was constructed at Fletton recreation ground and later at

Woodston recreation ground, Celta Road, Orton Avenue and Orchard Street.

Peterborough received a large influx of population from the London evacuation areas. At the beginning of September over 5000 evacuees arrived in Peterborough. Woodston placed 308 and nearby Fletton placed 385 into local families. Due to a vast increase of people to the area it caused very difficult times for the local shop keepers.

The arrangements for the billeting of evacuated children in the city are under the direction of the local authority, and the scheme has been completed by the Mayor and the City Treasurer, in conjunction with the school teachers. Mr Hankins, Woodston, is the reception officer under the scheme.

During December of 1939 an air raid precaution exercise for all services took place at Woodston. The rescue squad under Mr T Ashcroft received the first call to the corner of Celta Road and Belsize Avenue where a house had been struck. Here they rescued a trapped air raid warden and erected supports for the wall of the damaged house. The second call was received by the Fire Service for a fire at Botolph's Bridge.

A report in the Peterborough Advertiser dated 22nd September 1939 stated:-

"The Sinking of H.M.S. Courageous by Woodston Able Seaman.

A graphic description of the sinking of 'H.M.S. Courageous' has been given to the Advertiser by Able Seaman William Albert Hill, of 95 New Road, Woodston, who was a member of the ship's crew.

"I was in the galley at about five to eight on Sunday evening washing up plates after supper when I heard two distinct explosions. One followed the other almost immediately and I was thrown violently against the steel bulkhead and everything went black for a few seconds. When I came to I realised we had been torpedoed for the ship was already at an angle and in complete darkness. I made for the doorway fumbling around in the darkness for a few moments until I discovered some ammunition hatches. I climbed up these past two decks and made my way on to the lower flight deck where our planes took off in rough weather. When I got to the deck I saw that the ship was already listing at an angle of 20 degrees and the port side of the deck on which I was standing was already under water. There were a number of decks below the lower flight deck and for the water to have encroached on to that so soon the ship must have listed very rapidly. As soon as I was on deck I saw plenty of other fellows standing on the deck. Some were smoking and laughing and no where did I see any panic.

As the ship tilted more I realised that I should soon have to go into the water. I took all my clothes off and hung on to the starboard guard rail. The ship was all the time settling deeper into the water and the deck was tilting more and more. I hung on until the last moment and when I let go of the rail and slid into the water the deck was almost vertical. All this had taken only ten minutes and as soon as I got into the water I was almost numbed with the cold. I struck away from the ship as fast as I could so that when she went down I should not be drawn down with her by the suction. I did not see her go down but I certainly felt the suction.

Swimming was very difficult for there was a lot of oil fuel on the surface. This clung to my body, and I also swallowed some and it made me feel very groggy. After a while my strength began to flag, and although I tried to make the destroyer I just could not do it. There were two destroyers accompanying the 'Courageous' but as soon as the explosion occurred one of them steamed after the submarine.

One destroyer stood by to pick up survivors and an American liner and an English merchant man soon appeared on the scene. It was this destroyer that I could not swim to so I turned around in the water and saw a raft some 200 yards away. I nearly failed to get to this but with the help of a drifting spar I managed to get on to it.

There were several of us on this raft and we were picked up by a lifeboat from the merchant man about twenty minutes past nine. I was so weak that I had to be carried up the ship's ladder, and when we got on board we were rubbed down, given hot rum and put to bed.'

Mr Hill reached port on Tuesday afternoon and arrived home on Thursday lunch time. He is now enjoying fourteen days survivors leave."

<u>A report in the Peterborough Advertiser dated 27th October 1939 stated:</u>

"Service Honours were paid by a Royal Air Force detachment at the funeral of Boy Herbert Michael Bradley of H.M.S. Southampton which took place at Woodston Cemetery on Friday afternoon, as recorded in our last issue , Bradley, who was the youngest son of Mr & Mrs J.W. Bradley of 12 Tower Street New Fletton, was killed in the air raid on the Firth of Forth on Monday last. About two hundred people assembled at Woodston Cemetery. R.A.F. station police preceded the cortège and kept a clear space round the grave. The funeral party and firing squad with arms reversed marched in slow time before the coffin which was borne by six airmen. After the committal the firing party fired three volleys over the grave and a bugler sounded the Last Post and Reveille."

Photograph shows the mourners at Herbert Michael Bradley burial, he was the first fatality for Peterborough.

A FEW REPORTS REGARDING WOODSTON MEN AT WAR

<u>A report in the Peterborough Advertiser dated 18th August stated:-</u>
On the first anniversary of his joining the Army Private. Peter O'Dell, husband of Mrs P.R. O'Dell of Cavendish Street was wounded in Normandy. Aged twenty one he is the youngest son

of Mrs O'Dell of 1 The Crescent Woodston and of the late Roger O'Dell and was formerly a gauge inspector at Newell's Engineering in Peterborough. He is in hospital in England making a good recovery from severe wounds.

A report in the Peterborough Advertiser dated 6th October 1944 stated:-
Mrs Dixon of 163 Oundle Road Peterborough was notified on Wednesday of the death of her husband Lance Corporal. John T.Dixon in Italy on September 17th. An Old Deaconian Lance Corporal. Dixon before joining the Army five years ago was employed by Aveling Barford of Grantham. He leaves a daughter aged three years.
A later report stated Mrs Dixon lived at 119 Oundle Road.

A report in the Peterborough Advertiser dated 3rd November 1944 stated:-
Mr and Mrs Wilkins of 188 Oundle Road have received information that their son Private. Dick Wilkins, the Hampshire Regiment, has been posted missing. Previous news was received that he was wounded on September 4th and had returned to the line, but he was posted missing on October 2nd Private Wilkins joined the army as a boy of fifteen in 1939.

COUNTRY CELEBRATES WORLD PEACE

A report in the Peterborough Advertiser dated Friday August 17th 1945 stated:-
Palmerston Road Celebration – Palmerston Road children were given a fish and chip tea on Wednesday evening. Mrs Hoyles and Mr and Mrs Rycraft being host and hostess. Games and sports were held in the road, and baby V.Golder broke the toddlers 5 yards record in six minutes and three fifths of a second.
Lusty cheers were given when Mrs Dunkley brought out the ice-cream kindly supplied by Mr Miller, and even louder cheers when Mr Miller announced that a free picture show would be given on Saturday afternoon.
For the sports and games £6 was given in prizes and gifts to the children. From 9 o/clock to1.30am there was dancing in the road for which Mr R. Wright was M.C.

A report in the Peterborough Advertiser dated 12th October 1945 stated:-

Homeward Bound – Private A.W. Underwood, eldest son of Mr and Mrs A.W.Underwood of Aboyne Lodge, Palmerston Road. A prisoner in Japan since the fall of Singapore is at Manila waiting for a ship. In a letter received by his parents on Wednesday Private Underwood said he was travelling in a home-ward ship on September 18th but was held up with malaria in a U.S. hospital ship in Nagasaki. He later however travelled to Okinawa by ship and on to Manila by plane. He adds that he has met a few of 'The Old Regiment' – the Peterborough Royal Artillery. During his captivity Private Underwood says he received one letter in February 1944 and that was posted in England in August 1942. He was formally at Newell's.

THE SECOND WORLD WAR FATALITIES IN WOODSTON

Ronald Cecil Bee – A Lance Corporal with the Royal Marines who died 18th August 1945 whilst hitch-hiking in England

Kenneth Sidney James Church - A Private in the 1st Cambridgeshire Regiment, Suffolk Regiment who died in a Japanese prisoner of war camp on 28th June 1943 aged 23.

George Frederick Cocker – A Private in the 7th Royal Norfolk Regiment who died in Normandy 7th August 1944 aged 19.

Sidney Arthur Ellender – A Sapper in the 252 Field Company of the Royal Engineers who died in Italy 20th January 1944 aged 20.

Walter Gerald Hitchborn – A Trooper in the 5th Royal Tank Regiment who died in the Middle East on 29th November 1942 aged 30.

George Frederick Hornsby – A Gunner with 70 Medium Regiment Royal Artillery who died in Austria on 28th July 1945 aged 28.

Albert Law – A Corporal in the 1st Oxfordshire and Buckinghamshire Light Infantry who died in Peterborough hospital from an ulcer caused by starvation whilst being held a prisoner of war by the Germans aged 35.

Elsie Kathleen Norris – A Corporal who died in Belgium 13th January 1945 aged 24.

George W.Ruff – A Railwayman, aged 37, who died on 16th January by a bomb whilst on duty.

Alex James Smith – An Aircraftman, 1st Class, with the Royal Airforce Volunteer Reserve who died 12th August 1940 aged 26.

<u>Reginald Adolphus George Steels</u> – A Gunner with the (Honourable Artillery Company) Regiment, Royal Horse Artillery who died in the Middle East on 23rd January 1942 aged 26.

<u>Percy Hudson Thimblebee</u> – A Flight Sergeant with the Royal Air Force Volunteer Reserve who died 27th May 1942.

<u>Sidney Richard Tinkler</u> – A Sergeant with (F.N.S.) Squadron, Royal Air Force Volunteer Reserve who died whilst on air operations on 14th May 1942.

<u>Leslie Bertram Toogood</u> – A Marine on HMS Hood of the Royal Marines who died 24th May 1941 when his ship was sunk by the Bismarck.

<u>Arthur Percival Wardle and Ezra Frank Wardle</u> – Able Seamen on HMS Vengeance in the Royal Navy – Twins who both died of alcohol poisoning after celebrating their 21st birthday on board ship in a Scottish port.

<u>William West</u> – A Gunner who with (The Northumberland Hussars) Lt.A.A./Anti-Tank Regiment, Royal Artillery who died in the Middle East on 10th September aged 28.

A photograph of the War Memorials plaques on the Lych Gates of St Augustine's church.

Thanks go to David Gray who allowed me to use these details which have been taken from his Peterborough War Memorial website:- www.pboro-memorial.com

Woodston Home Guard.